The Cambridge
CAE
Course

Mary Spratt & Lynda B. Taylor

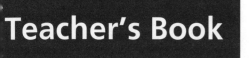

PUBLISHED BY THE PRESS SYNDICATE OF THE UNIVERSITY OF CAMBRIDGE
The Pitt Building, Trumpington Street, Cambridge CB2 1RP, United Kingdom

CAMBRIDGE UNIVERSITY PRESS
The Edinburgh Building, Cambridge CB2 2RU, United Kingdom
40 West 20th Street, New York, NY 1001–4211, USA.
10 Stamford Road, Oakleigh, Melbourne 3166, Australia.

Acknowledgements
The authors would like to thank the staff at Cambridge University
Press, Geraldine Mark and Liz Sharman in particular, for the
guidance and care with which they have supported this project.

First published 1997

Printed in the United Kingdom at the University Press, Cambridge

A catalogue record for this book is available from the British Library

Library of Congress Cataloguing in Publication data

ISBN 0 521 44709 7 Student's Book
ISBN 0 521 44711 9 Teacher's Book
ISBN 0 521 44710 0 Self-study Student's Book
ISBN 0 521 44712 7 Set of 3 cassettes

Introduction

The *Cambridge CAE Course* prepares students thoroughly for the Cambridge Certificate in Advanced English examination and, at the same time, helps them to improve their overall command of English and communication skills at this level.
The *Cambridge CAE Course*:

- **familiarises students with the content and format of the CAE exam.**
- **gives students extensive practice in carrying out CAE exam tasks. The final section of each unit and three separate Revision Exam Practice units concentrate solely on CAE question formats and exam-attack skills.**
- **provides ample and stimulating opportunities for speaking and writing English.**
- **contains a wide variety of authentic reading and listening material on engaging and unusual topics.**
- **develops the various subskills that are particularly important at this level, e.g. understanding textual cohesion, using language appropriately, and reading for detail.**
- **contains systematic language study with regular vocabulary extension activities, a focus on pronunciation and functional language, and grammar activities. These latter are divided into Grammar reminder and Grammar analysis slots which offer respectively revision of previously studied grammatical areas and examination of aspects of grammar which may be new to students at this level.**
- **contains a Ways of learning feature in each unit that encourages students to reflect on their approaches to learning and to exam preparation.**

Who is the *Cambridge CAE Course* written for?

The *Cambridge CAE Course* was designed with two kinds of students in mind – firstly, those studying for the CAE exam, and secondly, any advanced students of general English who wish to improve their overall command of the language and their communication skills in English.

What is the level of this course?

The CAE examination is taken sometimes one year after the First Certificate in English examination and sometimes two years after. This course would be suitable for either group of students as many of its activities adapt to the level of their user, and it is possible to use the Student's Book either by working through it or by approaching it selectively according to students' needs. General students of English will benefit most from using this course if they are at a good upper intermediate level or are beginning to achieve a certain proficiency in the language.

What are the aims of this course?

This course has five main aims:

1. **to improve students' all-round command and level of English**
2. **to familiarise students with the content and format of the CAE exam**
3. **to give students adequate practice in carrying out CAE exam tasks**
4. **to increase students' confidence in their ability to learn and master English**
5. **to increase students' awareness of how to improve their own language and make the most of their own learning styles**

What are the components of the *Cambridge CAE Course*?

The course consists of three separate books and supporting recordings: a set of 3 cassettes.

- **Student's Book**
- **Teacher's Book**
- **Self-Study Student's Book**
- **Three Cassettes**

The Student's Book

What are the contents of the Student's Book?

The Student's Book contains five main parts:

1 Map of the Book
2 Starter Unit
3 Units 1–15
4 Revision Exam Practice (after Units 5, 10 and 15)
5 Exam Tips

The **Map of the Book** is designed to help both teachers and students plan a learning syllabus and design a route through the materials in accordance with students' needs.

The **Starter Unit** is unlike the other units in that its focus is the content of the course as a whole (ways of learning, communication and the CAE exam). It serves as an introduction to each of the strands of the course. The three blocks of **Units (1–5, 6–10, 11–15)** develop particular features of language, particular communication skills, approaches to the different parts of the exam, and an awareness of ways of learning. (See the Map of the Book for details.) Each unit is designed around a topic of general interest that could well be covered in the CAE exam.

Revision Exam Practice units occur after each block of five units, and contain additional practice of the exam formats presented in the preceding five units. They are also based on the topics of these units. In this way they aim to provide opportunities for revision, checking and consolidation.

Exam Tips is a brief supplementary section at the end of the book that aims to summarise the recommendations of the CAE Examination Reports produced by the University of Cambridge Local Examinations Syndicate (UCLES). (See below.) The tips are presented paper by paper.

How are the units in the Student's Book organised?

Each of units 1–15 contains three sections (Section A, Section B and Section C). Sections A and B contain a similar structure and focus. Each develops a different aspect of the topic of the unit, and contains a focus on reading, listening, speaking and/or writing, grammar and vocabulary. Activities on pronunciation, style, register and functions may also occur in these sections. Section B ends with a Vocabulary Summary, which aims to give students opportunities to review key vocabulary items encountered in the unit.

Section C focuses on the CAE exam. Each Section C looks at one or two different exam tasks by introducing their content and aims, giving practical advice on how to approach the tasks, and providing extensive practice.

The subskills practised in any unit (e.g. reading for gist, listening for specific information, fluency practice, practice of word stress etc.) will vary. They reappear in more than one unit in order to ensure consolidated attention and practice. The skills and subskills related to reading and listening are focused on through a wealth of authentic texts. The reading texts are taken from a wide range of sources and normally reflect the text types used in the exam. The listening extracts also vary widely in type, so as to reflect the range covered by the exam. One special feature of the listening extracts is the emphasis on authentic speech that they contain. This has been achieved by recording unscripted text where this is appropriate to the text type.

Grammar is treated in two ways: through Grammar reminder and Grammar analysis slots. Grammar reminders cover structures or grammatical items which students have probably been taught many times before yet continue to make mistakes with. These mistakes happen not so much because students don't know or understand rules (either consciously or unconsciously), but more because they fail to apply them – possibly as a result of influence from their first language. Grammar reminders are intended to act as memory jogs to help students overcome these recurring mistakes.

The Grammar analysis activities are more exploratory in nature. They require students to think about the use of particular structures or grammatical points and work out rules of use. They focus on grammatical items whose meanings and use students may not yet have encountered or fully explored, and aim to increase students' knowledge of the meanings and use of these items as well as to provide practice in them.

The grammar selected for coverage in the course is central to the requirements of the CAE exam.

The Ways of learning slot in each unit will be related to a learning theme of the unit, and often to an aspect of the exam task focused on in Section C. The aim of these slots is to increase students' awareness of what makes up communication (e.g. interactive language, appropriate language) and the different approaches to learning (e.g. how to read for different purposes, strategies for dealing with listening in an exam context). Students are encouraged to reflect on these and evaluate their own behaviour with a view to modifying it if they need to.

How does the Student's Book focus on the CAE exam?

The Student's Book focuses constantly on the CAE exam, though not always in an explicit way. Sections A and B aim particularly to develop students' general level of language and communication. In doing this, they focus on the exam in an implicit way by aiming to bring students' general language proficiency up to the required level. However, the book does also focus on the exam in a number of explicit ways:

1   All Sections A and B contain at least one exam practice activity. In the Student's Book they are marked by the symbol ✳. The number of such tasks in the sections increases as the book progresses.
2   Section C of each unit focuses on one or two different exam tasks, so that the book as a whole contains a detailed breakdown of all components of each of the CAE papers.
3   The Revision Exam Practice units consist only of exam tasks. These are presented in the same format as in the exam.

How should the Student's Book be used?

This book has not been designed with one fixed approach in mind. It would be possible to use it in several ways. You could, for instance:

- work through the book from beginning to end
- select units that meet particular needs and interests
- select sections in accordance with particular needs and interests

The Map of the Book will help you find your own route through the book. You will find some cross-referencing to other units in the teaching notes where this is appropriate. You will also find that there is an increasingly explicit focus on the exam as the book progresses.

The Teacher's Book

What are the contents of the Teacher's Book?

The Teacher's Book contains:

- A unit-by-unit guide
- Answer keys for the Revision Exam Practice units
- A Map of the Student's Book
- CAE answer sheets

The unit-by-unit guide contains:

- The aims of each block of activities
- For each activity (where appropriate):
  - background information on exam tasks or other features of the exam, language skills, grammar, cultural information etc.

- teaching tips
- tapescripts and answer keys

The Self-Study Student's Book

What are the contents of the Self-Study Student's Book?

- Tapescripts
- Notes to help students understand exercises and keys as appropriate
- CAE answer sheets

Symbols used in the course

[▪▪] indicates Listening

✳ indicates Exam Practice Activities

Materials available from the University of Cambridge Local Examinations Syndicate (UCLES)

What CAE exam materials does UCLES produce?

From UCLES you can obtain copies of old exam papers for each exam session, e.g. the version of CAE administered in summer 1995 or the version of CAE administered in winter 1996, etc. You can also obtain copies of the once-yearly CAE Examination Report. This contains an analysis of candidate performance in the exam as a whole, as well as on the individual papers. It also contains recommendations for candidate preparation. These publications as well as a publications order form can be obtained from:

Marketing Division
UCLES
1 Hills Road
Cambridge CB1 2EU
UK
Telephone: 01223 553311
Fax: 01223 460278

The authors hope that you enjoy working with this course, that it provides you with the support you need in guiding students, and that your students find it clear, comprehensive and motivating.

Starter

The general aim of this unit is to get students settled into this book, their course, being with one another, and being with you, their teacher. Unlike the other units, it doesn't focus on general aspects of their language language or skills improvement. It focuses instead on language learning, communication, and the contents of the CAE exam. Students will become aware of what the course and the exam involve, and work out learning goals for the course which can then act as a foundation for their study. They will find this easier if they don't have to worry yet about how to express themselves – this will come in later units.

A

Ways of learning

Starter activities

Aims
To build up students' awareness of their preferred style of learning.
To introduce a range of learning styles and their possible strengths and weaknesses.
To introduce the notion of developing different ways of learning for different learning purposes.

1 This activity is designed to make students aware of how they like to learn, and to get them to start talking to one another about themselves. Make sure the students actually tick the methods they prefer so as to give them a firm basis for discussion. This activity will also give you, the teacher, some useful information on how your students differ from one another, and the learning styles of different students.

As this is the first discussion in the course, it would probably be a good idea to have a discussion in pairs followed by a whole class discussion. In this way students can gather their confidence in pairs before holding forth in front of their classmates.

NB There is of course no 'best' way to learn languages – people will prefer and need to learn in different ways according to habits and abilities they have developed from previous learning. They can of course also adopt new learning styles.

2 These descriptions are ones used by researchers to describe different kinds of learners. They are not exhaustive, as research into learning styles is still in its early stages.

After students have completed the matching activity you could start the discussion of 'which best describes you' by talking about yourself – how you learnt languages, and how you like to learn languages. After students have talked about their own descriptions, you could briefly elicit their opinions on the possible advantages or disadvantages of different learning styles. This will prepare the way for the discussion in 'Your thoughts'.

NB More than one description may be suitable for any one person.

3 This activity involves listening for gist, so students do not need to understand every word in the conversation to complete the task. The emphasis in this unit is on the message of the unit rather than on language.

4 This activity involves listening for detail. It presents students with further ways of learning to think about. The recording is an authentic conversation between two people talking about their actual learning experiences. Ensure that each student completes the third column. This should give rise to a meaty discussion as students talk about whether they like these ways of learning. Listen in so that you can find out about your students' learning patterns and difficulties.

Tapescript

Man: I'm thinking of learning Italian. [Oh] Are you erh ...? Don't you speak ...? I thought you had ...

Woman: Well, I did, I used to go to erm ... adult classes ... to do Italian.

Man: Yeh. Really!

Woman: Oh, I loved it. I loved it. It was wonderful.

Man: Is it easy?

Woman: Well, erm, erm, it ... it is quite easy because I think particularly in Italian, they have one word that means an awful lot of things, and it's such an expressive language [yes] that, that the way that you say a word means all sorts of different things.

Man: Yeh, what about the grammar? I mean is that ... ? I've heard that's quite tricky and ...

Woman: Well, it's not, it's not [not particularly] ... I mean the truth is I've forgotten an awful lot, which is the awful thing because I haven't, I mean I used to go to Italy quite a lot and I haven't been for a long time, so er, when I'm there I find I pick it up really quickly.

Man: So you find it easier actually in the country?

Woman: Oh, much easier. I mean I have kind of worked there very briefly, but well, for a couple of months and by the time I came back I was wonder ..., I mean I was really excellent.

Man: The thing is I want to, I want to get to know it, to be able to speak it quite well first [yes], so that I don't kind of make a fool of myself when I go out there, because I don't particularly like making mistakes.

Woman: Oh, you shouldn't worry about making mistakes, that's ridiculous ...

Man: No, I suppose not really, I should be a bit more adventurous really ...

Woman: Well, and also I tell you, it's completely different when you're there. [mm] I mean when you hear people talking naturally and at the sort of right speed and everything it sounds so different. And also, and also when you have to, when you have to do things [mm], you know if you go into a shop and you have to buy something you have to communicate [yeh], so you just do it, I mean you just learn how to do it.

Man: And what about, what about, I mean, vocabulary and things? Do you, if they're words you don't know, I mean how did you look them up and then translate them back into ... ?

Woman: Yeh, yeh. [you carried it ...] I mean I used to have a wonderful time, I used to always go back and get really frustrated by something I wanted to say and then go home and look it up, and work out how to say it [yeh], and I'd be really pleased with myself, that I'd come up with this phrase that, you know, somebody might understand.

Man: When you learnt, did you have ... was it one to one? Did you have a teacher and just you or other people in the class ... ?

Woman: Oh, no, no, it was a big class.

Man: So, you all used to do conversation with each other and ...

Woman: Yes, I mean she'd she'd kind of take ...

Man: I think I prefer that.

Woman: Yes, yes. And also, I mean it can be great fun. I mean if they're sort of a nice bunch in the class and everything, it can be very funny. [yeh] And also when you get it wrong, it's a hoot [yeh]. I mean, and you get homework. I mean, it is a bit like going back to school, but it's erm. No it's great fun, and they used to do things like you'd go to erm an Italian restaurant, say, and you'd all have to speak, order your food in Italian and do ... or cook a meal or something, so that it wasn't just sort of sitting behind the desk, you know, repeating the grammar.

Man: Yes, that's the way to do it, yes.

Woman: Oh, it's lovely, lovely. I think you should do it.

Man: I will.

Woman: Definitely.

Key

2   1 C   2 E   3 A   4 B   5 D   6 F

3   (a) They are talking about evening classes for learning Italian.

   (b) The woman definitely enjoys learning. The man does too but he has some reservations.

4

Way of learning	Woman	Man
Learning in the country where the language is spoken	✓	?
Learning the language before you go to the country	✗	✓
Making mistakes in public	?	✗
Being challenged	✓	?/✗
Using a dictionary	✓	?
Learning with others in a class	✓	✓
Doing homework	✓	?
Lessons involving real-world activities (e.g. ordering food in a real restaurant)	✓	✓
Repeating grammar	?	?

The woman would seem to be a risk-taker, possibly a translator, and a child-like unconscious learner.

The man is possibly a systems person and a teacher depender.

Your thoughts

You will meet 'Your thoughts' sections throughout this book. They are designed to round up discussion of a topic or a text and to activate relevant language. You will need to decide how many of the discussion points to cover and in which order, and also whether to conduct the discussion in pairs, groups, or as a whole class. You may wish to vary your approach.

Ways of learning and this book

This introduces students to the 'Ways of learning' sections in each unit. It also introduces them to the Map of the Book. If students can get used to using the Map of the Book, this will help them direct their own learning and show them how to make use of the coursebook for reference in their homework and revision.

B

What does 'communicating' mean?

> **Aims**
> To increase students' awareness of various elements which make up 'communication'.
> To increase students' awareness of their own mastery
>   of the different elements of communication.
> To allow students the opportunity to set themselves learning goals for communication.

Students may be used to thinking in terms of improving their English language rather than improving their communication in English. However, to be fully successful in English – as well as in the CAE exam – they will need to be good at both. Language is only one element in communication. This section aims to broaden students' awareness of different aspects of communication, in preparation for work in the rest of the course and for the CAE exam.

1 None of the responses are 'wrong'. They each focus on a different aspect of communication. After the discussion is finished you could ask students to identify these different aspects for you to write up on the board.

You could conduct the discussion first in pairs and then with the class as a whole.

2 This activity is a warm-up to the reading text in activity 3. Try to elicit from the discussion the main points that are made in the text. This is important, as the text is not easy to read, and needs the support of the photos and this prior discussion to help students understand it.

3 To encourage students to read this rather long and

serious article for gist (rather than word for word for language), you could set a time limit for reading (e.g. 2 minutes) and explain that the next activity will ask them to read the text in more detail. The completed sentence summarises the contents of the passage.

4 This is a kind of multiple matching activity, in which students have to match the photos to the elements of communication, and then both of these to the text.

Key

2 Possible answers:
Mother and baby – depend much more on non-verbal signals; baby is learning means of communication, mother has to work at trying to interpret baby's meanings

2–3-year-old at family table – child will try to make sense of what he/she hears, parents will possibly see themselves as still teaching child to talk

School child – learning to talk in more formal settings, learning new vocabulary, learning how to get attention and to take turns in talking

Woman talking at business meeting – probably using quite formal language and possibly specialised language (technical jargon) too; dress and body language probably important elements of communication in this setting; use of appropriate language also important

Boy and girl – non-verbal communication, eye contact and physical gestures, intimate exchanges

3 (1) expression   (3) negotiation

4 1 negotiation
    2 appropriate use of language, understanding facial expression, learning intonation, learning to get attention
    3 writing, learning to get attention, stating views, learning to take turns in talking, appropriate use of language
    4 appropriate use of language, awareness of body language, technical jargon, dress
    5 appropriate use of language, understanding facial expression, awareness of body language

5 These activities are designed to make the topic of communication personal to the students and their own communicative abilities. You could ask students to write their own report for homework using the report here for guidance. You may wish to add in other elements of communication. Students might need to discuss what is meant by 'appropriate use of language' and 'negotiation in speaking', particularly as these are important focuses of this course and of the CAE exam.

Elements of communication and this book

As with the final part of Section A, this section is designed to get students familiar with using the Map of the Book. It also shows students where they can look for guidance on the areas of communication they identified as their weakest in activity 5.

C

The CAE exam

> **Aims**
> **To familiarise students with the general content of the CAE exam.**
> **To give students an opportunity to reflect on the contents of the CAE exam.**
> **To allow students an opportunity to set themselves learning goals for the CAE exam.**

In each unit Section C focuses on part of the CAE exam. It is these sections which contain explicit preparation for the exam's targets and techniques, while Sections A and B concentrate more on improving students' general language and communication skills to bring these up to the level required. Section C always contains an 'exam practice' section in which students practise an exam task in an exam-like situation.

What is CAE?

1 Students may want to hear the recording twice to complete their answers to the questions. NB Throughout the course students may need to hear tapes twice. This could require you to rewind tapes and play extracts again. Answers should be in note form only. If you have copies of a CAE exam (available from the University of Cambridge Local Examinations Syndicate (UCLES) – see page 5 for the address), you could show them to the students after this listening task to help make the exam more real for them.

2 This activity aims to start students thinking about their learning goals in relation to the exam. The students' answers to these questions will probably give you clues to their individual learning needs.

If your students have sat the First Certificate in English exam you could discuss how much the CAE exam differs from or is similar to that exam.

Tapescript

1st woman:	Jane … I know you've already taught CAE, isn't that right?
2nd woman:	That's right, yes, I've just finished a course actually.
1st woman:	Well, I've er, just got my timetable for this term and I've discovered that I've got a CAE class and I've, well, I've never

taught towards it before, and I wonder if you could sort of fill me in because I really don't know much about the exam at all.

2nd woman:	Well, you know what it stands for, don't you? CAE?
1st woman:	Cambridge something or other …
2nd woman:	Yes, well, no, actually it is a Cambridge exam, you're right, but … CAE actually stands for the Certificate In Advanced English.
1st woman:	Right, so, Certificate In Advanced English, O.K.
2nd woman:	What else would you like to know about it?
1st woman:	Erm, well I suppose really, what sort of level it is, you know, if it's divided up into papers, and what the different papers are.
2nd woman:	Erm, sure. Well, it's a fairly high level examination [mm] and I suppose it was really designed as a final qualification in English for people who wanted to use English in their jobs or possibly to go on and use English in a study environment. [hm, hm] Erm, it focuses quite a lot on using the language in real world tasks reading articles or writing letters; that type of thing. [hm, hm] So, it has a practical side to it.
1st woman:	So, it's not erm … not a sort of academic exam?
2nd woman:	No, no, it's … I wouldn't say it's a very high level academic exam, but I would say it has practical application when you're using English in a job or study context. [aha] So, it's of relevance to a lot of students who've been studying English for a number of years and want some final qualification which gives an indication of how well they can speak and use the language.
1st woman:	Oh right, so a lot of the sort of work that you do in the classroom … kind of authentic tasks and things like that [mm], what they'd be relevant, would they?
2nd woman:	They would, yes. In the course that I taught we used a lot of authentic materials from newspaper articles, magazines, listening tasks based on things I'd recorded off the radio; that type of thing. [hm] And then, a lot of the writing tasks we did were based around the sorts of writing that you'd very often have to do in, in a job situation or possibly in a study situation; writing a formal or an informal letter, drawing up a short report or writing a description perhaps for a guidebook, that type of thing.
1st woman:	Hm, so no composition writing?
2nd woman:	Oh, no.
1st woman:	Thank goodness, oh, that's a relief. So there's writing in it?
2nd woman:	Yes, there's a writing paper.
1st woman:	So, there's a writing paper.
2nd woman:	And then, there's a reading paper.
1st woman:	Oh now hold on, writing, reading, yeh

2nd woman:	And, then, of course, the other two skills: listening and speaking.
1st woman:	Right so, each of them are papers, are they?
2nd woman:	Yes, yes that's right.
1st woman:	How do you have a speaking paper?
2nd woman:	Well, it's it's more like an oral test, I suppose. [oh right] In fact, it's quite unusual because er, instead of just the usual sort of interview which you often get in a speaking test where you have an interviewer and one candidate; in this case there are two examiners and two candidates present all at the same time [mm]. Which means that it's not just a situation where the interviewer's talking to the candidate, not just sort of that one way type of interaction. But there's the opportunity for the two candidates to talk to each other.
1st woman:	Yes, I don't know, but I can imagine that lots of students would find that a bit more relaxing.
2nd woman:	Well, I know the students in my class actually quite enjoyed it because we do a lot of pair work in class anyway, and it just meant that when it came to the exam, they were doing something very similar to what they were used to.
1st woman:	Mm ... right so from what you've said, it sort of ... the exam doesn't seem to be ... the kind of work you'd need to do for the exam doesn't seem to be very different from a lot of the work you'd do in class anyway.
2nd woman:	I think that's right, and that certainly made my life a lot easier obviously, in teaching the class, because many of the things the students had been used to doing, they find turn up in the exam in terms of activities.
1st woman:	So, there's the four papers?
2nd woman:	No, there's actually five [oh]. There's a fifth paper, and that's called the English in Use paper.
1st woman:	English in Use, right. Grammar?
2nd woman:	Yes, it's er, it has grammar in it, but it's not rigidly a grammar paper. It includes work on vocabulary as well, so it's grammar in the widest sense. And not just at the sentence level either, but grammar through a text. [hmm] Erm, it also looks at things like style, choosing the right words to use in the right situation, erm, and all sorts of aspects of English that we use in everyday situations. [mm] So, it's not just a matter of students showing how well they can use grammatical rules. And actually, we did some interesting work in class on that, not just going through a grammar book.
1st woman:	Right, well, thanks very much. Er, well, can I come and ask you more questions later on maybe?
2nd woman:	Do, yes, yes, and if you want to borrow

any materials you're welcome to use them just let me know.

1st woman: Right, thanks very much.

Key

1 Certificate in Advanced English

2 fairly high level

3 people who want to use English in their jobs or possibly to go on and use English in a study environment; people who want a final qualification

4 language in real world tasks

5 5

6

Writing	Reading	Listening	Speaking	English in Use
practical writing e.g. writing a formal or an informal letter for a job or study situation; report writing; writing a description for a guidebook etc.; no compositions	articles from newspapers and magazines	listening based on off-air recordings	two examiners and two candidates present; like pairwork	grammar and vocabulary; grammar at sentence and text level; style; choosing appropriate words

Exam practice

This could be done in class or as homework. It is an opportunity for students to think about and formalise their learning goals for their English course and for the CAE exam.

Exam study and this book

This section again aims to familiarise students with the Map of the Book and to encourage them to direct their own learning. You could explain to students the difference between:

1 the exam practice activities in Sections A and B. These familiarise students with exam task formats in the context of their general learning.

2 the exam focus in Section C. This focuses explicitly on the aims and content of different exam tasks.

3 the Revision Exam Practice units. These give students an opportunity to revise the language of the preceding five units, while at the same time providing extra practice in the exam tasks that have been focused on. The exam tasks in the Revision Exam Practice units are presented as they would be in the exam.

One

A

The way we live

Starter activities

> **Aim**
> To start students thinking about the topic of how we live.

Key

1 A Egyptian   B Aztec   C Roman   D Greek

2–3 Encourage students to discuss as much as possible in these activities.

Listening

> **Aim**
> To practise listening to radio extracts and rapidly identifying their content.

1 Students should not be concerned about unknown vocabulary when they listen to these extracts the first time. They will be able to carry out the matching task without recognising every word. Point out to them that it is useful to develop skills in identifying content for listening to the radio.

2 Ensure that your students only take notes on relevant points. This is <u>not</u> a dictation!

3 There are no correct answers to this activity. Its aim is to get students to give their opinions and utilise some of the language they have heard in the extracts.

Tapescript

Excerpt 1

Early schooling was the responsibility of mothers and nursemaids. Most girls and boys went to primary school at seven to learn reading and writing, but primary school teachers were not much respected and most pupils were only taught to learn by heart, with frequent use of the cane.

A smaller number of children went on to grammar school, where the main subject was literature – Greek as well as Latin. A still smaller number of boys finished their education at a school of rhetoric. There they were taught the subjects necessary for a career in public service, such as public speaking and the ability to conduct a debate or legal argument. Most educated citizens could speak Greek as well as they could speak Latin.

Excerpt 2

Each god served a particular need. Some originated in ancient tribal traditions, such as the sacred bulls worshipped at Apis, or the cats dedicated to the goddess Bastet. Others, such as the sun god Ra, developed out of their reverence for nature. Some gods looked human, others had the heads of animals and birds. One important religious belief was the idea of *ma'at*: justice and good order. People believed that the gods ruled the world, and it was people's duty to live according to their will and to maintain *ma'at*, so far as was possible.

Excerpt 3

Demokratia meant government by mass meeting. In Athens a general assembly was held on average once in nine days and every ordinary male citizen was free to attend, speak and vote. In practice, normal attendance at an assembly was about five to six thousand. The city was governed by the votes of this crowd.

Excerpt 4

Understanding time was crucial to them. They needed to know practical things such as when to plant and when to harvest. Much more importantly, these superstitious people wanted to know which days were lucky and which were thought unlucky. They had two calendars. One of these, the solar calendar, was very like ours with 365 days. Five of these days were thought to be very unlucky – it was believed that arguments that started during the 'nothing' days could last for ever, and that children born then would never amount to anything. During this time the Aztecs stayed at home and did nothing.

The other calendar was the sacred calendar, the Count of the Days, which was important for priests and astrologers. This calendar was used mainly for making prophecies and deciding which were lucky days.

Key

1 Excerpt 1: Roman
Excerpt 2: Egyptian
Excerpt 3: Greek
Excerpt 4: Aztec

2 Possible answers:
Roman education: early education = responsibility of mothers and nursemaids; most children went to primary school where learnt reading and writing; pupils learnt by heart, cane used; small number of children went to grammar school where studied literature; smaller group of boys went on to school of rhetoric where learnt skills of speaking.

Egyptian gods and religion: many gods to serve different needs; some gods looked human, others like animals; very important religious belief = *ma'at* i.e. a belief in justice and good order which it was everybody's duty to maintain.

Greek democracy: mass meetings which any ordinary male could take part in; held frequently and regularly; decisions taken as a result of the meetings' votes.

Aztecs concerned about time, particularly about lucky and unlucky days; had two kinds of calendar, ordinary one and sacred one; ordinary one helped them to know which days were lucky; sacred calendar was used by priests for making prophecies and deciding on lucky days.

Reading

Aims
To encourage students to begin talking about themselves and to get to know one another.
To encourage reading both for gist and for detail.
To give guided practice in deducing meaning from context.

1 Make sure students write **M W** or **N** etc. against each chore before they begin discussing. This will give them a firm basis for discussion.

3 This demands quite careful reading. You could ask students to underline the parts of the text containing the answers if they seem to be making a lot of mistakes.

Key

3 1 T   3 T   5 F   7 T
  2 T   4 ?   6 F   8 F

4
disinclined	= unwilling
lift a finger	= help/work
emerge	= be revealed
take the lead	= take on responsibility
overwhelmingly	= above all
confined	= limited
top the league	= come first
all-round	= general
stoutly maintain	= strongly affirm
fellows	= men
chores	= boring domestic work
prone	= inclined

✳ Writing

Aims
To give students the opportunity to use some of the language they have encountered in the unit.
To give students the opportunity to reflect on and develop some of the issues presented in the unit.
To practise the kind of task students might encounter in CAE Paper 2 (Writing) Section B.

You might want to hold a short class discussion about the kinds of things to include in the letter so students have a clear idea of what is expected of them.
As this is essentially a revision task, you may prefer to ask students to do it for homework rather than in class. This could help you diagnose the level of written English of each of your students. Alternatively, as this writing task occurs early on in the course, you could do it as a class activity with small groups or pairs writing the letters. In this way you could have some discussion on the format and style of letter-writing, if you think your students need this.

Grammar reminder: prepositions

> **Aims**
> To raise awareness of the importance of
>   prepositions in accurate language use.
> To develop awareness of the range of grammatical
>   contexts in which prepositions can occur, and their
>   varying grammatical functions.
> To allow students an opportunity to work out a
>   learning strategy for tackling prepositions.

The correct use of prepositions, and understanding of
their correct use, is important for the CAE exam. They
are tested directly or indirectly in Papers 1 (Reading)
and 3 (English in Use), and contribute to effective
communication in Papers 2 (Writing) and 5 (Speaking).

Key

1 fixed expressions: *to lift a finger round the house;
three out of four; in charge of; they left it to women; at
their best*

adjective + preposition combinations: *responsible for;
confined to; based on; due for*

verb+preposition combinations: *long for, to take the
lead in; took part in; looking at; treated with; to care for;
to mark with; reconciling with: interviewed about*

noun + preposition combinations: *view of; sort of;
availability of; exit from*

passive constructions: *dispatched by Brussels;
challenged with; confirmed by; marked by*

prepositions of place: *in the United Kingdom; escort
children to playschool; to school; among the most
domesticated; in Portugal; at the kitchen sink; in Europe;
in Denmark*

2 All the fixed expressions.

Vocabulary

> **Aim**
> To give students an opportunity to play with words
>   and see the great number of words that can be
>   generated by the prefix and suffix system of English.

This activity is intended as a game. You might want to
organise it on a team basis the first time round, and
then in pairs or as individuals as students grow more
confident.

Key

responsible	*irresponsible, irresponsibility,*
	responsibility, responsibly, irresponsibly
incline	*inclined, disinclined, inclination,*
	disinclination
liberate	*liberated, unliberated, liberation*
likely	*unlikely, likelihood*
concern	*concerned, unconcerned*
affect	*affected, affectedness, unaffected,*
	unaffectedness, affectedly, unaffectedly
overwhelm	*overwhelmed, overwhelming,*
	overwhelmingly
willing	*willingly, unwilling, unwillingly,*
	willingness, unwillingness
domestic	*domestically, domesticated,*
	undomesticated, domestication
usual	*usually, unusual, unusually*
enthusiasm	*enthusiastic, enthusiastically,*
	unenthusiastic, unenthusiastically
common	*uncommon, uncommonly, commonly,*
	commonness
public	*publicise, publicly*
available	*availability, unavailable, unavailability*
hope	*hopeful, hopeless, hopefulness,*
	hopelessness, hopefully, unhopefully,
	hopelessly
agree	*agreement, disagree, disagreement,*
	agreeable, disagreeable, agreeably,
	disagreeably

B

The way we are

Starter activities

> **Aims**
> To start thinking about the topic of lifestyles.
> To activate vocabulary related to physical description.

1 This should give rise to discussion as the students try to justify their answers.

2 The students give personal details about themselves. They may prefer to do this in small groups rather than as a whole class.

Listening

> **Aims**
> To practise listening for gist.
> To practise an exam-type listening task.
> To revise and/or extend students' knowledge of the vocabulary of physical appearance and personality.
> To allow students continue getting to know about one another.

✱ 1 Ask students to justify their answers to see how much relevant language they recall from the recording.

2 Ensure the students only note down the required language. This is not a dictation.

3 This should involve students using other expressions for personality and physical description.

Tapescript

Woman: That's me in the bath with my brother. We loved bath times actually; we normally shared the bath together. But erm, I'm surprised I'm sitting at the taps end because erm I was 18 months older than him, and was a much stronger character and could normally force him to sit at the taps end. My mother always used to throw lots of toys in for us and that always sort of took away the pain of having our hair washed which I hated and used to fight against, but it had to be done.

Woman: This is a picture of us at our dance class and looks like some good time is going on. I seem to be day dreaming as normal; my attention has been taken off the camera ... mean maybe we were taking a bit of time for it all to happen; I don't know, but I'm not quite there ... seem to remember doing that a lot in my childhood, sort of being half there and half not, very taken with my own thoughts, not really paying much attention to anybody else ... wasn't nasty, I was just made like that.

Woman: Oh, look at that, I remember that was taken at my friend Susie Wallis's 5th birthday. And whenever I used to go to somebody's birthday party I always used to go straight for the birthday cake, and try and eat it before anybody else got their hands on it. I used to love cake. I mean, I'm just eating it there with my bare fingers and my sister's next to me, just watching me sort of hammer away at this cake. I loved food more than anything. I think I loved it more than playing or anything like that. An I've sort of grown up quite similar actually. I've a terrible weight problem.

Man: Yes, Smiley, they used to call me or Spotty, but I wasn't then really 'cos I must have been about 5?. My hair was lighter; it's darker now; and that's a really dodgy jumper; yeh, I think that was erm, er one of my granny's birthday presents. Yeh, 'cos you used to get loads of those. The one my brother's actually in is worse; but, yeh, I don't know, I always seemed to have a grin on me face and be kind of cheeky but I don't know, I paid attention at school when I got older and I kind of grew up quite boring really.

Man: Yeh, this is a picture of me next door with the two little girls who lived next door, being forced to play with paints; and erm, this was sort of a punishment, and also to keep me in check because I was a bit of a wild boy; and, in fact, I've got very short hair in this photo and it's because I'd come off my bike about two months before and had a quite nasty er gash on my head, and erm they just thought I was I was playing with boys that were older than me and rougher, and erm, so I was forced to play these sissy games, as I saw them next door, and er, that's why I'm not looking very happy, I think.

Key

1
    speaker 1 – Picture 2
    speaker 2 – Picture 3
    speaker 3 – Picture 5
    speaker 4 – Picture 1
    speaker 5 – Picture 4

2
    Possible answers:
    1st woman: *strong character*
    2nd woman: *day dreaming; not quite there; being half there and half not; not really paying much attention to anybody else*
    3rd woman: *I loved food; I've a terrible weight problem*
    1st man: *Smiley; a grin; my hair was lighter; it's darker now; cheeky; grew up quite boring*
    2nd man: *wild; short hair; gash on my head; not looking very happy*

Reading

> **Aims**
> **To practise reading magazine articles (a very common text type in the CAE exam).**
> **To illustrate a light and personal style in a magazine article.**
> **To continue the theme of finding out about people's personal lives.**
> **To practise reading for gist, detail and specific information.**
> **To raise awareness of word stress in English and how stress is presented in dictionaries.**

NB In the paragraph in the text about Maeve's childhood birthday parties, she refers to 'cakes with hundreds-and-thousands on them'. *Hundreds-and-thousands* are tiny pieces of multi-coloured sugar which are sprinkled (usually generously) on various kinds of cakes.

1 This is a prediction exercise to warm students up to the topic and language of the article. Encourage students to give as many ideas as they can.

2–4 The three activities demand different approaches to reading: reading for gist, reading for detail, and reading for specific information. Try to ensure that students don't read in the same way for each task. You could also take this opportunity to discuss different ways of reading, and how they relate to different purposes for reading.

5 Check that students have understood the meaning of the adjectives and nouns. Make sure they don't confuse *self-conscious* with *self-confident*. In some ways these are opposites to one another.

6 Use this activity as an opportunity to discuss how word stress operates in English – i.e. words carrying lexical meaning generally carry the main sentence stress(es) whereas grammatical words tend not to be stressed. Individual words will often have main stress and secondary stress.

If you have access to dictionaries in class, ask the students to see what other ways are used to present stress. You could set students a further set of words for homework, asking them to look up in the dictionary the word stress for each word.

Key

3 Possible answers:
brought up to think she was centre of universe; received lots of love and attention; jolly mother; lots of comfort; maid who became a friend; religion; some good teachers; summer holidays

4 **Occupation:** teacher, then writer
Country of origin: Ireland
Father's occupation: barrister
Mother's occupation: nurse, then housewife

Religion: probably Catholic
Type of school attended: convent
Physical description: big and fat (as a teenager)
Personality (as a child): (possible answers) self-confident, goody-goody, extrovert, placid, quick-minded, fanciful, devout, content, innocent, not very academic, lazy

Grammar analysis: the simple past and present perfect tenses

> **Aims**
> **To revise some distinctions in the use of the past simple and present perfect tenses.**
> **To encourage students to analyse language by themselves.**

2 The purpose of this exercise is to show that there is a difference in meaning between the two tenses, so misapplication of one of the tenses can produce not only inaccuracy of form but also inaccurate meaning.

3 Encourage students to discuss the answers amongst themselves as much as possible. They should refer to the sentences in activity 2 for clues to the answers.

Key

1 present perfect, simple past.

2 **1** Both a and b are grammatically correct; b is factually correct.

2 a is grammatically correct and factually correct; b is ungrammatical and therefore also factually incorrect (it makes no sense).

3 Both are grammatically correct; we don't know if a is factually true; b cannot be true as it implies that Maeve is dead.

4 Both are grammatically correct; both are also likely to be factually correct – it is clear that Maeve's childhood is still important to her, so a is correct, and it is likely that she regarded it as important while she was a child, so b is also probably correct, though we don't know for certain.

5 Both are grammatically correct; we don't know if a is true; b is true as she says so in the article.

6 Both are grammatically correct; a is true; b is not factually correct as it implies that she is yet to become a writer, which is not the case.

7 Both are grammatically correct; a is true but we don't know if b is – it implies that they still spoil her.

8 Both are grammatically correct; both a and b could be true. a implies that her childhood no longer inspires her writing, while b implies that it continues to do so.

3 (1) actions   (3) just   (5) past
(2) time   (4) past   (6) effect

Speaking: asking for personal information

> **Aims**
> To allow students to continue getting to know one
>   another.
> To give practice in the language and activity format
>   required by CAE Paper 5 (Speaking) Phase A

✳ 3 Students could walk round the classroom as if they were meeting one another at a party of some kind. This might help them to relax and get to speak to people who don't sit near them.

Key

2 Possible answers:
Name: What's your name?
Occupation: What's your job? Do you have a job? What do you do for a living?
Father's/mother's occupation: What does your father/mother do for a living? What's your father's/ mother's job?
Religion: What religion are you? Are you religious?
Physical description: What do you look like?
Country of origin: Where do you come from? Where are you from? What country do you come from?
Type of school attended: What kind of school did you go to? Where did/do you go to school?
Personality: What kind of person are you? What are you like?

Vocabulary summary

> **Aim**
> To revise the main vocabulary fields of the unit.

By the time students have compared their answers, in pairs and then in groups, they should have reviewed a large amount of vocabulary. Make sure they categorise the vocabulary correctly. Discussion of the categorisations should bring out the meaning of the words. You could do some further work on word stress once students have collected together their group lists of words. This could consist of dictionary work checking stress, and/or repetition work for pronunciation.

Key
Possible answers:
Domestic chores: *shopping, washing up, cooking, cleaning*
Personality: *goody-goody, extrovert, placid, quick-minded*
Physical description: *strapping, big, fat, lovely*
Childhood: *school, birthday parties, homework, summer holidays*

C

Paper 1 (Reading): Multiple choice

> **Aims**
> To practise doing multiple choice comprehension
>   questions, and through this to reflect on the best
>   ways of doing multiple choice.
> To practise the reading comprehension multiple
>   choice exam format.
> To build up awareness of the strategies employed for
>   different reading purposes.
> To build up awareness of the fact that the CAE exam
>   does not require students to read every word in a text.

Introduction

The multiple choice reading text does not always occur in the same place in Paper 1, but it does always occur somewhere. It is usually the second or the third part of the paper. You might want to tell your students this. Make sure you ask your students to reflect on what they are doing as they do the task. It might be better to ask the students to do this task individually. After they have finished doing the comprehension work, encourage them to talk about <u>how</u> they went about answering the questions, so that activity 2 will be more meaningful.

Key
1 1 C   2 D   3 B   4 D   5 A

How to approach multiple choice questions

1 Answers 1, 2, 5 and 9 are clearly wrong, whereas the other answers depend on various factors: the kind of reader you are, how good you are at reading, the kind of text being read, and the kind of reading the question requires. For this reason, there is no one right way to answer multiple choice questions. Weaker readers, though, would probably be well advised to take a cautious and systematic approach.

2 This activity is designed to encourage students to do some serious thinking about how to answer multiple choice questions. It also acts as a conclusion to the previous activities. Leaflet-writing is a possible task in CAE Paper 2 (Writing).

Moving from pair work to group work should enable the discussion to develop. When comparing their leaflets students could compare the format as well as the content. Give students the opportunity to read all the leaflets once they have been displayed, and let them add points later in the course if more occur to them.

This activity could function as useful revision before going on to the Exam practice.

Exam practice

You will see that each Section C contains an Exam practice. This is designed to expose students to tasks that are presented exactly as in the exam in terms of their content and layout. You may choose to do these sections under exam-like conditions in the classroom, or to do them as homework. Or you could do them as a communicative activity with a view to familiarising your students with the exam format in a less formal way. Which way you choose will depend on your students' needs, and possibly on how close they are to doing the exam.

When the examiners mark Paper 1, they add up candidates' scores across all sections, so it is not necessary to pass every section. You may want to give your students this information.

Key
1 B　　2 D　　3 C　　4 A　　5 A　　6 D

Ways of learning: approaches to reading

As an introduction to this section, you could ask students to tell you some of the kinds of texts they have read recently (in whatever language), e.g. novels, comics, magazine articles, advertisements, newspaper articles, study books, menus, telephone directories etc., and then ask them if they thought they had read each in the same way. How you read a text will depend on what kind of text it is and what you as a reader want to get out of it. Even at this level students sometimes approach texts in English as if they were a mine of linguistic information rather than something with a message to convey. Texts are, of course, a mine of linguistic information, and it can sometimes be very useful to look at a text in this way. To do so all the time, however, especially in exam conditions, would get in the way of reading for the message(s) of the text and slow the reader down. It is worthwhile pointing this out to students.

Two

A
Voyages of discovery

Starter activities

> **Aim**
> **To start thinking about the topic of travel and exploration.**

1 It does not matter if students are unfamiliar with the vocabulary for the types of transport shown in the pictures. Encourage them to think about what the purpose of each vehicle was/is, and in what ways they are similar.

2 If your students have difficulty thinking of any explorers themselves, you could make use of the following information. Put up the details randomly on the board and ask students to match each explorer with the correct dates and achievements.

Marco Polo	13th/14th C	travelled all over Asia and to China
Ferdinand Magellan	15th/16th C	commanded first ship to sail round the world
Roald Amundsen	19th/20th C	first man to reach South Pole
Edmund Hillary and Tensing Norgay	20th C	first men to climb Mount Everest

Key
1 All the pictures show vehicles which were/are designed and used by human beings for the purposes of exploration.

Reading

> **Aim**
> **To practise reading quickly to find specific details.**

1 Encourage students to share what they know about Christopher Columbus, e.g. dates, nationality, occupation, travels, achievements, etc.

✳ **2** Ask students to look carefully at the questions before they start reading the text. Then they will know what sort of specific details to look out for during their reading. Explain to them that they will not need to read and understand every word in the text.

Key
1 Christopher Columbus – Italian – 1451–1506 – sailed across the Atlantic – reached the New World in 1492 – undertook three more voyages

2 1 A Guanahani, Cuba, Haiti
      B Jamaica, Puerto Rico
      C Trinidad, Mainland America
   2 A Santiago
      B San Salvador
      C Trinidad
      D San Juan Baptista
      E Hispaniola
   3 A–E gold, spices, birds, pineapple, tobacco (in any order)

Your thoughts

Some people believe Columbus showed great bravery and faith in setting out on such journeys, and that he contributed to the 16th century's knowledge of the world, of mapping techniques and of navigational skills. Others believe his actions led to the destruction of a civilisation. Encourage students to share with a partner their personal reactions to Columbus' 'achievements' and then discuss their views together as a class.

Grammar reminder: *so* and *such*

> **Aim**
> To revise the use of *so* and *such*.
> To practise using *so* and *such*.

Ask students to read through the reminder box with the examples. You may like to check their understanding of the general rules by eliciting from them two or three of their own examples before moving on to the practice exercise.

Key

1	so + e	5	such + a
2	such + d	6	so + c
3	So + b	7	such + h
4	so + g	8	such + f

Listening

> **Aim**
> To encourage listening to interpret opinion.
> To encourage intensive listening for detail.

1 Use this introductory discussion question to help students activate some of the vocabulary they are likely to hear in the listening extract. Ask them to work in pairs first, though you may like to go on to list possible reasons for the whole group. Check the pronunciation of any vocabulary items to help them recognise the words more easily when they come to listen to the recording.

2 Check the pronunciation of any new items of vocabulary.

* 3 Make sure students understand what sort of detailed information they should be listening for. The pronunciation of the names is as follows: Michael Palin ['maɪkəl 'peɪlɪn] and Brian Blessed ['braɪən 'blesɪd].

Tapescript

V1: It must be difficult being an explorer nowadays because there're very few places left to explore, but I'd really fancy, I mean would you like to be an explorer, Nigel? I mean would ...

V2: I don't know. I don't think I would really, it doesn't appeal to me. I like home comforts too much. I mean what motivates people to want to go off and discover something no man has found before, you know ...

V1: Yes ...

V3: I think people explore for different reasons these days, I mean for instance they can raise money for charity [mm] ...

V1: Yes ...

V3: Um, you know, every step, um, [it's] a certain [yes] amount of money is given.

V4: I understand that if you're doing it for a reason but I mean it's the people who, they seem to do things for no reason at all ...

V1: Well, it must [which is] be very exciting, I mean ...

V2: And the desire for fame and wealth, I suppose ...

V1: Well yes, I suppose so, but how many famous explorers are there, really famous, nowadays?

V4: And how much, you don't really get any – I mean you have to be wealthy to go ...

V1: Mm ...

V4: Now, don't you? I mean ...

V3: You have to be well sponsored.

V4: It's a wealthy person's game really.

V2: Well, that TV presenter – um – what's – Michael Palin [mm], you know, he travelled from the North to the South Pole, didn't he? And the camera crew went with him and the TV series was made about it – that would be a good way to do it.

V4: Well, that'd be great [yeah], be great – you'd get paid as well.

V2: Yes.

V1: But imagine the excitement standing on the top of Mount Everest or whatever, compared with most people's lives which is just – you know – going down the pub or whatever.

V4: Yes I know, but [well], I mean it must be terrifying, must be terrifying [isn't it – mm], climbing a mountain like that, absolutely petrifying.

V3: But there's some actor at the moment – what's his name – Brian somebody, um ...

V4: Blessed.

V3: Who wants to ...

V4: Brian Blessed. Blessed, that's right. He wants to climb Everest and, um, he wants to be the oldest person ever to climb Everest.

V4: Yes.

V2: But it's nice to get away from all the kind of, the modern, the modern world and cars and conventional jobs and [escape the, the routine of everyday life] earning money. It's completely different, isn't it [yes, yes]? Well I can see the attraction of that.

V3: Mm, it must be exciting to think that you might be treading somewhere where no-one has ever trod before [mm]. I think that must be [yes] ...

V1: And you don't know what you'll find. I mean when they went to the moon they didn't know whether they would find all sorts of cures for sicknesses or ...

V3: Yes.

V2: That's true.

V4: But do you think it's because now as well we don't really experience very much physical danger in our lives, do we, because it's all kind of sorted for us [yeah], so to actually go off and really pit yourself against the elements is something [mm] [mm] that we don't in our daily lives do. We're all so protected [yes].

V2: Go excitement seeking like.

V3: Yes, yes.

V2: Wouldn't appeal to me though, I don't think.

Key

3 1 few places left (to explore)
   2 costs (of exploring)

	1 Michael Palin	2 Brian Blessed
Job	TV presenter	actor
Project	travel from North to South Poles	climb Everest
Purpose	make TV series	be the oldest person to do so

Speaking: discussing opinions

Aims
To build up awareness of phrasal stress and
  intonation.
To practise phrasal stress and intonation.

1 Begin by eliciting from students their own suggestions of common phrases that speakers use when discussing opinions. Play the first two or three phrases and then check students' answers before continuing.

2 Show students how to mark in the intonation and stress on the first two or three examples before continuing with the rest.

3 After practising the stress and intonation patterns with the cassette, extend the practice by asking students in pairs to use the phrases in longer sentences, e.g. 'It must be difficult being an explorer today because … etc.'

Tapescript
V1: It must be difficult being …
V2: I mean would *you* like to be
V1: I don't know, I don't think I would really …
V2: I mean, for instance …
V1: It doesn't appeal to me …
V2: well yes I suppose so but …
V1: that would be a good way to do …
V2: well that'd be great …
V1: but imagine …
V2: yes I know but …
V1: well I can see the attraction of that …
V2: that's true
V1: but do you think it's because …
V2: wouldn't appeal to me though I don't think …

Key

it must be difficult being …	well that'd be great …
I mean would you like to be …	but imagine …
I don't know, I don't think I would really …	yes I know but …
I mean, for instance …	well I can see the attraction of that …
it doesn't appeal to me …	that's true
well yes I suppose so but …	but do you think it's because …
that would be a good way to do …	wouldn't appeal to me though I don't think …

✱ Writing

Aim
To practise writing an article.

You may want to spend some time helping students to prepare their article. Encourage them to look back over the Reading and Listening activities for ideas and vocabulary. They could finish writing the article for homework or do it as a timed written exercise in class.

B

Holiday travel

Starter activities

> **Aims**
> To start thinking about the topic of holiday travel.
> To activate vocabulary related to the topics of
> holidays, travel etc.

1 Follow up the paired discussion with a class poll to find out which of the holiday destinations shown would be the most/least popular, and why.

2 Before listening to the speakers, revise vocabulary for various types of holiday – *beach/seaside*, *mountain*, *activity*, etc. – and the sorts of reasons why people choose them.

Tapescript

V1: Well my – perfect kind of holiday is a walking holiday in beautiful, sunny hilltops around the Mediterranean ... I'd say the South of France or ... er ... perhaps Spain or northern Majorca, p'haps the hills round Tuscany. Beautiful, beautiful countryside, walking, drinking, sleeping, lovely ...

V2: I like contrasts so, I love sailing and being completely isolated, just the wind blowing and the sea and the colours of the sky, and then arriving somewhere in the evening and having all the bustle and joining in with people and then being able to get away from them again so you can relax in two different environments ...

V3: I go to my friend's cabin in northern Vermont, near the Canadian border, park the car, walk about 5 miles in – nearest civilisation is a little country store with a wood stove – storekeeper with a check shirt, and you have to really go out of your way to see people ...

Key

2

	Type of holiday	Reasons
Speaker 1	walking holiday	beautiful countryside, walking, drinking, sleeping
Speaker 2	sailing holiday	relaxing in contrasting environments
Speaker 3	cabin in the countryside	being away from other people and from civilisation

Reading

> **Aim**
> To practise identifying different text-types and their functions.
> To revise and extend knowledge of adjectives.

1–2 Set a time limit of about 1½ minutes to make sure students read the short texts quickly and superficially when doing these exercises. Follow up with a brief discussion of the clues they used to decide their answers, e.g. content, layout, style.

3 Students can take more time to read the texts for this exercise.

Key

1 A travel guidebook
    B holiday postcard
    C modern novel
    D advertising brochure

2 1 C   2 A   3 B   4 C   5 D   6 D

3 B interesting, lovely
    C warm, velvety, beautiful
    D irresistible, exotic, familiar, luxurious, unpretentious, palm-fringed, lush, scenic, superb, tranquil, undeveloped, bright, delightful, special, world-class, exciting

Grammar analysis: the present simple and continuous tenses

> **Aims**
> To revise and analyse the use of the present simple and present continuous tenses.
> To practise using the present simple and present continuous tenses.

1–2 You may wish to begin by reviewing with students very briefly the forms of the present simple and present continuous tenses, especially if it is some time since they did any formal grammar work or used the formal terms for the tenses. This will ensure there is no confusion about which verbs to underline in the extract. For example, ask them to find the first use of the two tenses in the extract from the novel (present continuous – *is wearing out*, and present simple – *enter*). Check quickly how they form the verbs for all the persons. For the present simple, make sure they remember the third person singular '–s'.

NB The present continuous is also sometimes referred to as the present progressive.

3 Discuss the examples with students. They are based on the novel extract in activity 1.

Some students may ask about the difference between *What do you think?* and *What are you thinking?* If necessary, point out briefly that there are a number of verbs which appear more often in a present simple than a present continuous form. These are known as the 'stative' verbs and usually express a <u>state of affairs</u> rather than <u>a dynamic action</u>. They include verbs of 'being' or 'having', e.g. *What do you think? You have a one in six chance …* Such verbs can appear in a continuous form, in which case they indicate that a state is only temporary or incomplete, e.g. *What are you thinking about (right now)? He's having his injection at the moment but he'll be back shortly.* Reassure students that there will be intensive practice of the present simple for stative verbs in Section A of Unit 3 (page 42). You may also wish to remind students that both the present simple and the present continuous can be used to refer to the future: *The plane leaves on Tuesday; I'm seeing her after school tomorrow.* Attention is given to this in Section B of Unit 13 (page 174).

4 Point out that adverbs and adverbial phrases can often give a strong clue about which tense to use, *at the moment, currently* (indicate present continuous); *normally, always, often* (indicate present simple).

5 Check the students' example sentences if possible.

Key

1 is wearing out, are being damaged, enter, are eroding, bring, are rotting, is killing/causing, is, have, swim, are, is, is, aren't enjoying themselves, go, are engaging in, 's, 's

2 The present simple tense is generally concerned with the characteristic or permanent nature of things. The present continuous tense is generally concerned with present instances rather than general characteristics.

4   1   present continuous (b)
     2   present continuous (c)
     3   present simple (d)
     4   present simple (c)
     5   present continuous (a)
     6   present simple (b)
     7   present continuous (d)
     8   present simple (a)

✳ Speaking: describing a situation

> **Aim**
> **To practise describing a situation in the past and the present.**

Encourage students to practise using the present simple and present continuous tenses in their descriptions.

Ways of learning: choosing and using a grammar book

> **Aim**
> **To develop students' confidence in choosing and using a grammar book.**

1–2 These activities could be done individually, in pairs or groups, or as a whole class. They could also be set for homework, and the findings discussed in a later lesson. During the course try to give students access to a selection of different grammar books and make use of them from time to time to compare explanations or collect examples. Some recommended titles are:

Collins Cobuild English Grammar (Collins)
English Grammar in Use (CUP)
Oxford Practice Grammar (OUP)
Heinemann English Grammar (Heinemann)
Longman English Grammar (and accompanying Exercises) (Longman)

Vocabulary summary

> **Aim**
> **To revise the main vocabulary fields of the unit.**

1–2 Set in class or for homework. You could combine individual efforts into a wall display for the whole class.

C

Paper 2 (Writing): Section A

Aims
To familiarise students with the content and format of CAE Paper 2 (Writing), Section A.
To encourage students to organise their preparation for writing.
To encourage students to consider their reason(s) for writing.
To encourage students to select information relevant to their writing purpose.
To encourage students to consider their audience.
To raise awareness of the need to choose an appropriate tone and style.
To help students to structure content logically and coherently.
To practise a Paper 2 (Writing) Section A task.

Introduction

1 This activity is to help students focus on what is important for them to remember about this task.

Key
1 Produce one or more pieces of writing
approximately 250 words
response to a substantial reading input
Presentation, register and style should be appropriate
tasks ... set within a context
purpose and intended audience ... made clear

How do I begin?

There is no 'correct' order of steps, but some steps may fit more logically before or after others. Encourage students to think about what they already do when producing a piece of writing in their own language.

Key
Possible answer:
1 read the input to identify the relevant information
2 decide on the reason for writing
3 identify the audience you're writing for
4 organise the information in an appropriate way
5 choose an appropriate style and tone
6 produce the final piece of writing

What information is relevant?

Point out to students that their first task is to identify the issue or problem which is being raised. Once they have done this, their task is to search for any information which could help to address the issue or solve the problem.

Key
1 flying
2 possibility of choosing smoking/non-smoking seats if desired
papers, magazines, blankets and other useful items usually available on board
cabin crew always ready to help
good idea to drink plenty during flight to prevent dehydration (preferably non-alcoholic)
yawning/swallowing helps reduce discomfort during climb/descent
don't remove tight-fitting shoes

What is my reason for writing?

Remind students that there will often be more than one reason for writing. If they can clearly identify their reason(s) for writing at the start, then it becomes easier to check at the end whether they have achieved their aims.

Key
to reassure, to give advice

Who am I writing for?

It is not possible to be certain of these details, but explain to students that their writing may be more convincing if they build a mental picture of the person(s) to whom they are writing.

Key
Possible answers:
Sex: female?
Age: 60+?
Occupation: retired?
Other information: slightly anxious?

How should I organise the information?

1–2 Make sure students check back over the information they collected earlier in this section. Show them how the different points may be grouped, e.g. advice on smoking/non-smoking, advice on comfort, reassurance about airline staff/facilities. Encourage them to add their own additional advice/ideas if relevant.

What style and tone should I use for the reply letter?

Remind students that choosing an inappropriate style and/or tone can have a negative effect on a reader. Written in the wrong style or tone, their letter could upset/anger/amuse a reader so that it fails to achieve its intended goal.

Key
neutral, reassuring

Exam practice

You could ask students to do this exercise as a timed class activity or to do it for homework. Remind them to make good use of all the preparation work they have done.

Key
An adequate letter of reply would probably include the following:
- thanks for the letter
- reference to taxi rank/car rental
- reference to shuttle buses to airport hotels – Gerda may be staying there?
- location of railway station and details of access to it
- regularity of trains to Amsterdam Central Station
- expression of hope for good journey and pleasure at meeting again

Three

A

Family matters

Starter activities

> **Aim**
> **To start students thinking about the topic of family relationships.**

1 Encourage students to use their imagination and past experience as children to build a story based on the pictures.

2 *Squabble* is another word for *quarrel* or *argue*. People, and especially children, often squabble over/about trivial or unimportant matters.

Listening

> **Aims**
> **To practise listening for detail.**
> **To practise identifying speakers' opinions or feelings.**
> **To practise short conversational phrases.**

✱ 1 Before playing the extract, give students enough time to read the gapped text about Dave and Celia so they know what to listen for. You could speculate with them on the sorts of details or opinions they might hear.

2–3 Work through two or three examples with students before asking them to write down, mark, and practise aloud the remaining phrases.

4 Remind students that the phrases in activities 2 and 3 help a conversation run smoothly. Encourage them to practise them in their own conversations with a partner.

Tapescript

Celia: So Dave, um, have you got any brothers or sisters?

Dave: Yeah, I've got a sister.

Celia: One sister, [yeah] and is she older or younger?

Dave: She's four years younger ...

Celia: Right ...

Dave: ... but for a couple of months or something – so, the baby sister.

Celia: Right [laughter] – and do you treat her like the baby sister?

Dave: Well, I suppose I did as a kid, because er [yeah] she was, I used to kind of look after her, you know – but I always used to get in – in trouble; it was always me that got the blame, I think it was because I was older ...

Celia: Yes, yes ...

Dave: ... do you know what I mean?

Celia: I do know what you mean.

Dave: She used to get away with an awful lot.

Celia: Yeah.

Dave: Like she'd hit me [laughter] and it'd be all right because she was, you know, the baby, kind of thing [yes] and if I clumped her back then I was in big trouble which ...

Celia: And did she used to blame you for things that you didn't do, as well, or did she never go quite that far?

Dave: Yeah, well, she kind of did naturally [yeah], I don't think she was scheming about it, she just kind of, you know, the way to get out of trouble was blame big brother [yeah – laughter – yeah]

Celia: And what about when you were a bit older, did you, um, what about like sort of teenage ...

Dave: Teenage [...years?] was the biggest problem actually.

Celia: Was it?

Dave: Yeah.

Celia: Why?

Dave: Well I hit teenage first – so I wasn't interested in a little sister, as you can imagine.

Celia: Right.

Dave: And then when she hit teenage she was really a rebel, much more than I was ...

Celia: Yes

Dave: ... and caused a hell of a lot of trouble, and 'cause I was on my parents' side which was er, you know, 'cause I couldn't believe she was being so naughty ...

Celia: Oh, really!

Dave: Yeah.

Celia: So was there a bit of a split between you?

Dave: Yeah – for a couple of years it was really bad; and in fact that's why I left home ...

Celia: Oh really?

Dave: 'Cause I just couldn't live with my sister any more.

Celia: Oh, no.

Dave: Yeah.

Celia: So and are you back, are you ...?

Dave: And now we're fine, we get on really well 'cause we don't see much of each other ... [right – laughter]

Dave: Have you got any?

Celia: Well I have actually, I've got two sisters; but it's funny the thing you said about like being the oldest and sort of getting blamed ... for ...

Dave: Are you the oldest as well?

Celia: I'm the oldest as well and so I know. I know exactly what you mean.

Dave: Yeah, you have to guard against that if we have children, you know, you have to [yeah] try and think, yeah, I remember it happened so often.

Celia: What it was like – mm.

Dave: My parents were good I'm sure, you know, you can't blame them but ... it's a natural thing.

Celia: Yeah, yeah, absolutely. But um, I mean and I was the same as you, my, I've got two younger sisters and the middle one I was, I think I was very jealous of when she arrived so I used to be horrible to her ...

Dave: Oh, yeah.

Celia: ... most of the time.

Dave: How many years younger is she?

Celia: She's eighteen months younger, so not very much at all.

Dave: Oh, quite close.

Celia: Yeah, and then er, the youngest one, Suzanne, she's five years younger than me and er, we were very close in the first place, but er ...

Dave: Oh, yeah.

Celia: ... but we're all very close now, I think you go through, I think everyone probably goes through that patch, don't they, particularly like sort of – ten onwards, perhaps mid-teens ...

Dave: It's that growing up thing, isn't it?

Celia: ... yeah, exactly.

Dave: Changing, and you know, ...

Celia: ... getting your own personalities together and things ...

Dave: ... yeah.

Key

(2) *younger*

(3) *into trouble/the blame/ blamed*

(4) *teenagers*

(5) *naughty/rebellious/ a rebel*

(6) *parents*

(7) *leave home*

(8) *(very) little*

(9) *(really/very) well/fine*

(10) *oldest/eldest*

(11) *jealous/envious*

(12) *middle sister*

(13) *close*

(14) *younger*

2–3 **expressing agreement** – *yes; yeah; absolutely; mm;* **expressing surprise/shock** – *oh really?; oh, no;*

seeking further information/explanation – *why? and do you? what about ... ? who was there? what?*

checking listener's understanding – *do you know what I mean? you know ... ? you know the kind of thing;* also question tags

confirming understanding – *yeah; right; I know exactly what you mean; I do know what you mean*

Reading

> **Aims**
> **To extend knowledge of idiomatic phrases.**
> **To practise reading for detail.**
> **To practise note-taking.**

1 This activity introduces the topic of the newspaper article – *Sibling Rivalry*. Check that students can pronounce the term correctly.

2 Before reading the text in full, you could try eliciting students' own ideas or experiences relating to avoiding build-up of tension, dealing with conflicts, and punishing bad behaviour. This will help them have a clearer idea of the sorts of things they are looking for. After reading the text, list the suggestions in three columns for all to see. Follow up by discussing students' reactions to the suggested methods.

3 If students have special difficulty with any of these phrases, they could try using the dictionary to help them. Encourage students to practise the phrases by putting them into full sentences. You might like to start a class list of collocations and idioms met during the course. Keep the two halves of a collocation or idiom on separate cards in two bags or boxes, and from time to time ask a student to take a card out of one of the boxes. The rest of the class must try to recall the full phrase.

Key

1 **sibling rivalry** [ˈsɪblɪŋ ˈraɪvəlrɪ].

2 • **organising an outing, going for a walk, all-age activities**

 • **offer of chocolate/trip to the park/send child to grandparent's/friend's/diversionary activities like drinks/alternative activities/encourage children to sort out their problems between them**

 • **send children to separate rooms/withdrawal of treats/child to tidy up room**

3 *fight like cat and dog*   *be at each other's throats*
  retain your sanity   *come up with a solution*
  break the rules   *take it in turns*
  ease tension   *tell someone your side of*
  lose face   *the story*

Grammar analysis: stative verbs

> **Aims**
> To analyse the use of stative verbs.
> To practise using stative verbs.

1–2 Point out that the verbs in activity 1 are all in the simple form, not the continuous. In activity 2 discuss why sentences 1, 3 and 4 are incorrect – i.e. the verbs should be in the simple form as they are in sentences 2 and 5.

3–4 Check the meaning of the listed verbs by asking students to give an example phrase or sentence for each one. Make sure they use the verb in a simple rather than continuous form. Point out that there may be more than one possible answer for some of the gaps.

5 You may want to give students time to think about and write down example sentences before they use them to talk about their own childhood or family relationships. They can talk in pairs or groups.

Key
1 *was, was, had, belonged, don't think, was*

2 1 She *believes* that her parents love her baby brother more than her.
   3 Psychologists *agree* that sibling rivalry is quite normal.
   4 Most parents *love* their children equally.

3 • *see, hear, smell, sound, feel, taste*
  • *want, need, mean, like, wish, hope, forget, think, imagine, love, remember, understand, know*
  • *advise, deny, confess, say, doubt, agree*

4 1 *like/love*
  2 *mean/want/wish*
  3 *confesses/admits*
  4 *believes/thinks*
  5 *advises*

B

Habits and customs

Starter activities

> **Aims**
> To start thinking about the topic of habits and customs.
> To raise awareness of differing cultural views on what is acceptable or unacceptable behaviour.

1– ✱ 2 Encourage students to think carefully about what is actually happening in each cartoon picture before they decide whether they think it is acceptable or unacceptable.

Remind students that some types of behaviour may be acceptable in some circumstances or cultures but not in others. If you have a multicultural group, there may be possible sensitivities, which require students to be respectful of another culture's ways of behaving.

▣ Listening

> **Aim**
> To practise listening for detail.

✱ Before doing the listening activity, ask students if they have ever travelled abroad (or even to a different region within their own country) and been surprised or shocked by habits or customs they found there. You might like to conclude with a brief discussion on how best to deal with these sorts of situations and reactions.

Tapescript
Speaker 1 Er, about 3 years ago I was on a, a tour sort of round Africa and er we, we'd already been to several, er, countries, and um this was the fifth country that we visited; and it soon became very clear that Nigerians have a, a great fondness for making speeches at almost er the drop of a hat; um, you could be just going for a cup of tea with somebody, and somebody would have to make a speech about how nice it was to have you for a cup of tea and then somebody else would get up and say how nice it was for them to have made the speech to welcome you and give you a cup of tea and – and then somebody would get up and say that somebody else would be making a speech later – it's very, it's very, um, it's a great love of sort of um performance and um sort of making a great formality on any, anything how, however casual it was supposed to be, there would be this feeling that it was a very formal event and this is the way it, it is ...

Speaker 2 I'm from Swansea in South Wales, and a couple of years ago I went on a trip, um, around the Greek islands and, er, we ended up on a tiny island called Siphnos; and, um, we stayed in a little village room which was on the back of, a gentleman called Angelos, on the back of his house; and, er, we found out that they were very hospitable and in Greece they have a tradition not only of having, um, a birthday but also a saint's day; and, er, in fact it was the daughter of the house's saint's day while we were there; and, um, what they did was invite us in to, er, their home, and they make a special cake of, er, honey, I think is in it, and almonds, and um also, er, the wife of Angelos, um, she actually produces her own, sort of distils her own wine, um, and er we had a few glasses of this and the home-made cake. So there you not only have, as I say, birthdays but also saints' days as well which they celebrate on completely different ...

Speaker 3 Well my first visit to Britain was when I was fifteen and it was with, with a school exchange, I was staying with a family for three weeks, and, well I used to go to school with this girl, she was my penfriend in these days, and, um, well we took a double-decker bus every day to go to school and I was very surprised when I, on the first day, when I saw these girls wearing school uniforms; well at, at school everything was more or less normal and like in my country, but the very funny thing was that they stayed at the school over lunch and had all these sandwiches and crisps with different flavours, vinegar and salt, and things like that, and this white floppy bread, it was really, it was an experience for me because in my country you can, you go home for lunch, you have cooked lunch because you don't have school in, every, every afternoon, so you can just go home and be, be with your mum who has cooked a fine, very nice lunch for you; so this was something, something very different from what I was used to ...

Key

	Country visited	Habit/custom
Speaker 1	Nigeria	making speeches
Speaker 2	Greece	celebrating saint's day
Speaker 3	Britain	school uniforms/lunches etc.

Reading

> **Aims**
> To practise reading quickly to identify the topic.
> To practise reading for detail.

✱ **1** Before doing the reading activity, you may wish to explain that many British magazines contain a section with letters from readers. These letters often ask for advice on a variety of issues from gardening matters to problems in personal relationships. The four letters in this activity all ask for advice concerning 'good manners'. Set a time limit of about one minute for this activity.

✱ **2–3** Encourage students to look for vocabulary clues to help them with the matching activity.

Key

1	1 a	2 d	3 c	4 b
2	1 C	2 A	3 D	4 B
3	1 d	2 c	3 b	4 a

Grammar reminder: -ing or infinitive?

> **Aims**
> To revise the use of the *ing* form and the infinitive with *to*.
> To practise using the *-ing* form and the infinitive with *to*.

1–2 Encourage students to look out for more example sentences showing how these verbs are used to mean different things according to their form. If possible, keep a class list of such examples so students can add to it as they come across them. You might also like to point out that when it is used for making comparisons, *prefer* is normally followed by the *-ing* form.

Remind students that there are also some common verbs which are always followed by the *-ing* form: *enjoy, mind, dislike, adore, finish, can't help* etc.
e.g. *I don't mind removing my shoes when I visit a Japanese home.*
Do you enjoy learning about a culture different from your own?

Key
1   1 b   2 f   3 d   4 e   5 h   6 a   7 c   8 g

Writing

Aims
To revise phrases used for giving strong and tentative advice.
To practise writing a letter of advice to a friend.

1–2   It is quite difficult to draw a strict line between what is 'strong' and what is 'tentative' advice-giving. The distinction between the two lists below is only a very general one. Remind students that whether advice sounds strong or tentative can also be affected by features like intonation, voice tone etc.

✱ 3   With a monocultural class, the preparation for the letter could be done as a whole class and the writing up done in groups or for homework. In a multicultural class, this activity could lend itself to some interesting discussion about different wedding traditions.

Encourage the students to read the instructions for the task carefully, and to use the phrases practised in activities 1 and 2 when they come to write their letters. They could look back at the guidelines on writing given in Unit 2 Section C (page 36) if they wish.

Key
Possible answers:

Strong advice	Tentative advice
You ought to ...	If I were you I'd ...
You must ...	You could always ...
You'd better ...	Why don't you ... ?
It's best to ...	What about ... ?
	It might be a good idea to ...

Additional possibilities suggested by students might include:

You mustn't/shouldn't ...	You might as well ...
Don't ...	It's not such a good idea to ...
Make sure you ...	How about ... ?
	Try to ...

Ways of learning: talking about grammar and vocabulary

Aim
To familiarise students with commonly used grammatical terms and their meaning.

1–2   You could start by eliciting from students any grammatical terms they are familiar with already, e.g. noun, verb etc. Then ask them to look at the full list in this section and do the activities.

Key
1

1	adjective	7	noun
2	adverb	8	participle
3	conjunction	9	preposition
4	article	10	pronoun
5	infinitive	11	verb
6	modal	12	verbal auxiliary

2

manners – noun	*calmly* – adverb
be – verbal auxiliary	*polite* – adjective
wheeled out – participle	*can* – modal
for – preposition	*or* – conjunction
goes – verb	*it* – pronoun
the – article	*to be* – infinitive

Vocabulary summary

Aims
To revise the main vocabulary fields of the unit.
To practise using grammatical terms.

C

Paper 3 (English in Use): Section A

> **Aims**
> To familiarise students with the content and format of CAE Paper 3 (English in Use), Section A.
> To identify helpful approaches for completing the multiple choice cloze task in Paper 3.
> To practise completing a multiple choice lexical cloze task.
> To identify helpful approaches for completing the open cloze task in Paper 3.
> To practise completing an open structural cloze task.
> To review and consolidate approaches for completing Paper 3 Section A.

Introduction

Encourage students to find key words in this short passage which identify the important information to remember i.e. *two blank-filling exercises, authentic texts, vocabulary focus, multiple choice items, structural focus, 15 blanks, 250 words per text.*

Choosing the best words to complete a text

1–3 These activities introduce some of the thought processes needed when selecting from several options the best word to complete a gap in a text. In activity 2 students should start by drawing on their own knowledge of the meaning of options **A–D**. They can go on to consult a dictionary if they still have difficulty distinguishing between them. Emphasise that, although all four options fit the gap grammatically and are similar in meaning, there is one which fits properly in terms of collocation, meaning within the sentence, and meaning across the text as a whole.

Key
1 They are all nouns in the plural form, and they are all words describing people who watch or see something.

2 'Spectators' are people who watch sporting events.
'Witnesses' are people who report in a law court on what they have seen.
'Observers' are people who watch something and comment on it.
'Audiences' are people who watch or listen to a play, film, opera, concert etc.

3 D

Exam practice 1

This gives students an opportunity to work through a longer text with ten items. Encourage them to use the approaches previously identified and discussed, and to be aware of the ways in which they select the best option as they work through the task.

Key
1	B	6	D
2	A	7	C
3	C	8	D
4	D	9	D
5	A	10	A

Finding the missing words in a text

1–2 These activities encourage students to think about the different approaches which will help them replace missing words in a text. Follow up the activities with a discussion about the occasions during activity 1 when individuals used specific approaches mentioned in activity 2.

Key
1 (1) *as* (2) *in* (3) *more*

Exam practice 2

The text is a continuation of the text used for Exam practice 1.
This is another opportunity to work through a longer text with ten items. Encourage students to use the approaches previously identified and discussed, and to be aware of the ways in which they select the best option as they work through the task.

Key
1
(1) *as*   (6) *this*
(2) *who/that*   (7) *what/all*
(3) *everyone/anyone*   (8) *if*
(4) *what*   (9) *and/or*
(5) *them*   (10) *much*

Ways of learning: strategies for completing gaps in a text

1–2 Activity 1 could be prepared for homework and then followed up by activity 2 in class. Display all or some of the posters for everyone to see. Finish by compiling with students a final version which is photocopied and distributed to everyone for future reference.

Four

A

Health on holiday

Starter activities

> **Aims**
> **To start students thinking about the topic of health on holiday.**
> **To give opportunities for vocabulary learning and revision.**

Your students may have problems with the meaning and stress of the vocabulary. Use their answers to check whether their understanding of the meanings is accurate. It may be helpful to elicit the equivalents of these words in their own language when possible. Point out that words in isolation usually carry only one main stress – this will be practised under Listening below.

1–4 You could do these as individual, pair or group activities, or as a combination. Invite students to ask you for the names of any illnesses or remedies they do not know in English.

4 Your students may have some interesting and/or funny stories to tell one another. Encourage these.

Key
1 **Possible answers:**
   broken arms/legs/limbs, sunburn, sunstroke, skin rashes, stomach bugs (from polluted water), food poisoning (from unfamiliar food), tropical diseases

Listening

> **Aims**
> **To encourage intensive listening.**
> **To build up awareness of word and sentence stress.**
> **To practise word and sentence stress.**

1 These questions are short and need to be reacted to immediately. Warn students what to expect, and encourage them to listen attentively. Let students shout out the answer, rather than selecting one person. This may help students to relax and enjoy the activity. Do the activity a couple of times if you wish.

2 If your students find it hard to imitate the stress pattern, point out that unstressed vowels in English often reduce to schwa /ə/. You could get the students to beat the rhythm of the words out with their hand or foot as they say them. Students may feel more comfortable repeating the words as a group initially.

3–5 Point out that English sentences normally have only one or two words carrying the main stress. Other words carry secondary stress, and others carry no stress at all. Which words carry stress will depend on the focus of the meaning, but they are usually the main content words rather than structural words. Content words usually carry the most meaning. Again, beating out the rhythm of the word or sentence with the hand or foot can help with the pronunciation.

Tapescript
1   1   **To stop mosquitoes biting, would you wear dark colours or cover yourself with cream?**
    2   **What would you do if you got sunstroke?**
    3   **Can you fly if you're pregnant?**
    4   **Would you drink tap water abroad?**
    5   **What would you do if you got food poisoning?**
    6   **Would you need a bandage or some elastoplast if you sprained your ankle?**
    7   **When things start going wrong on holiday – for example: losing your passport, having your passport stolen, sleeping in a noisy hotel etc. etc.,**

you can begin to feel quite stressed. What's the solution to holiday stress?

8 Acute sunburn can be very dangerous. How can it be avoided?

9 How would you manage to pay hospital charges after a skiing accident?

10 What diseases should you have injections against before travelling to some countries?

11 What should you do before going on holiday to a place where there's malaria?

12 Do you think it's worth taking out a health or accident insurance before going on holiday?

2 accident, bandage, mosquito, aspirin, chemist, sunburn, insurance, elastoplast, poisoning, injection, medicine, pregnant

3 1 You can buy elastoplast at a chemist or supermarket.
2 Go to see a doctor if you get food poisoning.
3 You need a bandage if you sprain your ankle.
4 You shouldn't go in the sun between 12 and 3 o'clock.
5 Insurance cover can pay for holiday accidents.
6 You can't get injections against malaria.
7 Aspirin isn't much good against travel sickness.

Key

1 There is no one correct answer to these questions.

2 The stress on these words is as follows:

'accident	in'surance
'bandage	e'lastoplast
mos'quito	'poisoning
'aspirin	in'jection
'chemist	'medicine
'sunburn	'pregnant

3 2 doctor, food
3 bandage, sprain, ankle
4 sun, 12, 3 o'clock
5 insurance, cover, holiday, accidents
6 can't, injections, malaria
7 aspirin, good, travel sickness

5 Nouns, adjectives, verbs and adverbs (i.e. content words) tend to be stressed more often than structural words (e.g. articles, prepositions, negatives) because content words play a greater role in communicating meaning. Structural words can sometimes be stressed though, e.g. put it on the cupboard not in it

Grammar reminder: modal verbs expressing obligation and permission

> Aim
> To remind students of the difference in meaning between certain modal verbs.

Your students may well put forward different answers. This is useful as it can lead to discussion of the range of meaning in the answers.

Reading

> Aim
> To practise reading for details.

1 You might write your students' answers to this question on the board, or just write up any vocabulary from their answers that is related to holiday stress. You could do some repetition practice with the vocabulary to practise sounds and word stress.

2 Encourage the students to read the text for detail by following the task instructions. Five minutes should be sufficient reading time.

3 Students could attempt to use their own knowledge first, and then go to the text to check and/or complete their answers.

Key

2 The text mentions the following as possible sources of holiday stress:
• having to deal with problematic relationships in an unknown environment
• holiday preparations
• crowded airports, delayed flights, packed hotels i.e. crowds, queues, delays
• compromising on what you want
• chores
• disappointment with the holiday
• worry about security
• spending lots of time with the same person/people
• difficulty in relaxing
• other people having a better time than you
• taking holidays at the wrong time

3 high blood pressure
family relationships
vicious circle
crowded airports/flights
delayed flights
physical fitness
deeply disappointed
recharge your batteries
tackle problems
high hopes

4 a heart disease, high blood pressure, severe aches and pains (neck and backache)
b cancelling the milk and the newspapers, boarding the family pet, last minute shopping, securing your home from burglars, self-catering, cooking, looking after children, doing chores
c absenteeism, pressure, tense, mini-stresses, a stress factor, strain, over anxious + all the illnesses mentioned

Your thoughts

Encourage students to recount any stressful holidays they have been on. This will prepare them for the following writing activity, and possibly lead to activation of some of the vocabulary of the text.

✱ Writing

> **Aims**
> To extend comprehension of the text (*How to beat holiday stress*).
> To familiarise students with, and give practice in, a CAE Paper 2 (Writing) task: writing a leaflet.

You and your students could bring in some real leaflets before this task. These don't have to be in English. You could then compare the layout and styles of the different leaflets, discussing how they present information and the kind of language they use.

NB Generally speaking, the language contained in leaflets is simple and concise and the tone is often neutral. Information is often presented as a series of independent bullet points or paragraphs with headings. You could show the students the possible answers given in the key. These could be used as a model to follow, a piece of work to criticise, or a check against any work produced.

If possible, why not get the students' leaflets word-processed? They could then be displayed in the classroom and discussed.

Key
Some possible answers:
- Tackle your problems before you go. If you're not getting on with someone, talk it through with them.
- Plan your holiday well in advance and try to get those last minute jobs done early too.
- If you don't like crowds try going on holiday outside the high season, travel mid-week even if it does mean you miss a day or two of holiday, or simply go somewhere quiet.
- If there's work to do round the house on holiday, make sure everyone understands before they go that they have to help out. It's everybody's holiday.
- Don't rely on your holiday to solve all your problems or expect too much of it. What if it's a disappointment?
- Think hard about who you go on holiday with. You may love someone's company in short bursts, but what if it's all the time?
- Just relax and enjoy yourself.

B

Health around the world

Starter activities

> **Aims**
> To draw students into the topic of 'health around the world'.
> To stimulate students to think about regional differences in health, and the reasons for these.

To get students involved in these activities, it might be better for them to do them individually first before moving on to pair, group, or whole class discussion.

Key
1   1   **North America**
    2   **Central America**
    3   **South America**
    4   **Greenland**
    5   **Western Europe**
    6   **Africa**
    7   **Asia**
    8   **Australia**

🔘 Listening

> **Aim**
> To practise listening for detail and taking notes.

Before listening, encourage general discussion about Algeria and the UK with regard to climate, health provision, wealth of country, geographical factors etc.

Tapescript
Man: Yes, talking about illnesses, I'm quite surprised to see that in the U.K., illnesses are very different from those in Algeria ... to some extent. For instance, in the U.K. people seem to suffer from heart disease and [yes] stress, quite a lot [right, right]; whereas in Algeria they seem to er ... suffer from bowel problems more often than in Britain by the sound of it; [hmm] the reason for it being I think erm is diet, is connected with diet; in the way people eat, in Algeria they tend to eat hot, spicy food [peppery things]; peppery things, very hot things; which I can't take myself, but the tendency is to eat hot food, and it seems to result in that.

   If you look at the pace of life in Algeria and in Britain you'd find that this explains quite a bit of the differences in terms of illnesses. Erm, in

Algeria, people, I think, lead a much slower pace, because er life is less hectic [yes], less industrial for a start [yes] erm, and, so they don't tend to get erm this type of illnesses that are related to stress, such as heart attacks.

Woman: Do you get ... what else do you get here? You get quite a bit of cancer.

Man: Cancer? Well, cancer exists there as well; but I think it's more frequent in Britain than it is there. Erm, the reason for it I think is mainly to do with pollution, the levels of pollution that Britain has. It goes again with industry, stress, [yes] ... Algeria is slightly developed in the North, and that's where we record I think, I'm not an expert in the matter, most cancers; whereas the South is pretty healthy. Erm, so there's that kind of illness that is recorded there, but not very frequent; erm, other types of illnesses that people suffer from, especially young children here is asthma [there's a lot of asthma].

There's a lot of asthma; it's on the increase [yes definitely]. Erm, in Algeria it exists also; but it seems to affect the north, the northern strip, the Mediterranean strip of it rather than the South [yes]. The reason for it is that it's damp. It's also the part of Algeria that is developed, so if we're to relate it to [to pollution] to pollution then perhaps there is a little bit of that [yeh]. Whereas the South is, is meant to be erm exempt from asthma.

When it comes to other types of illnesses, like er psychological disturbances, psychiatric related problems erm, it appears to me that in Britain people erm are more mad than in Algeria.

Woman: Really?

Man: It seems to be so; in the sense that less people go to the psychiatrist in Algeria than here. Is it a fashion? Is it a true reflection of a state of society? I'm not sure.

Woman: Are there more psychiatrists here?

Man: Oh, far more psychiatrists here than in Algeria, yes. Yes, and people in Algeria would resort to a psychiatrist almost as a last resort for a ... for mental illnesses. They tend to rely on the family, because the family structure is again very different from that one in Britain.

Woman: Much stronger.

Man: It's much stronger, so the family would tend to support or even hide in some cases their mentally ill, and try to help them within [yeh]; often by ignoring their illness; saying you are normal, therefore behave normally and that's what's expected from you ... seems to work [yeh] seems to work.

But when you move away from these cases or psychological problems, you, you end up, you fall erm into the category of normal medicine, like if you have a broken limb you end up in hospital and you find hundreds of people with broken limbs [yeh], being treated the same way as they would be treated in Britain [right], really. Erm 99% of the cases will be treated the same way as in Britain [the same way]. Yes, perhaps one thing to mention is that people use herbal medicine; or used to use herbal medicine more than in Britain, but I think now Britain uses it quite a lot as well.

Woman: Well it certainly has developed, yes.

Man: It has developed, hasn't it? Yeh, erm, the recipes may differ [mm], people there you know they all seem to have their secret recipes coming down from their granny whatever, but [right] if you analyse them, you'd find that ... that the same ingredients for the same cures come and crop up in the books of herbal medicine [yes] yeh [yeh].

Key

1. a **Algeria – bowel problems, some cancer, some asthma in the North**
   UK – heart disease, stress, cancer, asthma, psychiatric problems
   b **The hot spicy food in Algeria causes the bowel problems. The damp in the north of the country causes asthma. The hectic pace of life in the UK, pollution and possibly fashion are given as causes of its illnesses.**
   c **People in both Algeria and the UK go to hospital and use herbal medicines. Algeria uses psychiatry less than the UK.**

Reading

> **Aims**
> **To practise reading both for gist and for specific information.**
> **To consolidate students' proficiency in using expressions with numbers.**

If you find students are trying to read this article word for word, encourage them to read it just for the purposes given in the tasks. They will need to read selectively and purposefully for the exam.

1 Encourage students to spend no more than 3 minutes reading the text for gist.

2 Students should not spend more than 3–4 minutes on reading for this task. Their answers should be in note form rather than in sentences.

3 Even at this advanced level, students often have problems with numbers. If this exercise shows this is a weak area for your students, do some regular practice on expressions with numbers, e.g. fun 'filler' activities such as 'numbers bingo', maths quizzes, sums competitions etc. There is further practice in Unit 14 (page 182).

Tapescript

3 a third, ninety one percent, four thousand three hundred and sixteen, thirty nine percent, eight out of ten women, ten percent, seven out of ten men, men aged between sixty five and seventy four, forty percent, the year nineteen eighty, two thirds, a half, forty eight percent, thirty two percent, the year two thousand.

Key

1 c

2 1 men

2 men

3 70% men, 80% women

4 more exercise

5 using stairs instead of lifts; walking and cycling instead of taking the car

Speaking: agreeing and disagreeing

> **Aims**
> **To develop and practise fluency.**
> **To revise and/or extend students' use of expressions of agreement and disagreement.**

1 Students should do this activity alone and not discuss their answers until after they have done activity 2.

Key

2 **Some possible answers:**
   agreement: *ok, right, that's right, yeh, I couldn't agree more, I entirely agree*
   disagreement: *that's nonsense, that's not really the case, I don't think so, not really*

Grammar analysis: the definite article

> **Aim**
> **To consolidate understanding and use of the definite article.**

At this level, students still often make mistakes with the definite article, usually through inserting it where it is not required. Often students understand the use of the definite article in English, but force of habit brought about by different uses in their own language allows these mistakes to persist. Use a variety of approaches to give students repeated reminders about the use of the definite article if they are still making mistakes with it.

1 This is an exam practice task as occurs in Paper 3 (English in Use). In the exam this task sometimes focuses on one particular area of language.

Key

1	1 ✓	8 ✓	15 *the*
	2 ✓	9 ✓	16 ✓
	3 ✓	10 ✓	17 *the*
	4 ✓	11 *the*	18 ✓
	5 *the*	12 ✓	19 ✓
	6 ✓	13 ✓	
	7 ✓	14 ✓	

2 (a) *before/previously*   (f) *countries*
   (b) *mentioned/talked about* (g) *the Amazon/etc.*
                                  (h) *the Seine/etc.*
   (c) *specific*   (i) *ranges*
   (d) *in general/generally*   (j) *the*
   (e) *must*

Vocabulary summary

> **Aims**
> **To consolidate and revise vocabulary encountered in the unit.**
> **To encourage students to revise vocabulary.**
> **To provide an entertaining end to the section.**

Remind students that all the words required as answers have occurred in Sections A or B of this unit. Ask students to review the vocabulary in the unit before playing the quiz.

Carry out this activity as a team game. Play one question at a time. The first team to answer correctly gets a point. You then go on to the next question etc.

NB Don't forget to keep a tally of the scores.
You may wish to add in other clues of your own about other words that have cropped up during your study of the unit. Students could also make their own clues in teams for the same or other words.

The quiz questions all begin with *what* plus a letter or letters from the alphabet. This does not mean all the answers will be nouns. It reflects a conventional way of asking questions in this type of quiz. You may want to point this out to your students.

Tapescript
Number 1.
What 'b' do mosquitoes give you?

Number 2.
What nasty 'u.s.' can unwashed fruit or vegetables give you?

And number 3.
What 'h.o.' means you drank too much alcohol?

Next number 4.
What 'b' do you wrap around a sprained ankle?

Number 5.
What 'v' means you're bouncing with health and energy?

Moving on to number 6.
What 'd' means you're down?

And number 7.
What 'i.r.' can help keep mosquitoes away?

Followed by number 8.
What 'm' is a tropical disease?

And number 9.
What 'i' do cautious people take out before going on holiday?

And number 10.
What 'v.c.' means you're tied up in knots?

Moving right along to number 11.
What 'r.y.b.' keeps you going that much longer?

Followed closely by number 12.
What 'b' is a nasty pain in your back?

That brings us to number 13.
What 'l.m.' means you really should have remembered before?

Number 14.
What 'c' means dreary housework?

Followed by number 15.
What 'o.a.' means you're worrying too much?

And number 16.
What 'h.h' means you're very optimistic?

And number 17.
What 'c' is a country's money?

Followed by number 18.
What 's' is a study of behaviour or an overview?

And number 19.
What 'q' is a half of a half?

And finally number 20.
What 'b' is a good thing you get from something?

Key

1	*bites*	11	*recharge your batteries*
2	*upset stomach*	12	*backache*
3	*hangover*	13	*last minute*
4	*bandage*	14	*chores*
5	*vitality*	15	*over-anxious*
6	*depression*	16	*high hopes*
7	*insect repellent*	17	*currency*
8	*malaria*	18	*survey*
9	*insurance*	19	*quarter*
10	*vicious circle*	20	*benefit*

C

Paper 4 (Listening): Sections A and B

> **Aims**
> To provide students with information about the content and purpose of Sections A and B of CAE Paper 4 (Listening).
> To make students aware of strategies they can adopt to improve their listening in exam conditions.
> To give students an opportunity to reflect on what they find easy or difficult about listening in exam conditions.
> To give the teacher the opportunity to boost students' confidence in their ability to handle Paper 4.

Introduction

1 Sections A and B of Paper 4 receive equal weighting when they are marked, and the examiners' reports indicate that candidates don't find Section B any more difficult than Section A. This may be because, even though the extract is only heard once, all key information is generally repeated or paraphrased in some way.

If it is appropriate, remind your students that, although they may often worry about their performance in the listening paper and say they find it difficult, in fact there is nothing in the examiners' reports to suggest that students do poorly or have particular difficulty with listening. What is, of course, frustrating in a recording-based listening exam is that you have no control over, or power of intervention into, what you hear. It may well be this feeling of powerlessness which is at the root of students' worries.

2 This acts as a warm-up to later activities which develop its themes. It aims to ensure that students have understood, assimilated and evaluated the information provided in activity 1.

Tapescript
1 Examination information
Sections A and B of Paper 4

Section A
Section A is a monologue so you only hear one voice. You hear the monologue twice and it lasts approximately two minutes. The monologue may be taken from a range of possible text types; for example it could be an announcement or a radio broadcast, a recorded telephone message, a talk or a lecture. You will be tested on your understanding of details of the text as well as the text as a whole. The types of exam exercise that will be used in this section include note-taking, box ticking, multiple choice etc.

Section B

Section B is essentially a monologue, though you may hear short contributions or prompts from a second speaker. You hear this section just once and like Section A it lasts approximately 2 minutes. It also covers the same range of text types as Section A with the possible addition of conversations. The exam exercises are the same as in Section A.

General information on CAE Paper 4

Timing

You are given time before each section to read it through, and there is a pause after each section. Then at the end of the paper, you are given ten minutes to transfer your answers to an answer sheet.

Writing your answers

You can write your answers in pencil or pen. While you are listening you write your answers on the question paper, then after all the sections of the listening are finished, you transfer your answers from the question paper to the answer sheet. You're given ten minutes transfer time for the whole paper.

Key

1 (1) *voice*
(2) *twice*
(3) *two*
(4) *broadcast*
(5) *lecture*
(6) *details*
(7) *whole*
(8) *ticking*
(9) *prompts*
(10) *second*

(11) *once*
(12) *approximately*
(13) *conversations*
(14) *before*
(15) *pause*
(16) *ten*
(17) *answer sheet*
(18) *paper*
(19) *transfer*
(20) *whole*

Exam practice

Encourage students to think about what strategies they employ, to prepare for the Ways of learning Section.

Tapescript
Section A

You will hear the boy in the photo talking about his illness. As you listen, complete in a few words the information for questions 1–7.

I have haemophilia, which is a hereditary blood clotting disorder. You get bruises inside your body which bleed, but you can't see them. To stop myself having a bleed I inject myself about three times a week. I take bottles of clotting agent to school and, if I need to, I inject myself.

I can usually sort the bleed out before it really starts to hurt. It's a special kind of pain – more than an everyday pain but nowhere near as bad as having broken a leg. It's not too bad when it first starts but, after a couple of hours it can really hurt. I used to have bleeds every week, but now it's only once a fortnight.

I don't mind people knowing about it. I think you should

be open about these things. After all, no-one's perfect, are they? And I can do most sports. Not rugby and football though. I play tennis and I'm in the chess club at school. And last year I went away with my school to Spain and only had one bleed. We did everything: water skiing, canoeing … If you don't go for it, life can be really boring. Some people are born ugly or get spots. You can't change what you have, so you have to live with it. Some people at school call me 'a little bleeder', but I don't mind. Maybe some of them have learning difficulties and don't understand. Haemophilia has made me really positive. I think it's made me more sympathetic and certainly more determined to enjoy life.

When I'm older, I want to play for England in table tennis which I'm good at. I want to be a 'Grand master' at chess too. And I'd like to help to find a cure to haemophilia; even if it's not for me. I want to help the Royal Free Hospital in London in their work on gene therapy.

Now you will hear the piece again. (repeat)

That is the end of Section A.

Section B

You will hear an extract from a radio programme about the voice problems suffered by some famous singers. Listen to the recording and then complete the information for questions 8–14. Listen carefully as you will hear this piece once only.

The radio programme mentions various factors which affect a singer's voice. Tick the correct column, according to whether the programme indicates that each factor is good or bad for the voice.

Presenter: Forget drink and drug abuse. Rock stars now face a new hazard: voice abuse. After last week's announcement that Genesis singer, Phil Collins, might give up touring because live concerts are ruining his voice, doctors are counselling stars about the do's and don'ts of voice care. Here in the studio with us today we have Mr. Paul Phillips. Mr. Phillips is a consultant laryngologist at the Highfield Hospital, London and counts many pop and rock stars among his clients. Mr. Phillips, What advice would you give to singers facing voice problems?

Mr. Phillips: If pop singers have got voice problems they really need to be more selective about where they work, they shouldn't work in smokey atmospheres, and, of course, they shouldn't smoke themselves. They also need to think about resting their voices after a show, for instance, they should rest their voices instead of straining them at parties or chatting to fans. Something else they need to be careful about is medicines; aspirin, for example. Singers should avoid aspirin, it thins the blood, and if a singer coughs this can result in the bruising of the vocal cords.

Presenter: And, is it true that some singers use steroids before concerts to boost their voices when they have voice problems?

Mr. Phillips: Yes, this does happen on occasions. They're

easily available on the Continent; and they're useful if a singer has inflamed vocal chords and has to sing that night. But if they're taken regularly and long term they cause a thinning of the voice muscle. Most pop singers suffer from three things: lack of training, overuse and abuse of the voice, especially when they're young. They have difficult lives; when they go on tour they do a vast numbers of concerts, sing in smoke-laden places, and they go off to the next gig in an air conditioned bus or on a plane. Now both of these have low humidity; and this damages the vocal chords. Then they're expected to do very long tours – three months or so; no opera singer would ever dream of doing a tour that long, and they abuse their voices by forcing them so as to be heard over background noise.

Presenter: So what advice would you give to rock and pop singers?

Mr. Phillips: Warm your voice up before a show, and warm it down after.

Presenter: So, whereas late parties, pill popping and cigarettes used to be de rigueur for pop and rock stars, they're now recommended to warm up their voices before a concert and go straight home to bed with a cup of nice hot cocoa after.

Key

Section A

1 Symptoms: pain, bruises inside the body
2 Medicine: clotting agent
3 How medicine is taken: (by) injection
4 Frequency of illness: once a fortnight
5 Activities not allowed: rugby, football
6 Activities he does/has done: canoeing, water skiing
7 Attitude to illness: positive

Section B

	Good	Bad
8 chatting with fans		✓
9 taking aspirins		✓
10 regularly taking steroids		✓
11 air conditioning		✓
12 low humidity		✓
13 long tours		✓
14 warming your voice down	✓	

Ways of learning: dealing with listening in exams

The CAE Examination Reports analyse candidates' behaviour on these and other sections of Paper 4, and on the other papers as well. They also give advice for candidate preparation for the examination. They are a useful resource for teachers and students, and can be obtained by writing to the Marketing Division of the University of Cambridge Local Examinations Syndicate (UCLES) at the address given on page 5.

Five

A

Animal communication

Starter activities

> **Aim**
> **To start thinking about the topic of animal communication.**

1–2 Begin by eliciting the names of the animals shown in the pictures. Alternatively, write up the six names and ask students to match each one to a picture.

To help students talk about the way animals communicate, remind them of the common use of the gerund: *Whales communicate with one another by ____ ing ...*

Key

1 Grasshoppers rub their back legs together.

   Bees dance to inform the hive where the honey source is.

   Monkeys make a series of sounds and calls.

   Peacocks call and display their tails.

   Whales make a series of calls, clicks etc.

   Rabbits drum their back legs on the ground as a warning.

   Other examples: Fish use colour, snakes/lizards use smell/taste, insects use sound vibration etc.

2 Possible answers:
   to attract a mate
   to recognise other members of the same species
   to warn other members of the same species
   to inform other members of the same species
   to frighten an attacker

Reading

> **Aims**
> **To practise reading both for gist and for detail.**
> **To develop knowledge of collocation and word-building.**

1 Set students a time limit of about $1\frac{1}{2}$ minutes to encourage them to read the text quickly the first time. Remind them that when reading for gist they don't need to read and understand every word. They only need to get a general idea of what the text is about and where different types of information are located within it.

 2–3 Give students more time to read and locate the relevant details. Once again they won't need to read the text in full. They should return to those sections which specifically describe the treatment of Gua, Viki and Washoe.

4 Collocations with *language* could be collected by the group as a whole.

For the table completion, students should start by drawing on their own vocabulary and word-building knowledge. They can refer to dictionaries subsequently if they wish. You could briefly review some of the principles for word-building after the students have done the activity.

Key

1 chimpanzee

2 1 A, B, D, E
   2 D, H
   3 C, F, G

3 1 *sweet*   3 *flower*
   2 *funny*   4 *toothbrush*

4 e.g. *to acquire/teach/learn language*
      language development
      true/sign/human language

Verb	Noun	Adjective
construct	*construction*	*constructive*
acquire	*acquisition*	*acquisitive, acquired*
understand	*understanding*	*understanding/ understandable/ understood*
speak	*speech/speaker*	*spoken*
mean	*meaning*	*meaningful/ meaningless*
communicate	*communication*	*communicative*

Listening

Aims
To practise listening both for gist and for detail.
To practise identifying a speaker's opinion.

1 Tell students not to worry when they first listen about understanding the details of the experiment being described. Instead they should focus on the general results and on the speaker's views.

✱ 2 Give students plenty of time to look at the diagrams showing the two stages of the experiment. Make sure they know what details to listen for. You could end the activity with a discussion about their own reactions to the experiment.

Tapescript

V1: (male, radio host): It's obvious that a number of attempts have been made over the years to try and teach dolphins to speak – can you tell us something more about them ... ?

V2: (female, guest): Well I suppose one of the most interesting experiments with dolphins must be one done by Dr Jarvis Bastian. What he tried to do was to teach a male dolphin called Buzz and a female called Doris to communicate with each other across a barrier. The important thing was that they couldn't actually see each other through this barrier.

V1: So how did he do it exactly?

V2: Well first of all he kept the two dolphins together in the same tank and taught them to press paddles whenever they saw a light. The paddles were fitted to the side of the tank next to each other. If the light flashed on and off several times, then the dolphins were supposed to press the left-hand paddle followed by the right-hand one. If the light was kept steady, on the other hand, then the dolphins were supposed to press the paddles in reverse order – in other words, first the right and then the left. Whenever they responded correctly they were of course rewarded with fish. All right so far ... ?

V1: Sounds terribly complicated ...

V2: I know ... well that was the first stage, and once

they had learned to do that correctly, Dr Bastian moved on to the second stage. In this stage, he separated the dolphins into two tanks. They could still *hear* one another but they couldn't actually *see* each other. The paddles and the light were set up in exactly the same way, except that this time it was only Doris who could see the light indicating which paddle to press first. But in order to get their fish *both* dolphins had to press the levers in the correct order. This meant of course that Doris had to *tell* Buzz which this was – whether it was a flashing light which meant left-hand and then right-hand, or whether it was a steady light which meant the opposite.

V1: So did it work?

V2: Well – amazingly enough, the dolphins achieved a 100% success rate – even over thousands of attempts at the task. It really did seem that dolphins could talk and that Doris was actually communicating new information to her partner through the barrier.

V1: You sound a bit sceptical – er, do you have some doubts about the experiment?

V2: Yes, I think there *was* a problem, and later it became clear that things weren't quite as the researchers had hoped. You see, while the dolphins were still together in the same tank, Doris had developed the habit of making certain sounds when the light was flashing and *different* sounds when it was continuous [ah]. Um, after the dolphins were separated, she continued the habit. And Buzz had, of course, already learnt which of Doris' sounds to associate with which light. So although it's true to say that they were communicating, you can't actually say Doris was "talking creatively" ...

Key

1 a The experiment was successful.
  b The speaker is sceptical about the results.

2 (1) *(the) same/one/(a) single*
  (2) *light*
  (3) *left (hand)*
  (4) *right (hand)*
  (5) *fish*
  (6) *separate/two/different*
  (7) *Doris*
  (8) *Doris*
  (9) *Buzz*
  (10) *fish*

✱ Speaking

Aim
To practise a CAE Paper 5 (Speaking) task.

Go through the instructions with students so they are clear what to do.
Remind them during the activity to:
• **provide their partner with as full and detailed a description as they can.**

- listen carefully to the description their partner gives.
- ask their partner questions if something in the description is confusing or unclear.

Key

1 Student A has the second picture in Student B's set of pictures.

2 Student B has the fifth picture in Student A's set of pictures.

Grammar reminder: prepositions of position/direction/time/manner/purpose

> **Aims**
> To revise the use of prepositions of position, direction, time, manner and purpose.
> To practise using such prepositions.
> To practise a CAE Paper 3 (English in Use) proofreading and text-editing task.

Prepositions are extremely common in English and can often cause difficulties for learners even at quite an advanced level. It may help to remind students of the different concepts which prepositions can be used to express in English. Remind them too that sometimes the same preposition can express more than one concept.

The examples are as follows: **a** position, **b** reason/purpose, **c** direction, **d** manner, and **e** time.

Key

1	*with*	6	*in*
2	*after/in/over*	7	*during/in*
3	*in*	8	*across/along*
4	*during/in/over; to*	9	*as, for*
5	*on*	10	*to, by, on*

B

Reading the signals

Starter activities

> **Aims**
> To start thinking about the topic of body language.
> To activate and extend vocabulary describing attitudes and feelings.
> To practise discussion and negotiation.

1–3 You may like to begin by doing one of the pictures together as an example.

Students may benefit from consulting a dictionary if they have exhausted their own vocabulary knowledge. Activity 2 ✱ is similar to a CAE Paper 5 (Speaking) task involving discussion and negotiation between students. You could extend the activity by discussing which of the adjectives in activity 1 carry a positive/negative connotation.

Key

3 They have a problem with their body language/the way they are standing.

Listening

> **Aim**
> To practise listening for detail.

1 Write up a selection of possible answers from student suggestions and discuss them together.

 2 Before listening to the extract, give students time to read the text then speculate with them on possible answers, especially the forms of words that are likely to fill the gap (e.g. symbol, adjective, adjective + noun). Reassure them that they will only need to write up to three words for each answer.

3 Discuss any differences in definitions and suggested effects of body language.

✱ **4** This is another task of the type found in CAE Paper 5 (Speaking) Phase C. The aim is for students to consider an issue in pairs and to arrive at a conclusion which they can report to others.

Tapescript

It's generally recognised today that one of our most important conversational skills comes not from the tongue, but from the rest of our body. Research over recent years has shown that, in actual fact, more than 70 per cent of our communication is non-verbal;

in other words, a surprisingly large percentage of the way we communicate involves the language of our bodies rather than the language we speak.

"Body language", as it has come to be called, often communicates our feelings and attitudes to people even before we open our mouths; and it gives other people a clear indication of how receptive we are likely to be towards them. Receptive body language normally involves open posture (such as keeping your arms and legs uncrossed), as well as plenty of eye contact, and a friendly smile. Most people with poor conversational skills don't realise that it is their non-receptive body language (closed posture, little eye contact, and no smile) which is often the cause of short conversations that fail to develop into anything more substantial.

Whether we like it or not, people very quickly judge us by the first signals we give; and if the first impressions are not positive and friendly, then I'm afraid it's going to be difficult to develop and maintain a good conversation.

Key

2 (1) *over/more than 70%* (6) *closed posture*
  (2) *feelings* (7) *no smile*
  (3) *attitudes* (8) *short*
  (4) *eye contact* (9) *positive*
  (5) *friendly smile* (10) *friendly*

4 Possible answers:
  put on a friendly smile, adopt a more open posture (uncover mouth, uncross arms), use more eye contact

Reading

Aims
To practise reading for gist.
To practise reading for detail.
To practise note-taking.
To extend vocabulary describing aspects of body language.

1–✱2 Encourage students to read the text quickly, setting a time limit if necessary.

These activities require them to identify the gist of each section of the text, and then to attach a suitable title and illustration to each section.

3 To save time, groups could be asked to focus on an individual section of the text and then report their findings for the benefit of everyone.

4 Using the example given in the grid, explain to students that the information in the text can be rephrased in terms of a more personalised message. They can then write similar messages based on the answers they gave in activity 3.

5 This could also be done by asking different groups to work on different sections of the text and to report back to the class as a whole.

6 You could adopt a team game approach. Set a time limit, and then award one point for each correct collocation identified using the text. The winning team is the one with the most points.

Key

1 A2 B3 C4 D1 E5

2 a5 b3 c1 e2 f4

4

Posture/gesture	Message
smile	'I am keen to communicate'
arms/legs crossed	'I prefer to keep to myself. Please don't talk to me.'
open posture	'I am interested in establishing contact.'
leaning forward	'I am interested in what you are saying. Please keep talking.'
leaning back	'I do not agree with/I am bored by what you are saying.'
warm handshake	'I want to show you that I have an open and friendly attitude towards you.'
nod of the head/eye contact	'I am listening and understand. Please continue.'

5 *phony face*
  open/closed posture
  crossed/uncrossed legs/arms
  thinking pose
  warm/firm handshake
  non-verbal gestures
  direct/natural/forced eye contact
  fixed stare
  aggressive behaviour

6 *strong indication*
  friendly/open/positive attitude
  conversational problems
  conversational/positive/receptive/non-verbal signals
  defensive frame of mind
  outside/first contact
  personal space
  social situations
  first step
  brief periods

  Adjectives collocating with *way* and *manner*:
  habitual, casual, natural, safe, positive, suspicious

Ways of learning: awareness of body language

> **Aim**
> To raise awareness of the role of body language in communication.

Variation according to cultural background

1 In a monocultural class, encourage students to draw on their own experiences of travelling abroad or simply meeting people from different cultures. In a multicultural class, you might like to select several different gestures, e.g. nodding/shaking the head, pointing the finger, shaking hands, kissing etc., and then compare around the class how these are used and what they mean.

2 In a monocultural class, you could ask students to discuss in pairs or groups and then as a whole class what should be the content of such a paragraph. In a multicultural class, you could ask single nationality groups to work together and produce a suitable paragraph. Display the results for everyone to read.

Grammar analysis: substitution

> **Aims**
> To analyse the use of referring words in text (substitution).
> To practise using referring words.

Substitution is one of the most important ways in which we make connections in written or spoken language. It avoids unnecessary repetition and should make comprehension easier. Explain to students that an awareness of how words can be used to refer backwards in a text will be a great help to them in their writing.

Point out to students that if they choose to avoid using *he/she* in 5/1 and use the now commonly accepted *they* instead, then it will be necessary for them to change the verb accordingly, i.e. *is* to *are*.

Key

1 1 a 2 d 3 a

3 a *they* b *his* c *that* d *one, another*

4 a *it, they, she, he, him, them*
   b *his, her, their, theirs, hers, its*
   c *this, that, these, those*
   d *one, such, another, so, some, many, then, there, the*

5 1 *it, he/she/they (are), him/her/them*
   2 *one, they*

6 *this – make connections in language between the things we say*
   they – various ways of doing this
   another – word or phrase
   this – replace or substitute one word or phrase with another

✳ Writing

> **Aim**
> To practise a CAE Paper 2 (Writing) Section B task.

You may wish to do some preparation with students for this task as follows:

1 Ask them to plan a rough outline of the points the speaker might have included in the lecture. They can look back at the Listening and Reading activities for ideas on content.

2 Ask them to make a list of four or five examples of 'good' body language and four or five examples of 'poor' body language. They can then decide which of the 'good/poor' aspects were demonstrated by the imaginary speaker. This could be partly determined by whether they have in mind a specific 'famous personality'.

3 Ask students to write their review, reminding them to include:

- **an explanation of who was speaking, when, where and on what subject**
- **a brief description of the points covered by the speaker**
- **personal impressions of the speaker's conversational skills (good and/or poor)**
- **conclusion about the value of the talk.**

Vocabulary summary

> **Aim**
> To revise the main vocabulary fields of the unit.

✳ **1** This activity practises a multiple choice vocabulary cloze similar to that found in CAE Paper 3 (English in Use) Section A.

2 If possible, encourage students to choose some of the words encountered in this unit.

Key

1
1	D	6	B
2	C	7	C
3	A	8	D
4	D	9	A
5	B	10	B

C

Paper 5 (Speaking): Phase A

Aims
To familiarise students with the content and format
of CAE Paper 5, Phase A.
To practise identifying the types of introduction.
To focus on common phrases used in personal
introductions.
To consider suitable topics for discussion during
introductions.
To focus on strategic phrases which help to maintain
a conversation.
To revise and practise the use of appropriate body
language and conversational techniques for
introducing/being introduced.
To familiarise students with the assessment criteria
for Paper 5, Phase A.
To encourage students to take personal responsibility
for their own language improvement.
To provide guidance on how to maximise performance
in Paper 5.

Introduction

1–3 Encourage students to read the descriptions of
Phase A and make a mental note of any details they
consider important.

Introducing yourself or someone else

1–2 You may prefer to play the first of the extracts
and work through it with the whole class as an example
before playing the other two for students to work on
alone.

3 After focusing on correct stress and intonation,
encourage students to practise using these phrases in
twos and threes with their own and others' names.

4 You may prefer to play the first of the extracts and
work through it with the whole class as an example
before playing the other two for students to work on
alone.

5 You could ask different groups to focus on a
different extract and simply note down the phrases for
their extract. Each person in the group could even focus
on one particular topic within their extract. Collate the
groups' findings for the benefit of the whole class.

Tapescript
1–2   Extract 1
Juliet: Hello, there.
Nick: Hello, yes, um [hi], we've not met, have we?
Juliet: No, [no] no I don't think so, I don't ...
Nick: I'm, I'm Nick.

Juliet: Oh, hello, I'm, I'm Juliet.
Nick: Nice to meet you [yes], um ...

Extract 2
CH: Er, Stephen, here's, er, somebody you should
        meet, this is [oh] Siriol Llewellyn. Siriol, this is
        Stephen Pacey.
SL: Hello.
SP: How do you do.
CH: You're going to be working on the same account.
        All right, I've got to leave you, I've got to find
        some other people. All right.
SP: Fine. I'm sorry, I didn't quite catch your name.
SL: Oh, it's, it's Siriol Llewellyn.

Extract 3
Mike: The street's a bit slippery.
Juliet: Look it's all right, have you got the bottle?
Mike: Yes, I've got it, don't worry.
Juliet: Oh, thank goodness for that, I thought you'd left
        it behind.
Jenny: Juliet!
Juliet: Jenny!
Jenny: Hi.
Juliet: How amazing to see you [hello], good god,
        I haven't seen you for ages!
Jenny: No, are you going to Graham and Barbara's?
Juliet: Yes, look [oh, good], this is my husband Mike.
Jenny: Oh, hello, how do you do?
Mike: Hi.
Juliet: This is Jenny. We were at school together, you
        know, Barbara, the three of us, we were ...

3
V1:   This is ...
V2:   Can I introduce you to ...
V1:   I'd like you to meet ...
V2:   Hello, I'm ...
V1:   My name's ...
V2:   How do you do.
V1:   Pleased to meet you.
V2:   Nice to meet you.

4   Extract 1
Nick: Nice to meet you [yes], um ...
Juliet: ... good party.
Nick: It's, it's great, isn't it [yeah, really nice], who do
        you know here?
Juliet: Er, well, Barbara [oh, right], yes I went to school
        with Barbara [oh, right, well I ...], what about you?
Nick: Well I work with her other half, Graham ...
Juliet: Oh do you, yeah [laughter].
Nick: He's a laugh, isn't he?
Juliet: Yeah, he is. What, what sort of, what sort of work
        do you do?
Nick: We work in an insurance office [oh, do you?], but
        he's, er, he's a rep so he's out a lot [yes] of the
        time and I sort of ...
Juliet: And what, what about you?
Nick: I work in the office all the time [mm], yeah ...
Juliet: Is that, is that interesting work?
Nick: Um, not really, it's not, you know, it's not what
        I've set my life aside to do but [no], it's good for
        now and because I've got a young family [yes] and
        it's quite, it's quite a stable job [mm], I feel quite
        secure, and, er, we live quite close to the office so

it sort of suits me not to be going out and about [yeah] like Graham, but er ... I mean, he's very much sort of a free spirit I think, isn't he?

Extract 2

SL: Oh, it's, it's Siriol Llewellyn.

SP: Llewellyn, presumably that's Welsh, is it?

SL: Yes, that's right, both my names are Welsh.

SP: Oh, right, you don't seem to have a Welsh accent.

SL: I suppose that's what comes of being middle class.

SP: Right. You've, you've lived in London for some time, have you?

SL: No, actually I've just been working for a company in Wales and I've been moved up here, [oh, I] promotion, so that's nice.

SP: I see [mm], how long have you been working for Boodle and Boodle?

SL: Well, um, about three years, before that I was working for Jordan and Mason.

SP: I see [mm], well as you know, I work for Ogilvy and Mather [yes] and, um, we're coming together on this project which should be quite exciting.

SL: Two good companies.

SP: Absolutely, yes [yes].

Extract 3

Juliet: This is Jenny. We were at school together, you know, Barbara, the three of us, we were ...

Mike: Oh, I see, the famous Jenny.

Jenny: That's right, three little maids from school are we (laughter).

Mike: That's right. You were involved in the incident with taking all the knobs off the doors, weren't you?

Jenny: Oh no, you haven't told him about that ...

Juliet: Course I have.

Jenny: ... my reputation goes before me.

Mike: You're infamous.

Juliet: So have you seen Barbara recently?

Jenny: Well, I bumped into her at a station actually [did you?] about three weeks ago and that's how I came to be coming to this.

Juliet: Oh, really, so you haven't been in touch with her really?

Jenny: No, well sort of off and on, you know, Christmas cards and sort of we keep in touch sometimes through mutual friends but, but yes so I thought I'd come along tonight ...

Key

1

	1	2	3
Introducing themselves	✓		
Introducing someone else		✓	✓

2

this is ...	✓
Can I introduce you to ...	
Hello, I'm ...	✓
My name's ...	
How do you do ...	✓
Pleased to meet you ...	
Nice to meet you ...	✓
I'd like you to meet ...	
Here's somebody you should meet ...	✓

4

	1	2	3
Family	✓		
Friends	✓		✓
Background		✓	✓
Work	✓	✓	

5 a oh, do you? oh, right; oh, really? did you? yeah

b yes, that's right; yeah, really nice; fine; absolutely, yes

c I see; oh, right; right

d not really ...; no, actually ... ; no, well ...

e I'm sorry, I didn't quite catch ...

What should my body language be on meeting someone for the first time?

1 Students can look back to Section B of this unit to remind themselves of useful tips if they wish.

2–3 These activities provide useful practice of what actually happens in the CAE Paper 5 test. If possible, encourage students to move themselves, move their chairs, walk in through a door etc. to try and create some of the conditions they will encounter in the test situation.

Key

1 DO: lean forward in an interested manner

maintain direct eye contact some of the time

shake hands warmly

nod your head to indicate understanding/ agreement

DON'T: sit with arms and legs crossed (i.e. closed posture)

cover your mouth/chin with your hand

stare hard at the other person

frown too much

What are the important features of speaking ability?

These are the five main assessment criteria used by the CAE examiners when assessing candidates for Paper 5. Discuss with students what each of them means and which they feel most/least confident about.

Key
1 B   2 D   3 A   4 C   5 E

How can I improve my speaking ability?

1–2   Reassure students that there are many practical steps they can take themselves in order to improve their speaking ability – some ideas are given in the table, and they may have their own ideas to share with the class. Encourage them to listen to each other's spoken language and give praise and constructive criticism where appropriate.

3   The annual CAE Examination Report gives some very useful guidance on student performance across the whole examination. It provides both encouragement and advice, as the extracts relating to Paper 5 demonstrate. Try to make sure you have access to the most recent report. (See page 5 for how to obtain a copy.)

Key

3 Possible answers:

	What I find encouraging	What I should remember
1	Candidates generally appear to work well together.	Ask for clarification or repetition if you don't understand something.
2	Candidates found working in pairs less stressful than a one-to-one interview.	Don't try to over-rehearse or memorise Phase A.
3	Phase A seems to put candidates at their ease.	Try to go beyond small talk and make interesting and original comments on topics raised.

Revision Exam Practice 1

The following activities have been included in the course for two reasons:

- **to provide further practice in the language of the topics of the preceding five units.**
- **to give further exam practice in the tasks that have been featured in Section C of the previous five units.**

All the activities are presented as they would be in the CAE exam.

You may choose to use these activities for homework, for practice in exam-like conditions in class, or simply to work through and discuss in class.

Paper 1 (Reading)

This task is taken from the multiple choice section of the Reading Paper. For information on how to approach this section of Paper 1, see the information and the facsimile questions on pages 26–28 of the Student's Book. The answer sheet for the Reading Paper is reproduced on page 138 of this Teacher's Book.

Allow approximately 20 minutes for this task.

Key

1 D   2 A   3 C   4 B   5 A

Paper 2 (Writing)

This task is taken from Section A of the Writing Paper. For information on how to approach this section of Paper 2, see the information and the facsimile questions on pages 36–38 of the Student's Book.

Allow approximately 1 hour for this task.

Marking guidelines

In assessing a student's written work, try to take account of the official assessment criteria used by CAE examiners. These relate to content (points covered), organisation/cohesion, range of vocabulary and structures, register (formality/informality), accuracy, and the effect on the target reader. On a rising scale of 1 to 5, give an impression mark based upon a combination of accuracy of language and task achievement. You may also want to mark up errors and add specific comments relating to accuracy, content, style etc.

The following questions may help focus your attention during the marking process:

Has the student thought about the purpose and the audience in terms of choice of appropriate language, style and layout?

The vocabulary and structure used should be relevant to the topic; the style should be appropriate to the target audience and purpose in writing; and the layout should be matched to the instructions.

Has the student succeeded in planning and organising their writing?

Well-planned and organised work leads the reader clearly through from start to finish and achieves its intended objective. Poorly planned and organised written work is usually confusing, exhausting to read and distracts from its purpose.

Has the student done everything the question asks within the specified word limit?

An underlength answer probably means that the task is incomplete in some way and that important elements have been omitted. An overlength answer could mean that irrelevant material has been included which may in turn have a negative effect on the target reader.

Has the student checked for accuracy of grammar, punctuation and spelling?

While occasional errors need not be heavily penalised, persistently poor spelling, grammar or punctuation can have a negative effect on the target reader and may adversely affect the achievement of the task.

Would the writing achieve the required objective?

Give an impression mark based upon a combination of accuracy of language and task achievement. Remember that clarity of handwriting can have an important effect on a target reader, so poor handwriting should be penalised.

Key

The version below is a suggested answer only, but it incorporates most of the elements that should be included.

Dear Sir/Madam

We are writing to complain about a holiday we recently spent at the Pacific Beach Hotel in Hawaii from September 12th–20th. The holiday was organised for us by your company and we had hoped it would be the "holiday of a lifetime"; instead it proved to be an expensive disappointment for a variety of reasons.

We were especially disappointed to discover that the hotel itself did not match the very positive description of it in your brochure. The rooms were described as all being comfortably furnished and having either full or partial views of the sea. In fact, we were unable to see the sea at all from our room! In addition, the air conditioning broke down twice during our stay, making life very uncomfortable in the tropical heat. The local town was described as being "just a short stroll away" but in reality it proved to be more than 30 minutes' walk up a steep hill!

Our holiday plans had included playing a lot of golf and one of our reasons for choosing the Pacific Beach Hotel was the fact that there were several good golf courses in the area within easy reach by car. Our original plans were disrupted as we were unable to hire a car until the third day even though car hire for the whole week had been included in the total price of the holiday. This also made it difficult for us to visit some of the famous sights on the island.

A further problem occurred when one of us was seriously bitten by an insect and tried to seek medical assistance. The hotel would not call a doctor and simply advised us to go to the local clinic in town. This is hardly the service one would expect of a four-star hotel, especially since it is described in your brochure as a "select hotel offering its guests the highest standards of personal care and attention".

We trust you will investigate our various complaints as quickly as possible and that you will be prepared to offer us substantial compensation for all the inconvenience and disappointment we experienced. At the very least, we would hope for some refund of the considerable cost involved in the holiday.

We look forward to hearing from you at the earliest opportunity.
Yours faithfully,

Paper 3 (English in Use)

This task is taken from Section A of the English in Use Paper. For information on how to approach this section of Paper 3, see the information and the facsimile questions on pages 47–49 of the Student's Book. The answer sheet for the English in Use Paper is reproduced on pages 139–141 of this Teacher's Book.

Allow approximately 30 minutes for this task.

Key
1 Multiple choice cloze

1	C	9	A
2	B	10	C
3	D	11	A
4	C	12	D
5	A	13	B
6	B	14	B
7	D	15	A
8	C		

2 Open cloze

16	*few*	24	*their*
17	*these/they*	25	*which/that*
18	*the*	26	*if/when*
19	*in*	27	*it*
20	*has*	28	*who*
21	*other*	29	*what*
22	*for*	30	*or/and*
23	*while/whereas*		

Paper 4 (Listening)

This task is taken from Sections A and B of the Listening Paper. For information on how to approach this section of Paper 4, see the information and the facsimile questions on pages 57–59 of the Student's Book. The answer sheet for the Listening Paper is reproduced on page 142 of this Teacher's Book.

Allow approximately 15 minutes for this task.

Tapescript A
(fade in) Right, nice to see you. Welcome to your first circuit training class. I hope you're going to enjoy it. Have any of you ever done any circuit training before? [no well a bit, but a long time ago]. Right then, well to start I I'll just tell you a bit about what you're going to be doing. Now you'll see round the hall there's all these bits of equipment and things right. Like over there there's some weights and over there are some other kinds of weights. There you've got a step at the back there. There's a weighted ball and in the corner there is just a pole. There's fifteen different activities in all. Some make use of equipment and others don't, and you'll see a notice by each one telling you what each one is OK? Now the idea is that you go round each of the activities and

do them one at a time. Ten of each first time, 15 second time and 20 third time [oh, you must be joking!, ah] Don't worry, I haven't told you the worst yet! You'll be working against the clock and in between each activity you'll all come together in the middle here to do some exercises together.

OK? Hope that doesn't sound too terrible. Has any body got any questions? [no, no] OK right now all of these exercise are designed to develop different muscles in your body to sort of well improve your muscle tone and of course your breathing. When you do the exercise the exercises in the middle, you may find yourselves puffing and panting a lot. You'll be doing stuff like skipping and running on the spot, star jumps, lunges – that's meant to help your breathing and your heart rate. Well you probably won't know what half these exercise are. You've got bicep curls for example, pressups, situps, stomach twists, back extensions. Anyone got any idea what they are? [no, don't tell me no] Oh well well don't worry. I'll give you a demonstration of each before we get going. And I'll be coming round to see if you're on the right tracks.

Now before you start, I'll just have to give you a bit of warning. It's a bit off putting maybe but it's meant at least to be for your own good. We just have to check that you really think you're fit enough to do all this you see. 'Cos exercise is good for you but, if you do the wrong kind, or at the wrong rate, or at the wrong moment, it can actually damage you. It ends up doing you more harm than good. So I'm just going to read a list of things out to you. If any of them is true for you, then you really shouldn't be doing any of this without seeing your doctor or having a word with me, right? So what you've got to watch for is if you've ever had any heart trouble, or any pains in your heart or chest. OK now what about blood pressure and things well? If you've often felt faint or dizzy or you've been told that you had high blood pressure, come and have a word. And watch it if you've ever had an injury, you know broken bones or any kind of joint problem that kind of stuff. If your doctor's told you that exercise can make these worse, then come and have a word with me before we get started.

Right, is that everything? No, hold on. Is anyone here over sixty five? [I feel it] It certainly [feel it] it certainly doesn't look like it? And last of all I just need to ask you if you've been doing any vigorous exercise recently? [no] Vigorous exercise? Right, well that doesn't mean haring around like a maniac or playing squash three times a day. No more like exercise for at least 20 minutes a time on a regular basis. So two or three times a week for two months or more? Even walking to college or work every day at a good pace? Right that means we need to take it slowly at the beginning and build up gradually [that's it]. Right. So you're all fit and healthy? [well, I think so, ah, mm] Good, then let's get started. I'll just show you how to (fade)

Tapescript B

Pat: And now for our regular health spot – the Doctor's Surgery. Doctor Ellie Field is back with us in the studio to help you out with anything you want to know about your health. Any problems you have or your friends or family, just give us a ring if you want to have a word. Remember, the number is 071 336 5730, that's right 071 336 5730. Ellie, it's nice to see you again.

Ellie: Thanks Pat. It's nice to be here and hello to all your listeners, it's good to be back with you too! As usual, I'll be here answering your letters and your calls. There's a pile of letters here waiting for me, so we'll start with them. Now, the first one is from Brian Quinn. That's Brian Quinn from Nottingham. Now Brian, you write that you have been feeling really low of late, low and listless. You say you've got no energy and you seem to be catching all the bugs around: 'flu, coughs and colds, stomach bugs ... You say you've always been very healthy and never had anything wrong with you. You play lots of sport – or at least you used to – and just can't understand what's going on. You say that you've felt like this for about 3 months now, but you haven't been to the doctor because you didn't want to make a fuss or waste his time. And last of all you give your age. You're 24.

Well, Brian. Um you're low and listless whereas you used to be full of go, and you're picking up bugs that have passed you by before. It's well it's hard to judge what might be up with you just from what you've said. What you need to look at first of all, I'd say, is if there have been any changes in your life over the last 3 months or longer even. Have you ever had any changes in diet, for instance? Or has your work been particularly stressful? Have you moved house? Moving house has been shown to be one of the most stressful things you could do, you know. It means pulling up roots and starting all over again and that can be hard and lonely. I don't know if that's the case but, if it is, your health could have suffered for it.

And what about other parts of your emotional life? Er, relationships for example. Have you had to break up with a partner or has anyone else left your life in any way? Lots of people, especially men, tend to think they should be able to cope with anything on the emotional front and even that it's a sign of weakness not to be able to do so. Well, that is definitely not the case. I mean, we're not machines, thank goodness. And and if and if anything goes wrong in our emotional lives, it can have an effect on our health. It's a blow to the whole system. So don't be afraid to admit it if something of that kind is wrong. Now, if there has been some kind of change in your life that has left you feeling low, you could maybe try talking to someone about it. A friend maybe, a counsellor or even me. I'd be pleased to talk about things with you. If you can't think of anything that has changed in your life, it might be worth going to the doctor for a checkup, you know, to get your blood pressure checked, for instance, or to have a few routine tests. Doctors aren't only there to repair broken bones or to get rid of excruciating pains you know. Lots of people go to the doctor when they're simply feeling under the weather as you seem to be. And a doctor will gladly see you with the kinds of symptoms you describe.

Well Brian I I I hope I've been able to give you some help. Do write again, or even ring if you want to talk things over a bit more, or give a few more details. It was good to hear from you and I hope things will soon start to pick up for you. And now Pat I believe we've got a caller on the line(fade).

Key

Section A

1	B	4	D	7	B
2	D	5	B	8	A
3	B	6	D	9	B

Section B

10 *listless*
11 *catching lots of bugs*
12 *he didn't want to make a fuss/waste doctor's time*
13 *good*
14 *work*
15 *relationships*
16 *admit*
17 *discuss (them)*
18 *a check up*
19 *ring Ellie*

Paper 5 (Speaking)

This task is taken from Phase A of the Speaking Paper. For information on how to approach this section of Paper 5, see the information and the facsimile questions on pages 68–70 of the Student's Book.

Marking guidelines

See 'What are the examiners looking for?' on page 133 of the Student's Book.

Instructions

Ask students to work in groups of three: one person to be the 'examiner', one person to take the part of Candidate A, and one person to take the part of Candidate B.

In Task 1 the assumption is that the two students already know one other, so they are asked by the examiner to introduce each other. Task 1 includes some of the questions the examiner is likely to ask. Decide in advance whether it is more appropriate for your students to use the first or second set of questions, depending on whether they are likely to take the examination in Britain or in their own country.

In Task 2 the assumption is that the two students do not know each other, so the examiner asks them to introduce themselves. The continuation will be the same as for Task 1 above.

Encourage students to practise both the Task 1 and Task 2 approaches. For the actual examination they may or may not be paired with someone they know already.

Six

A

Inventions

Starter activities

> **Aims**
> **To start students thinking about the topic of inventions.**
> **To practise a CAE Paper 5 (Speaking) Phase C task.**

1 You may wish to set this in advance of the lesson as a homework project. Students can then use library resources as well as their general knowledge.

✱ **2** This activity practises a Paper 5 (Speaking) task (Phase C). Even if individuals come up with different lists for the five most important 20th century inventions, encourage the pairs to discuss and reach agreement on a final list of five, and then to report their conclusions with some explanation for their choice.

Key
1

Invention	Name of inventor?	Where?	Which century?
telephone	Alexander Graham Bell	USA	19th
parachute	François Blanchard	France	18th
printing press	Johannes Gutenberg	Germany	15th
jet engine	Frank Whittle	GB	20th
microscope	Zacharias Janssen	Netherlands	16th
pendulum clock	Christiaan Huygens	Netherlands	17th

Listening

> **Aims**
> **To practise listening for detail.**
> **To build students' confidence in doing once-only listening tasks (CAE Paper 4 Section B).**

✱ Explain that one of the tasks in CAE Paper 4 (Listening) is a once-only listening task and that this is an example of such a task. Give students time to read the notes in the box, and then check they know what they are listening for. Remind them that they don't need to write very much – just a few words at the most for each answer.

After the task, you may like to replay the tape and point out those occasions when information is repeated within the conversation: e.g. Bell's dates – *1847–1922*; repetition of *States*; double reference to teaching the deaf – *that's what he did too* and *taught deaf children by day*; *telegraph instrument* reinforced by repetition of *instrument* and references to *telegraph project*; repetition of Thomas Watson's name. Point out that even in a once-only listening task, students may actually hear the information they need <u>more</u> than once because it is 'recycled' in a natural way by the speakers.

If 1875 is given as an answer for item (8), then explain that sometimes it is important not to focus in immediately on a possible answer (i.e. the date 1875), but instead to listen out for relationships between different points that are mentioned, i.e. the relationship between *it was 1875, but they had a lot of problems …*, *it wasn't really until the following year that …*, and *that's the officially recorded date*.

Tapescript
V1: (male): 835 7740 – Kevin speaking. [Oh, hi Penny]
V2: (female): Kevin … hi … it's Penny here! Listen, I've managed to do that background research we talked about for our class project [Oh, excellent]. Shall I give you the information so you can add it to what we've already got?

V1: OK ... fine ... let me just get a pen ... right, go ahead ...

V2: OK well, I found out quite a lot about Alexander Graham Bell ... you know we thought he was American ... well he was actually born in Scotland and only moved to North America in 1870 [oh] ... his family went first to Canada and later to the States ... I guess he must've been in his mid-twenties by then ...

V1: Have you got his dates there?

V2: Sorry, oh yes, eighteen forty-seven to nineteen twenty-two.

V1: (Writing) Eighteen forty-seven to ... nineteen ...

V2: ...twenty-two.

V1: OK ... go on.

V2: Well, apparently his father'd been a teacher for the deaf, and when Bell arrived in Boston in the States that's what he did too – he taught deaf children by day and did experiments with electricity at night.

V1: Right.

V2: He had this idea for a new type of telegraph instrument ... you know ... for sending messages. Anyway, he drew up some plans ... took them to an electrical shop in Boston to get the instrument made ... and that's where he met Thomas Watson [oh right]. They became friends and decided to work together on the new telegraph project.

V1: Hang on, hang on ... (writing) ... Thomas Watson.

V2: That's right; it took them several months but eventually they worked out a way of sending speech sounds along an electric wire; and after that they built what I suppose you could say was the first model of a telephone.

V1: So when exactly was this ... we'd better make sure we've got a date when the telephone was invented.

V2: Well by this time it was 1875, but [right] they had a lot of problems with the early version ... so it wasn't really until the following year that the first sentence was actually heard over the telephone – so that's the officially recorded date. Actually, there's an interesting story attached to this ... apparently the two men were working on the instrument ... one in one room and one in another room...when Bell suddenly knocked over a bottle of acid and spilt some on himself. He called for Watson to come and help him and Watson only heard him because of the telephone...at least that's how the story goes...anyway, that was it...they immediately patented the invention and the first telephone line ever was opened between New York and San Francisco in 1915. So will that be OK for the historical bit of the project?

V1: Yeah, I'm sure it will...thanks for doing the work on that section. I've typed up the part on how a telephone works...and I found some really good pictures of telephone designs through the 20th century which we can use...so I'll add this to the introduction and bring in a draft for you to look at tomorrow...OK? We can make any changes then.

V2: Fine. I'll see you tomorrow then...bye (fade out)...

Key

1 1922
2 Scotland
3 USA/America
4 teacher for deaf
5 electricity
6 telegraph instrument
7 Thomas Watson
8 1876
9 San Francisco

Reading

> **Aims**
> To practise reading for gist and for detail.
> To practise making notes on a text.
> To extend knowledge of the formation and use of compound nouns and adjectives.

1 Tell students not to worry about unfamiliar vocabulary in these two short texts. They are simply to look for the type of phone being referred to. (NB "whopper" is an informal word sometimes used to mean a big lie as in "he told me a whopper")

2 To save time, you may prefer to divide the class into two halves: one half reads and makes notes on the videophone, while the other reads and makes notes on the truth phone. Students can then work in pairs (one person from each half of the class). Using their notes they can exchange information they have gathered on the advantages and disadvantages of each type of phone.

3 This activity focuses attention on the formation of compound nouns by looking at examples taken from the texts. Students should be fully familiar with the terms noun, adjective and phrasal verb by now, but you could check just in case. Point out that in many cases both parts of a compound noun are stressed, while in others (especially those derived from phrasal verbs) there is a single, primary stress.

Part 5 focuses attention on the formation of compound adjectives by looking at examples taken from the texts. After looking at the examples, ask students to find 10 more examples and to write a similar explanatory definition for each one. You may like to point out that there seem to be many different ways of creating compound adjectives.

Tapescript

V1:		
satellite links	lie-detector	wrong number
read-out	front door	household appliance
close-up	peephole	videophone
civil rights	ear-pieces	best-sellers

Key
1 truth phone and videophone
2 Truth phone – advantages (A) and disadvantages
 (D)
 – tells the user when someone on the other end of
  the line is lying (A)
 – could be useful for surveillance/counter-
  surveillance in spying (A)
 – could be useful for checking employees' honesty
  (A)
 – could be useful for checking validity of insurance
  claims (A)
 – is very expensive to buy (D)
 – could be an invasion of personal privacy (D)
 – could be misused in the wrong hands (D)
 – depends on very careful procedures for use and on
  correct analysis (D)
 Videophone – advantages (A) and disadvantages (D)
 – you can see who you're speaking to (A)
 – could be a more personal and informative
  means of communication (A)
 – could reveal more than you wish (D)
 – could cause you to become preoccupied with
  how you look before answering (D)
 – could result in embarrassing breakdowns of
  communication (D)
 – conference calls could be hard to handle (D)
 – secretaries may find it harder to disguise the fact
  that their boss doesn't want to take the call (D)
 – not clear what will happen to picture quality on a
  bad line (D)
3 2 (a) satellite links, lie-detector, household
   appliance, peephole, videophone, ear-pieces
   (b) best-sellers, civil rights, front door, wrong
   number
   (c) close-up, read out
 3 'satellite 'links, 'lie-de'tector, 'wrong 'number,
  'read out, 'front 'door, 'household ap'pliance,
  'close-up, 'peephole, 'video'phone, 'civil 'rights,
  'ear-pieces, 'best 'sellers
 4 a 'telephone-'users, 'telephone 'console, 'bench-
   marks, 'modesty 'blind, 'conference 'call
  b 'digital 'reading, 'crossed 'line, 'retail 'outlet,
   'answering ma'chine, 'bottom 'line
 5 a pin-sharp
  b voice-only
  c pull-down
 6 long-awaited, widescreen, tell-tale, real-life, long-
  distance, well-known, would-be, much-vaunted,
  voice-stress, stress-free
 7 adjective + verb
  adjective + noun
  verb + noun
  adverb + verb
  verbal auxiliary + verb
  noun + noun
  noun + adjective

Ways of learning: deducing meaning from context

Aims
To suggest strategies for deducing the meaning of
 words from context.
To build confidence in coping with unfamiliar
 words and phrases.

1–3 Activity 1 presents students with a step-by-step
approach to working out the meaning of an unfamiliar
word using:
1) clues from the text
2) their knowledge of the way English works
3) their knowledge of the world

Reassure them that, even if they don't know a particular
word, they have these three tools to help them deduce
its meaning.

Key
1 a noun
 b red
 c shirt collar
 d married
 e apologising/saying sorry, inquisitive/curious
 f mark/stain
 g lipstick
 h ink

Grammar reminder: order of adjectives

Aims
To revise the ordering of adjectives before a noun.
To practise ordering adjectives.

1–3 You may wish to set this as a group activity,
or as a homework exercise to be followed up in class
later. Remind students that adjectives in a string are
sometimes separated from one another by a comma,
but there is never a comma between the final adjective
and the noun.

Key
2 1 a beautiful seventeenth century French castle
 2 exquisite traditional black lacquer plates
 3 important recent sociological studies
 4 clever new technological approach
 5 expensive new red Italian sports car

✳ Writing

> **Aims**
> To practise writing a short article designed to persuade.
> To practise CAE Paper 2 (Writing) Section B task.

Encourage students to make good use of relevant information from the texts they have read, and to draw on the views expressed during their discussions. Remind them to give careful consideration to their reason for writing and the likely audience. Refer them back to Section C of Unit 2 (page 36) for advice.

B

The art of persuasion

Starter activities

> **Aim**
> To start thinking about the topic of advertising.

1–2 These activities should encourage students to think about and discuss their own views and reactions to advertisements. If you are in a monocultural situation, you may be able to refer directly to contemporary adverts (on TV or in public places) of which everyone is likely to know.

📼 Listening

> **Aims**
> To practise listening for detail.
> To practise a CAE Paper 4 (Listening) Section B task (once-only listening).

✳ As usual, give students time to look at the table and to speculate on the likely content and form of the missing words.

Tapescript

Extract 1

V1: Have you ever actually done a commercial?

V2: I've done, yes I have, um, I've only done one, but it was, it was memorable in as much as, um, it was for um, a sort of yoghurty-custard um snack [right], and er, which was called "Heart", and um, it was um, it was a particularly disgusting product actually; um, but the, the catch for it was that they wanted, I had to dress up in this, in this sort of lion suit and er, I had to sing a song from, er, "The Wizard of Oz", um, the song that the cowardly lion sings [oh, yes, yes] "If I only had a heart" [Bert Lahr sing it] ; yeah, that's right, and um, and not only did I have to er, you know, dance as a lion, sometimes on all fours and sometimes on two legs, but I also had to sing this song; and um, and at the end I had to eat a spoon of this, um, this yoghurty-custardy product; and er, because there was so much um, you know, I had, I had to do so much coordination, very rarely did I actually get it right, um, but each time I had to eat a spoonful of this stuff; and, as the day wore on, I was getting sicker and sicker, and more and more tired, and er, finally, when on the final take I actually managed to get the steps, the dance, the song and the spoon in my mouth all together, and I was so relieved, that, um, I just threw up ... all over ...

V1: What, in front of the camera!

V2: Well, thankfully, you know, the camera had actually stopped running at that point [oh, right], but you know, it was, it was a, it was an embarrassing moment …

V1: I bet it was, yes.

Extract 2

V3: So what was it you were advertising again?

V4: Um, it was a, a skin preparation; um, it was in fact, it was before I was ever an actor or anything and er, my mother knew somebody that was er, worked for this advertising agency and they were looking for somebody with, er, with um, spots which I had at the time; and um, so I was sent up for this interview and er, it's sort of one of those before and after commercials and you know, "oh my confidence has grown since I used this product", I can't remember the name of it; and um, so I got the job because I was, as I say, I was covered in spots, you know the kind of thing, and um, almost sort of the day that they, they rang to say that I'd got it, it seemed that from that moment on they started disappearing; and er, come the day for the filming, I'd got a clear complexion; it was awful, you know, I thought I was going to walk in there and they'd um, they'd just tell me to get out, but um, they sort of they'd done a few of these commercials with other people and apparently it's not uncommon for this sort of thing to happen, and they had somebody standing by with make-up, so in fact they made up a lot of spots on me and um, it suddenly struck me that, you know, they could've used anybody in that case; you don't actually need anyone with, with spots if you've got somebody in the make-up but they made this horrific sort of acne rash on my face and then we did the first bit and then they washed them all off and um, so it was all faked really, when you think about it, it's actually sort of against the advertising code because I didn't actually have a skin condition that was improved by the product …

V3: But I suppose it would have been even worse for them if you had kept the spots and you'd used the product and then they couldn't have done the after if they hadn't cleared up

V4: Well, yes, mm, yeah, that's a, that's another point, isn't it? but …?

Key

	Actor 1	Actor 2
What was the product?	• a snack called Heart	• a skin product/ preparation for spots
Why was the actor chosen?	• acting/singing/ dancing experience	• suffered from spots
What did he/she have to do?	• dress up as a lion • sing and dance • eat a spoonful of the product	• be filmed before and after using the product
Were there any problems in making the advert?	• was very sick at the end of the filming	• spots disappeared before filming so needed to use make-up

Your thoughts

These questions are designed to encourage initial discussion of some of the ethical issues related to advertising and to set the scene for the reading task to follow.

✳ Reading

> **Aims**
> **To practise a CAE Paper 3 (English in Use) Question 5 task.**
> **To promote discussion on the subject of advertising.**
> **To extend vocabulary related to advertising.**
> **To develop awareness of connotation in vocabulary use.**
> **To practise identifying a writer's opinions.**

1 This is similar to a CAE Paper 3 (English in Use) Question 5 task. Students have to insert the correct sentence into each gap in the text. There are more sentences to choose from than there are gaps. Distracting sentences are often taken from later in the same text.

Ask students to read the whole text first. Encourage them to think not just about the meaning of individual words and sentences, but also about the way that the meaning of the text as a whole is constructed sentence by sentence and paragraph by paragraph. Tell them to look out for regular references backwards and forwards throughout the text which make it hang together logically and coherently, e.g. pronouns, contrastive expressions, lexical repetition. Then ask them to select the correct sentence to fill each gap.

Ask students what sort of clues they used to select each sentence. Elicit from them or point out to them specific clues that are in the text:

Item 1: *Its* must refer back to something already mentioned, i.e. *advertising* in the previous sentence; *primary function* sets up the expectation of *but … it also …* in the following sentence.

Item 2: *These images and lifestyles* refers back to *public images* and *lifestyles* mentioned in the two previous sentences.

Item 3: *This means …* must refer back to something previously mentioned, i.e. *they* and *advertising stories*.

Item 4: *But* offers a contrast with something already stated, i.e. *advertisements do not lie* two sentences previously; *they* refers back to *advertisements*; the emphatic use of *do* contrasts with *do not* in the first sentence of the last paragraph.

You may like to explain in a similar way why the distracting sentences would not fit into the gaps.

2–3 Here students review their own views on advertising and then consider them in relation to the views of the writer. Give them plenty of time to read the text carefully and identify the writer's opinions, as well as to change their mind on their own views in the light of what they have read.

4 This is designed to extend students' knowledge of some of the commonly used words and phrases relating to advertising, and to raise awareness concerning the connotation that a word or phrase may carry. Point out to students that although some words tend to carry a fixed positive or negative connotation (e.g. *reliable*, *devious*), the connotation of a word is very often dependent upon its context and on the perspective of the speaker or writer. In this text, particular words and phrases appear to have a positive or negative connotation attached to them partly because of their meaning in relation to the contemporary world of advertising, and partly because of the perspective of the writer.

A better discussion is likely to result in item 3 if students choose and bring in their own advertisements. An alternative approach would be for you to assemble a pile of magazine advertisements in class and ask students to choose one each to describe.

Key

1 (1) B   (2) F   (3) A   (4) D

3

	Writer's view
1 Advertising often promotes a particular lifestyle.	✓
2 Advertising usually distorts the truth.	✗
3 Advertising is incompatible with an environmentally sensitive lifestyle.	✓
4 Advertisements often project an imaginary world.	✓
5 Advertising can't sell anything to anyone unless they really want to buy it.	
6 Advertisements can create dissatisfaction with life as it really is.	✓
7 Advertisements often portray a product as a solution to your problem.	✓
8 Advertising changes people's behaviour.	

4 positive: *reliable, imaginative, green, rural, environmentally/ socially sensitive, carer-sharers, status, style, success*

neutral: *powerful, lifestyle, public, mythical*

negative: *urban, thrusting, self-satisfied, high-consuming, yuppie, escapist, contradictory, money grabbing, fairy tale*

✳ Speaking

> **Aims**
> **To activate some of the vocabulary from the unit.**
> **To practise a CAE Paper 5 (Speaking) Phase B task.**

1 Speaker A will see a picture of a family car with all the luggage unpacked. Speaker B has a picture of the same family car but with all the luggage packed inside.

2 Speaker B will see a picture of a young mother on the telephone. Speaker A has a picture of an old lady on the telephone.

Grammar analysis: cleft sentences

> **Aims**
> **To analyse the structure and use of cleft sentences.**
> **To practise constructing and using cleft sentences.**

1 Explain that cleft sentence structure enables the writer to focus on a particular part of a sentence and the information it contains. If you want to emphasise one noun group and make the whole clause say something about it, you can use the '*It …* 'structure: e.g. *It's people's value systems that advertising affects, not their buying habits.* It is also possible to focus on other clause elements if you wish to: e.g. *It's not people's buying habits that advertising affects, but their value systems.* If you want to focus on an action, you can use the '*What …* 'structure: e.g. *What most advertisements do is project an imaginary world.* Point out to students that *what* may appear not only at the start but also in the middle of the sentence, e.g. *An imaginary world is what most advertisements project.* In this case the focused information moves to the front of the sentence.

2 Work through the example so that students are clear about how the two parts fit together in terms not only of structure but also of meaning.

3 This exercise gives students further practice in manipulating cleft sentence structures. Warn students that there may be more than one cleft sentence structure which can be used to focus on the underlined information (see Key).

You may like to extend this activity by encouraging students to play around with each of the five sentences, and to see how many different cleft sentences they are able to produce by focusing on different parts of the sentence. You could divide the class into five groups and ask each group to work on one sentence.

You could go on to discuss in what context it would be appropriate to use each of the suggested sentence structures. Encourage students to imagine what the focus of a given paragraph might be, or what contrasts are being set up, e.g. what an <u>advertisement offers</u> contrasted with what a <u>product offers</u> etc.

4 This exercise offers practice in selecting a suitable cleft sentence to complete a text. Encourage students to consider carefully the focus that is being set up in each short text and how this might affect their choice. Point out that although both sentences would fit within the text, one is more appropriate than another in terms of emphasis of meaning.

A helpful approach in confirming the focus of a cleft sentence is to formulate a question to which the cleft sentence provides the answer, e.g.

Q: What was dominant in advertising in the 1980s? (i.e. focus on thing)
A: *It was images of successful, high-consuming young executives that were dominant in advertising in the 1980s.*
Q: When were images … dominant in advertising? (i.e. focus on time)
A: *It was in the 1980s that images of successful, high-consuming young executives were dominant in advertising.*

In this way it may be easier to determine which focus is more in line with the development of ideas in the text, and therefore which sentence is more appropriate.

Key

2 1 *What telephone engineers are working on now is a compact version of the videophone for the home.*
   2 *What is clearly going to be needed as a matter of urgency is <u>a videophone equivalent of the answering machine</u>.*
   3 *It's <u>in the business world</u> that the implications of the truth phone could be devastating.*
   4 *It's <u>personal privacy</u> which is an issue as much as anything.*
   5 *What people could be measuring is <u>your emotional response without you knowing</u>.*

3 *Possible approaches to changing structures: Advertisements offer their products as solutions to problems.*
   a) *What advertisements do is <u>offer their products as solutions to problems</u>.*
   b) *What advertisements offer is <u>their products as solutions to problems</u>.*
   c) *<u>Offering their products as solutions to problems</u> is what advertisements do.*
   d) *It's <u>solutions to problems</u> that advertisements offer through their products.*
   e) *It's <u>their products</u> that advertisements offer as solutions to problems.*
   f) *It's <u>advertisements</u> that offer their products as solutions to problems.*

   1 *It's as solutions to problems that advertisements offer their products.*
      What advertisements offer their products as is solutions to problems.
   2 *What market research does is uncover new social trends.*
      Uncovering new social trends is what market research does.
   3 *It's new social trends that market research uncovers.*
      What market research uncovers is new social trends.
   4 *What advertisers do is feed back to us versions of ourselves.*
      Feeding back to us versions of ourselves is what advertisers do.
   5 *It's versions of ourselves that advertisers feed back to us.*
      What advertisers feed back to us is versions of ourselves.
      Versions of ourselves is what advertisers feed back to us.

4 1(b) – *what advertisements for cars speak of* is being contrasted with *what advertisements for (most other) products tell you*

   2(a) – *images of successful, high-consuming young executives* are being contrasted with '*socially and environmentally sensitive images*'.

C

Paper 1 (Reading): Multiple matching

> **Aims**
> To familiarise students with the format of a CAE Paper 1 (Reading) multiple matching task.
> To identify useful techniques for completing a multiple matching reading task.
> To practise a Paper 1 multiple matching task.
> To review different examples of multiple matching activities.

Introduction

Remind students that there are three main formats for the reading tasks in Paper 1: multiple choice, multiple matching, and gap-filling. Multiple choice tasks were considered in Unit 1 and gap-filling tasks will be looked at in Unit 11. Here the focus is on the multiple matching format.

What does a multiple matching exercise look like?

1 Explain that multiple matching involves correctly matching one set of items to another. It could be matching a set of terms to their definitions, or matching a list of headings to their relevant paragraphs, or matching a series of solutions to a set of problems etc. Whatever the type of matching involved, the correct answer must be selected from a number of possible options available, hence the term multiple matching.

Use activity 1 to illustrate the format. Ask students to read the definitions one by one and then select the correct term for each one. Point out that although there are only five definitions, there are in fact eight possible options given to choose from. Some are therefore not used at all.

2 This activity illustrates another multiple matching format – matching headings to paragraphs. Ask students to read the introductory paragraph of the text on contact lenses. Then show them how **D** is the best option to select for paragraph 1 by highlighting the connections between the heading and the text. Ask them to follow a similar approach to identify the best heading for paragraph 2. When students are confident about the sorts of clues to look out for, they can complete the task with the remaining paragraphs.

Key

1 1 A   2 C   3 E   4 D   5 G

2 2 H   3 I   4 A   5 K   6 G   7 F   8 E   9 J

Exam practice

There are three slightly different multiple matching activities within this exam practice task: matching problem to source; matching opinion to speaker; and matching appropriate advice to the general situation. Ask students to make use of the techniques they have been discussing. When they have completed the task, discuss with them which parts they found most difficult and why.

Key

1	B, D	6	B
2	A, B, C, D	7	A
3	G	8	C
4	E	9	E
5	D		

What techniques help you to complete multiple matching reading exercises?

This section explains to students the different sorts of layout for multiple matching exercises which are commonly found in Paper 1. Look at the suggested examples with students and discuss how the layout might affect the order in which they read or process the questions, options, and text. The arrows suggest possible approaches:

- **For 'a' start from the answer options, then move to the text and refer back to the options.**
- **For 'b' start from the questions or statements, then move to the text and refer back to the questions or statements.**
- **For 'c' start from the questions, then move to the text and then refer to the separate answer options, finally checking back against the questions.**

Reassure students that clear instructions are always given at the start of each task. Point out too that very often the texts for this task are quite long and it is not intended that students should read and understand every single word. Instead they should read quite superficially, searching for those parts of the text which are relevant to the questions they have to answer or the task before them.

Reflections

You may find it useful to look at other examples of multiple matching tasks from past CAE papers or practice test books.

Key

1
- matching person to opinion/comment/attitude ✓
- matching paragraph to heading ✓
- matching paragraph/short text to name/content description ✓
- matching specific details to a set
- matching a person/object/event to a factual detail
- matching cause to effect ✓
- matching a problem to a solution ✓
- matching a person/object to an attribute
- matching a text/caption to a picture

Seven

A

What about getting a job?

Starter activities

> **Aims**
> To revise and/or extend vocabulary related to the theme of jobs.
> To start thinking about the topic of getting a job.
> To provide practice in word stress.

1 Ask students to carry out this activity in pairs or small groups to promote discussion.

2 You could use this activity for students to ask you the English for a particular job, including possibly their own.

3 Point out that words with more than two syllables usually carry secondary as well as main stress, particularly when the words are said in isolation. If students have problems pronouncing the weak syllables, you could show them how the weak sound often reduces to /ə/ (schwa). Get them to beat out one beat for each word, making sure the beat falls on the main stressed syllable. Encourage the students to listen carefully to one another's pronunciation, as this will increase their general awareness of stress and the kind of problems they have with it. Encourage them to correct one another as they carry out their pairwork.

4 This could be done in pairs, groups or as a whole class.

Key

1 Possible answers:
  1 solicitor, secretary, draughtsman
  2 librarian, author, translator, interpreter
  3 optician, chemist, speech therapist, pharmacist
  4 engineer
  5 (none)

  6 economist, systems analyst
  7 (none)
  8 architect, advertiser, actor
  9 policeman, dustman, customs officer, shop assistant
  10 barman

3
op'tician	'advertiser	in'terpreter
lib'rarian	'systems 'analyst	'actor
trans'lator	'pharmacist	'draughtsman
'builder	'architect	'sales repre'sentative
'customs 'officer	e'conomist	'barman
engi'neer	'dustman	so'licitor
'author	'speech 'therapist	'chemist
'secretary	po'liceman	'shop a'ssistant

Reading

> **Aims**
> To encourage students' interest in reading fiction so as to increase the amount of general reading they do in English.
> To stimulate students' imagination.
> To encourage extensive reading and reading for specific information.
> To practise the deduction of meaning from context.
> To practise a CAE Paper 3 (English in Use) gapped sentences task.

NB Fictional texts are not used in the CAE exam. However, wide-ranging reading can help students to perform better in Papers 1, 2 and 3, so it is good if students can develop a liking for reading either fiction or non-fiction in English.

1 Point out to students that they are about to read the beginning of a science fiction story. Remind them that *granny* is an informal way of saying *grandmother*. To maintain the humour of the story, don't tell students before they read that Dorcas is a monkey!

You could develop the discussion in various ways, e.g.

• **Is it right for animals to work for humans?**

- **Is it right for humans to train animals to do 'non' animal-like tasks?**

3 Students may well not know the meaning of these words. Encourage them to use the text to find clues to the meaning. They should only use a dictionary to check their answers.

4 Students will probably have listed different sets of words. By pooling their lists they can take advantage of their partners' words. They may have to justify why they think certain words are related to the topic of jobs.

✳ 5 Before students read the last part of the Dorcas story, you may like to ask them to predict the ending. They can then read to check their predictions.

This activity contains a cloze test like the ones students will meet in Paper 3 (English in Use). Encourage students not just to guess the missing words, but to use the clues to meaning and parts of speech in the text both before and after each blank. Students could do this task individually and then compare and discuss their answers with a partner, or do it straightaway in pairs.

Key
2

Employment record form	
Species:	chimp
Name:	Dorcas
Type of work undertaken:	domestic work
Qualifications:	Class A Domestic, plus Nursery duties, reasonable vocabulary,
Training:	trainable, amenable
Personality:	good-natured, conscientious
Competence for job:	strengths: good training, good at all domestic chores
	weaknesses: some annoying habits, a bit slow to learn certain things

3 Possible answers:
1 *snorted* – said abruptly and indignantly
2 *flipped* – turned over a series of pages quickly and for no particular purpose
3 *slurred* – not precise, indistinct
4 *squawked* – spoke in a loud, piercing way (like the noise a parrot makes)
5 *butt* – cigarette end
6 *wear off* – diminish, become less
7 *took her in his stride* – accepted her without fuss
8 *was taken off my hands* – taken away from my responsibilities/no longer my responsibility

4 Possible answers:
servants
trained
domestic work
routine manual labour
uniform
maid
jobs

5 (1) *no*
(2) *door*
(3) *from*
(4) *own*
(5) *so*
(6) *done*
(7) *intended/meant/involved*
(8) *throw/cast*
(9) *being/race*
(10) *only*
(11) *time/effort*
(12) *ever*
(13) *very*
(14) *obvious/clear/evident*
(15) *both*

Your thoughts

If students in your class have full-time or part-time jobs or have worked at all, this could be the opportunity to ask them to describe what they do or have done, and whether they enjoy(ed) it or not.

✳ Writing

> **Aims**
> **To activate language related to the topic of employment.**
> **To provide a conclusion to the Dorcas story.**
> **To practise letter-writing.**
> **To practise writing for a specific purpose to a specified audience in an appropriate register.**

Whether students carry out this task in class or at home, discuss with them beforehand what information to include in the letter, what order the information should go in and what style and register the letter should be written in. The letter should be relatively formal in style, as it is being sent to an unknown agency as a reference. You could also give students some useful expressions to include, e.g.

Thank you for your letter of (date) … or *With reference to your letter of* (date) …

I have known (Dorcas) *for X years* …

As far as her/qualifications/are concerned …

I have no hesitation in recommending Dorcas for …

Grammar reminder: words for linking sentences/clauses

Aim
To revise different ways of expressing contrast, exception, comparison and addition.

Key

1 *contrast:* despite, although, even though, in spite of

exception: apart from, except for

comparison: in relation to, in comparison with

addition: along with, besides, furthermore, apart from

1 *In comparison with/In relation to*
2 *apart from/except for*
3 *Along with/Besides*
4 *Along with/Besides*
5 *in comparison with/in relation to*
6 *Besides/Along with/Apart from*
7 *Despite/In spite of*
8 *Apart from/Except for*

Listening

Aims
To practise listening both for gist and for detail.
To familiarise students with exam-format tasks and texts.
To provoke thought and discussion about what makes a good job.

✱ 2 After this activity you could ask students to compare and justify their answers in pairs before letting them know the correct answers.

Tapescript

Presenter: Six months ago she was just another 17 year old hopeful modelling for teenage magazines. Today Lisa Green can earn £12,000 a day for her skills on the international catwalk, making her one of Britain's highest paid teenagers. But despite being the envy of thousands of schoolgirls, Lisa still longs for quiet days at home with her family in Tooting, South London.

Lisa: Yes, it can be quite lonely. Sometimes I would give up everything to be at home. Don't get me wrong, it's a good job, what what's fashion? It's just clothes. It's not about people dying and people getting Aids.

Presenter: While she enjoys the parties and the champagne lifestyle that come with the job, Lisa deliberately avoids the obsession with image that she sees in some of her rivals.

Lisa: You see, reality for supermodels is not the reality that normal people are used to.

They're rich, they're young and they're totally beautiful. For some people it can become an obsession. I know a few models who take pills for their skin – in fact a lot of models; but then it is your job. What I don't understand is how they can keep going so long. It sounds easy money being a catwalk model, but there are fittings and rehearsals as well as the show itself. I feel so tired. I've never been aware of the girls taking drugs to keep them going – but some probably do to keep up with the day.

Presenter: Lisa had this to say about the pressures on her following her meteoric rise to fame:

Lisa: I don't know about being an up and coming 18 year old. Sometimes this job makes you feel 50. You have to grow up fast doing modelling – it makes you older. You have to book flights, sort out your finances and get wise to people.

Presenter: Another concern of Lisa's is the bitchiness that inevitably accompanies a career on the catwalk. She admits she is still capable of being hurt by it (fade ...)

Keith Walker: There were two reasons why I applied for my first job – money and parental threats. Looking back to those first few days after leaving school my strongest memory is one of the sheer joy of being able to do absolutely nothing every day. I knew it couldn't go on, though, and after a while I started applying for jobs. My first interview was at the BBC where a fearsome personnel officer asked me questions that, to my surprise, I found I was able to answer. Anyway, I was given a six, yes six month contract to work on the night shift at BBC running copy to the presenters, photocopying and delivering cups of tea to those in need.

The two things I learnt were to rely on others' experience when you've got none of your own, and to do what you're told. The vast majority of the time I followed the routine, doing the tasks I'd been set, gradually getting to know the people I worked with and enjoying what I was doing.

Everyone was older than me, and it surprised me at first that it was possible to build up relationships with these people that were totally different from those I'd had with parents or teachers. Outside the BBC building in North London the world was quiet and dark, but inside, there we were, all working for the same end, giggling behind the presenters' backs, arguing and supporting each other like a, well like a large extended family.

I really enjoyed those six months, oh er apart from the times late in the evening when I had to leave my girlfriend and friends with the immortal words 'sorry, I've got to go to work'.

And I still remember the BBC for – of all things, the breakfast. At the end of the night's work I would head for the canteen with my work mates, buy a big breakfast and then we'd sit outside next to the river. We'd just chat and sit in the sun and know that when we left for home and a bit of sleep, everyone else would be just starting their working day. It was a wonderful feeling.

Key

1 (a) Modelling and working on a night shift (delivering copy and drinks).
   (b) They both enjoy(ed) their jobs.

2

	Lisa	Keith
a good salary		
interesting work		✓
good promotion prospects		
a good pension scheme		
acceptable working hours	✓	
good people to work with		✓
a good physical environment		
job security		
status and prestige		
freedom		

When students are discussing in pairs ensure that they both contribute roughly equally. No student should dominate, and people working with shy partners should try to draw out their opinions. This behaviour and language will count in the exam as part of 'interactive communication'.

Key

2 1 It's more important ... It's not so important ...
   2 It's much more important ...
   3 It's so much more important ... It's nothing like so important ... There's no comparison ... It's not half so important ... You just can't compare them ...

✳ **Speaking: ways of comparing**

> **Aims**
> To introduce or extend knowledge of some expressions useful when comparing, and to raise awareness of the differences in meaning between them.
> To build up fluency and appropriate use of language for ranking, a common task in CAE Paper 5 (Speaking).
> To familiarise students with the format of a Paper 5 task.

2 Before students begin the discussion task it may be useful to ask them to put some of these expressions into sentences so you can check that they use them properly.

The discussion work follows exactly the exam format of CAE Paper 5, Phases C and D, i.e. a communicative task, followed by reporting of conclusions, followed by a more abstract discussion. You may want to organise the whole discussion in pairs to practise for the exam.

B

Will I get a job?

✱ Starter activities

> **Aims**
> To prepare students for the topic and content of the reading text.
> To activate vocabulary related to the topic of employment.
> To practise a CAE Paper 5 (Speaking) ranking task.

Make sure students write numbers against each picture. This will help to ensure a committed discussion. This discussion could be done with the class as a whole or in small groups or pairs. If done in pairs it will follow the exam format. If done with the class as a whole it can be used as an opportunity to feed in vocabulary.

Reading

> **Aims**
> To practise reading long semi-serious articles.
> To encourage students to read both for specific information and for gist.
> To practise CAE Paper 1 (Reading) multiple matching and gapped sentence tasks.
> To think about and discuss job success.

1–3 This article may well look long and daunting to students, and they may be tempted to read it word for word trying to decipher the language as they go along. Point out that this will not necessarily help them to do activities 1 and 3, where it is quite possible to find the answers without reading or understanding every word.

1 It could be a good idea to give students a time limit (e.g. 3 minutes) to encourage them to read only for specific information.

▣ 2 This activity encourages students to use one another as a learning resource. If as a group they don't know words, encourage them to look in the text for clues rather than going straight for the dictionary or asking you.

The pronunciation exercise could be done with the whole class repeating together and/or students repeating individually.

✱ 3 This activity provides practice in a multiple matching task of simple design. When this design of task (with only one level of matching) occurs in the CAE exam it tends to be in the first part of Paper 1 (Reading). Encourage students to do this task quickly – even set them a short time limit (e.g. 2 minutes) so as to prompt them to work at gist level.

✱ 4 This is an exam practice task. Gapped sentences occur in CAE Paper 3 (English in Use). The techniques are similar to those that are useful for cloze texts, i.e. looking for clues both before and after the gap, and looking for clues that show both the meaning and part of speech of the missing language. In addition, students can read for gist to identify the general topic of each paragraph, which will help them to see which sentence is likely to go in which paragraph.

Tapescript

2 1. haphazard 2. a correlation 3. to inherit
4. affluent 5. to capitalise 6. plain 7. a peer
8. to rise through the ranks 9. awkward
10. a high-flier 11. to cope 12. a self-help manual
13. to forge your way to the top

Key

1 having wealthy parents
good looks
being tall
being good organisers
getting on with people
having a difficult childhood
going on courses
reading self-help manuals
trying different things when what you've tried hasn't worked
the right attitude and motivation
coping with disaster
leaving school early

2 Possible answers:
haphazard – chance
a correlation – a relationship
to inherit – to receive as an heir
affluent – well-off
to capitalise – to make the most of
plain – ordinary, unremarkable
a peer – someone of the same age
to rise through the ranks – to go up the ladder of positions until you reach the top
awkward – difficult, hard to get on with
a high-flier – an ambitious person who has made it to the top
to cope – to manage in difficult circumstances
a self-help manual – an instructional book that is designed for those learning on their own
to forge your way to the top – to fight your way steadily to success

3 A6   B15   C17   D4, 10
E10   F5   G9   H11, 12

4 1F   2E   3C   4A

Listening

2 This activity is designed to increase students' vocabulary and is not a test. It is therefore not very important for the students to remember whether the words were said or not. What is more important is thinking about and discussing the words and their meaning. You could conduct the activity as a game, with the person or pair who get the most words correct becoming the winners.

Tapescript

Presenter: Richard Price knows from bitter <u>experience</u> how fickle fortune can be. Last June he became the proud owner of a <u>degree</u> which he thought would be the key to a glowing future in broadcasting. Eight months on, he is unemployed and penniless; his only offer of a job in the past few weeks is to sweep the floor of an abattoir.

Richard's story is just one example of the downward spiral that has struck thousands of college leavers. <u>Unemployment</u> among them is suspected to be running at the highest level for nearly a decade; at anything up to 12%.

Jo Morris is another unemployed <u>graduate</u>. She graduated as a landscape architect. Here's her story:

Jo: Like most students I really worked hard for my final university exams, and then I got very drunk. And that was it. It felt as if I'd fallen off a cliff. Suddenly there was nobody to talk to. I was <u>lonely</u> and very isolated. It started to affect my opinion of myself. I could feel my <u>self-esteem</u> and <u>confidence</u> draining out of me.

Presenter: Gary Roberts is also a graduate, this time in international marketing. He's found the alienation of unemployment compounded by relatives and <u>friends</u> who can't understand why anyone with a degree should land <u>on the dole.</u>

Gary: Yeh, it's like having a physically disabled brother or something. People just don't realise how widespread graduate unemployment's become, so as far as they're concerned, I'm a <u>failure.</u>

Presenter: But these college leavers are still nourished by hope: Jo Morris is expecting to start a job soon in her chosen profession of landscaping, and Gary Roberts has kept on filling in <u>application forms</u> even though two of the jobs he was shortlisted for fell through before he got to interview. As for Richard Price, he's been bruised by the whole experience.

Richard: That's right. I just never thought it could backfire. I knew it'd be difficult to land my dream job, but it never occurred to me that I wouldn't be able to find any job at all. Well, I was stunned, to be honest. I've got no regrets though. I'd do it again. Those three years in college really developed my personality. I know I can do it now. I know I can achieve my <u>ambition</u> to be a director. I know I will get there … eventually.

Key
1 1 B, C, D, E   2 B, C, D, E   3 B, C, D, E

Grammar reminder: more words for linking sentences/clauses

Key
1

Reason	Purpose	Result
since	in order to	owing to
seeing as	so that	due to
because	so as to	
because of	in order that	
as	so	

2 b 1   c 3   d 7   e 6   f 4   g 2

Vocabulary summary

Aims
To revise vocabulary from the unit.
To encourage students to carry out vocabulary revision.
To provide some fun through a quiz.
To build awareness of collocation, and practise particular collocations.

1 Encourage students to review the vocabulary of the unit before they begin the quiz. The words in the quiz are no more important than those left out!

The first person to shout out the correct answer gets a point for their team. Don't forget to keep the scores [tallied up] on the board. The teacher or a student can act as referee. After the quiz is finished you could play the questions again and go slowly over the answers. You could write the answers on the board and then at the end do some pronunciation practice.

2 Make sure that students understand what 'collocation' means. If necessary, give some more examples, e.g. *to study hard*, *to pass an exam*, *industrial revolution*, and ask students to suggest some. Even use examples in their own language if this is helpful.

3 In this activity students should write down the names of people these collocations remind them of. It may be, for example, that *cigarette butt* reminds them of a relative who smokes a lot and whose ashtray is always full, or that *instruction manual* reminds them of a friend of theirs who is a computer freak etc. Sometimes a word may not remind them of anybody. In this case they should leave a blank.

The idea behind this activity is that a colourful association for the collocations may help students to remember them better. Be sure to explain all this to the students before you begin the activity to help them understand what on earth you are asking them to do and why!

Tapescript

1   Answer these questions as quickly as you can. We will give you a clue – just a letter – and you must say the word, for example:

What 'l' works in a library? The answer is 'librarian'.

Another example: what 't' means you've learnt how to do what you're doing? The answer is 'training'.

Now for the real quiz; let's begin:

Number 1.
What 'e' designs or makes engines or machines?

Number 2.
What 'd' makes drawings or plans for buildings?

And number 3.
What 's' gives legal advice to customers and barristers?

Followed by number 4.
This 'p' means you're on your way up.

And number 5.
These 'q's' help you get jobs.

And number 6.
This 'p' is a power to impress and influence.

Here comes number 7
Pigs do this 's' and so do some humans when they laugh.

And number 8.
This 's' means you're really not pronouncing clearly.

Followed by number 9.
What 'b.m.o.' means the way you did something?

Here's number 10.
What 'u.t.' means it all depends on you?

How about number 11?
When you are this 'a' you have a lot of money.

Try number 12.
This 'p' is the same age as you.

And number 13.
This 'c' means you can manage.

Followed by number 14.
What 'h.f' means you're rising and near the top?

Number 15.
This 'c' means there's a relation between things.

Followed closely by number 16.
This 'i' comes from your parents usually.

And number 17.
This 's.d.' certainly doesn't help you.

Number 18.
This 'b' means you have no money at all.

Next to last number 19.
You fill in this 'a.f.' to put in for something.

And finally number 20.
You get this 'd' when you complete a university course.

Key

1			
1	*engineer*	11	*affluent*
2	*draughtsman*	12	*a peer*
3	*solicitor*	13	*to cope*
4	*promotion*	14	*a high-flier*
5	*qualifications*	15	*a correlation*
6	*prestige*	16	*inheritance*
7	*to snort*	17	*self-destructive*
8	*to slur*	18	*broke*
9	*by means of*	19	*application form*
10	*up to*	20	*degree*

C

Paper 2 (Writing): Section A

Aims
To give further information on the content of Section A of CAE Paper 2 (Writing).
To raise awareness of strategies and language useful for completing the tasks.

Introduction

This section of Paper 2 (Writing) is designed to imitate real life situations in which people write texts after they have absorbed information from other texts. This is a very common real-world situation, e.g. writing a letter to a language school after you have read its brochure and brochures from other schools; writing a letter of application after you have read the job advertisement and job details; writing a book review for a teacher after you have read the book and a letter from a friend recommending it.

Section A of Paper 2 has various purposes:

*   **It allows candidates to write without having to think up many of their own ideas.**
*   **It allows the examiners to judge how good candidates are at selecting relevant information from source texts.**
*   **It provides an opportunity for the examiners to judge how good students are at handling different levels of formality in language; shaping what they write appropriately for the reader of the text (target audience); laying out texts in a way that is appropriate to their format; and getting their message across succinctly and fully using accurate language.**

When you read the assessment criteria for Section A of Paper 2, you can see that the examiners assess the writing not just in terms of its language accuracy but very much in terms of its communicative power. All the factors mentioned in the paragraph above contribute to giving a text communicative power, and students need to bear all of them in mind.

The CAE examiners' reports indicate that when students do poorly on this question it is normally for the following reasons:

*   **Failure to read the source documents carefully enough and extract from them the relevant information.**
*   **Too much indiscriminate lifting of text from the source documents.**
*   **Failure to structure the writing in a coherent order – possibly due to a lack of solid planning.**
*   **Failure to cover all the points required by the question – possibly due to inadequate reading of the instructions.**

*   **Failure to write in the register appropriate to the target reader and situation.**
*   **Inaccurate and/or limited use of language.**

The guidance you need to give follows closely on from the points above, i.e.

*   **Read the source documents carefully and extract the relevant information.**
*   **Don't lift text inappropriately from the source documents.**
*   **Plan your answer carefully, paying particular attention to the order in which you present information.**
*   **Read the instructions very carefully and make sure you carry all of them out. Each part and every word in the instructions is there for a good reason.**
*   **Ensure that you fully understand why you are writing and who you are writing to, so as to use appropriate language (i.e. formal, informal or neutral) and appropriate layouts for the types of texts concerned (e.g. leaflet, letter, note, report etc.).**
*   **Try to write as accurately as possible, using the full range of language that is appropriate to the task.**
*   **Always check your work for inaccuracies after you have finished it.**
*   **Pay equal attention to information content, appropriacy, and accuracy when writing your answers.**

NB The marks awarded for Section A come to the same total as Section B, so students should be advised not to spend all their time on Section A just because it looks longer. The timing of the paper has been calculated so as to give students enough time to do both sections.

1 Encourage students to remember in particular: the reading input (source documents); the need to select relevant information; the need to organise information carefully, and the need to bear the target audience of the text in mind in order to choose an appropriate style and tone.

2 Make sure that students realise that they don't have to do the tasks (yet). The purpose of this activity is to show that each text is included for particular reasons and contains information vital to the successful completion of the task.

Key

2 Possible answer:
In this task you have to read one or more introductory texts before you write your answer because the texts contain information about why you are writing, who to, what about, why, and in what style.

How to approach Section A tasks

Get students to learn by heart **identify–select–connect** as the three steps essential for carrying out Section A tasks.

Point out that while most of the information students need is to be found in the source texts, they will need to provide some from their imagination.

3–4 These are designed to raise awareness of the features of formal and informal language. Ensure that students realise that these tendencies are indeed tendencies rather than hard and fast rules. Although formal language is generally used in formal situations and informal language in informal situations, much language use is neutral. It is also true that people can use informal language in formal situations and vice versa, as we are not bound to obey speech and social conventions.

Key

1   **Some possible joining words:**
for sequencing: *first, first of all, firstly, then, next, finally, last of all*

for contrasts: *but, however, on the one hand ... on the other, in spite of ...*

for adding information: *and, what's more, in addition, moreover*

3   1   **You normally write informally to friends because you know them well. You write formally to people you don't know or to people in some kind of authority.**

2   **Informal writing gives the impression of friendliness, sometimes of lack of planning and improvisation; formal writing gives an impression of anonymity.**

3   **David's letter**
4   **David's letter**
5   **David's letter**
6   **David's letter**
7   **P. Simmons' letter**
8   **P. Simmons' letter**
9   **David's letter**

The letter from David is informal and the one from P. Simmons is formal.

4

Features of formal language	Features of informal language
longer sentences	shorter sentences
few contracted forms	more contracted forms
precise punctuation	loose punctuation
precise vocabulary	less precise vocabulary
more use of words derived from Latin	more use of Anglo-Saxon based words
more complex grammar in sentences	simple sentence grammar
more anonymous style	more personalised style

Eight

A
Crime and society

Starter activities

> **Aim**
> To start students thinking about the topic of crime and society.

1–2 Make sure students cover the pictures properly after looking at them. The key allows for some flexibility of interpretation about what is happening during the robbery. Students may have differing views on the likely age of the robbers, and on how many robbers were involved. Point out that this can be exactly the sort of confusion the police have to deal with when interviewing witnesses of a crime.

Key
1 1 an off-licence (i.e. a shop where you can buy – but not drink – alcohol)
   2 2 (+1 in the car?)
   3 30s–40s?
   4 dark trousers, anoraks/jackets, hats
   5 woolly hat, baseball cap, earring, stubble
   6 shotgun and bag
   7 8.00 p.m.
   8 car
   9 towards the city

Reading

> **Aims**
> To practise using the title of a text to speculate about its content, so aiding comprehension.
> To extend knowledge of vocabulary relating to criminal justice.
> To practise reading for gist.
> To develop awareness of how referring expressions contribute to text cohesion and coherence.

1 Write up the headline and discuss what clues it provides about the likely content of the text. Point out that by looking at the title of a text before reading it, we can activate a lot of useful information, including relevant background knowledge and related vocabulary. This will help our understanding. Remind students that titles, paragraph headings etc. are all potential aids to comprehension and should not be ignored.

2–✳3 The first activity focuses on some of the more specialised vocabulary in the text. By dealing with its meaning beforehand students will have a firmer base on which to carry out activity 3.

4 These activities are designed to raise awareness of how referring expressions are used in the text. Look first at the example given in part 1 and explain that the writer of the text has probably chosen to refer to the same person in different ways for a number of reasons. Identify the possible reasons with students from the suggestions given in part 2. Then ask them to practise on their own or in pairs in part 3.

Point out to students that a move from first mention of an item to subsequent mention is often reflected by a change of article from *a* to *the*. In addition, an item may be referred to very specifically (*an air pistol*) or in a more general way (*a gun/weapon*). Sometimes it may be appropriate to emphasise different attributes of the same item, e.g. *an 11-year-old <u>boy</u>*, *young <u>cyclist</u> – young <u>victim</u>*.

Key
1   firing an air pistol; the judge

2   1 G   2 H   3 F   4 L   5 D   6 I   7 K
    8 E   9 C   10 M   11 B   12 N   13 J   14 A

3   1 B   2 D   3 B   4 A   5 C

4   1   *a Colwood-area teenager, the accused teenager,*
        the 17-year-old boy, he, her client, the boy

    2   *a Colwood-area teenager – a*

        the accused teenager – d

        the 17-year-old boy – c

        he – b or e

        her client – d

        the boy – b or e

    3   *pellet pistol – a pellet gun, a handgun, a gun, a*
        weapon, an air pistol, the pistol

        an 11-year-old boy – his victim, the young cyclist,
        he, the boy, the young victim, the younger boy,
        him, the victim

        three young males – the group, the boys, the
        teenagers, them

        defence counsel – Dianne McDonald, she,
        McDonald

        a car – the vehicle, the car

Listening

> **Aims**
> **To practise identifying the content of short extracts.**
> **To extend vocabulary relating to crime and**
>   **punishment.**
> **To practise a CAE Paper 4 (Listening) Section D task.**

✳ 1–2   Before playing the extracts, check that students
understand the meaning of each of the crimes and
punishments listed. This will help to activate their
existing vocabulary, and you can carefully introduce
some of the relevant vocabulary from the tapescript to
aid their comprehension, e.g. *beheaded*, *punch* etc.

Tapescript
V1: At Liverpool Crown Court yesterday, two fifteen-
    year-old boys were found guilty of deliberately
    starting a fire. The fire last summer completely
    destroyed a children's playground in a city park and
    caused over 100,000 pounds' worth of damage.
    The boys were each sentenced to 100 hours of
    community service and the judge ordered them
    to help in the reconstruction of the play area.
V2: In Saudi Arabia this week, four Pakistanis were
    beheaded for smuggling drugs into the country. The
    severity of the sentence shows how seriously the
    Saudi Arabian authorities regard the crime of drug-
    trafficking and is intended to act as a strong warning
    to foreigners visiting the country.

V3: In the Philippines, a woman who killed a man with a
    single punch has been jailed for ten years. Jessica
    Arenasa punched Verdandino Redilosa after he
    teased her about her dress as he drank with friends.
V4: The Crown Court yesterday heard how a mother
    became angry when her son's school sent her a form
    to update. The woman, aged 32, attacked a secretary
    and bit a teacher's leg after being told that the
    headmistress could not see her immediately. She was
    given a two-year probation order.
V5: Michael Bassani was convicted at the Suffolk County
    Court this week of being at the wheel of a car while
    under the influence of alcohol and of causing
    criminal damage after he crashed into a telephone
    box in the centre of town. The judge stated that it
    was a miracle no-one had been hurt. Bassani was
    given a £200 fine and his licence was suspended for
    3 months.

Key
1   1 C   2 D   3 A   4 F   5 G

2   6 H   7 B   8 C   9 D   10 E

✳ Speaking

> **Aims**
> **To promote discussion of the relative seriousness of**
>   **different crimes.**
> **To practise a CAE Paper 5 (Speaking) Phase C task.**

1–2   There are no correct answers for activities 1 or 2
(Speaking). The results will depend very much on the
cultural backgrounds and personal views of individuals.

If you have a multicultural group, you may find some
large differences of opinion amongst students as
certain crimes are viewed as being far more serious
in some cultures than in others, and therefore carry
greater penalties.

Grammar reminder: reporting orders/requests/advice

> **Aims**
> **To revise the use of reported orders, requests, advice**
>   **etc.**
> **To practise reporting orders, requests, advice etc.**

Remind students that these reporting verbs do not
always have to take the person or people addressed as
their object, e.g. *he requested silence, she advised*
caution etc.

Key

1 a *ordered/the bank clerks* – 'Put your hands above your heads!'
  b *warned/them* – 'Don't touch the alarm!'
  c *told/the youth* – 'Your behaviour was/has been stupid and dangerous.'

2 2 The judge instructed the jury to disregard the evidence of that witness.
  3 The bank clerk begged the gunman not to shoot.
  4 The thieves commanded the shopkeeper to open the safe and put the money in the bag.
  5 The policeman advised the students to lock their bicycles whenever they left them anywhere.
  6 A/My friend urged me to report the theft to the police.
  7 The court forbade the young man to possess guns, ammunition or explosives for five years.
  8 The detective warned his men not to touch anything until they'd dusted for fingerprints.

B

Crime and the writer

Starter activities

> **Aim**
> **To start students thinking about the topic of crime in fiction.**

2 Ruth Rendell is one of Britain's most famous and popular crime novelists. She has won many awards and several of her novels have been successfully dramatised for British television. She has published some of her novels under her own name and others under her pseudonym, Barbara Vine. If you are in Britain, or in a country where her works appear in translation, you may like to ask students to find out the titles of some of the novels.

3 The term *blurb* is commonly used to describe the summary of contents which you find on the back or inside cover of a book. In the case of a novel, this usually tells you something of the story, and is designed to capture your interest so that you decide to buy and read the book. Discuss with students their own reactions to the blurb for *A Fatal Inversion*.

Reading

> **Aims**
> **To introduce the work of the British crime novelist, Ruth Rendell.**
> **To practise reading for opinion.**
> **To practise reading for detail.**
> **To practise making notes on a text.**
> **To extend knowledge of vocabulary relating to film and TV productions.**

1 Explain to students that the article they are going to read is Ruth Rendell's own account of the way in which *A Fatal Inversion* was dramatised for television.

Encourage them to read the article quickly, ignoring details for the moment and simply looking for Ruth Rendell's views on the success or otherwise of the project.

2 Ask students to read the article again more carefully, and to make notes in answer to the questions.

3 These activities focus on some of the vocabulary in the text which relates to novels, TV/film production etc.

They also deal with aspects of word-building. Before or after asking students to do part 2, you may like to briefly review with them some of the common suffixes used in word-building: e.g. *-ation, -able, -ility, -or, -er, -ive, -ivity, -ing, -ion.*

Key

1 She was very satisfied because the TV adaptation was faithful to the book.

2 1 the young man who came to design her conservatory
  2 her own garden
  3 Ecalpemos – 'someplace' spelled backwards
  4 its contemporary setting, the high level of suspense in the plot, the youth and vitality of the characters
  5 the choice of the house, the furnishings (carpets, curtains, pictures, ornaments), the design of the garden

3 1 a *setting, publication, adapted, plot, story*
    b *the small screen, shooting, cast, acting, performances, actors, video, viewers*
  2 *adaptation – to adapt, adaptable, adaptability, an adaptor*
    production – to produce, a producer, a product, productive, productivity
    setting – to set, a set
    film – to film, filming
    performance – to perform, a performer, performing (arts)
    actor – to act, an act, actress, acting, action, active, activity

Grammar analysis: relative clauses

Aims
To revise and analyse the use of relative clauses (both defining and non-defining).
To practise using relative clauses.

4–5 Point out the difference between a defining relative clause and a non-defining relative clause. The information contained in a defining relative clause is essential in order to distinguish clearly the main clause, as in example **a** where it distinguishes the young actress in question from all other actresses.

A non-defining relative clause (see example **b**) provides supplementary rather than essential information about a main clause and is normally enclosed in commas.

Key

1	first part	relative pronoun	second part
a terrace	*on which*	*there were statues*
the country house	*that*	*had been picked as the setting*

2 *who, whom, which, where, when, that, whose*

3 1 d *whose*
  2 c *where*
  3 e *where*

4 b *when*
5 a *who*

4 1b, 2a and 3a contain defining relative clauses.
  1a, 2b and 3b contain non-defining relative clauses.

Listening

Aims
To practise listening both for detail and for gist.
To practise listening to interpret meaning.
To provide an opportunity to listen for enjoyment.

This short story was originally published in a popular weekly magazine and has been recorded in the style of a short story broadcast for radio. It is divided into five sections. The activities attached to each section are designed to help students progressively understand and respond to what is happening in the story.

Before playing each section, make sure students have time to read and understand what they must do while listening. After listening to a section, check and discuss students' answers, replaying parts of the tape if necessary. Students will probably come up with different suggestions about what is going on in the story, but that does not matter. The important thing is that students are encouraged to set up their various hypotheses and then review them against subsequent sections, all the time making the necessary adjustments to their interpretation of what is happening. Try not to give the story away, even if some students seem to have worked out the twist before the end!

When activities 1–6 have been completed, and all the questions answered and discussed, make sure students have a chance to listen once again to the whole story just for enjoyment.

Tapescript
There it lay – small, black, business-like – on the centre of the table, the red cloth forming a backdrop like some exclusive window display. Light reflected off its shiny smooth contours. The man's fingers caressed the surface, tracing its outline, marvelling at its functional lines and economy of design. He picked it up and balanced it in the palm of his hand, enjoying the feel of it, and the way it adapted comfortably to his grip. The compact object was lighter than he'd expected. He pressed the catch that emptied it and then reloaded once again. This was the first time he'd used one but, now he'd got the hang of it, it seemed relatively simple. He was certainly getting better at each attempt. Satisfied, he finally slipped it into his jacket pocket. It was a snug fit. He patted his coat, confident that it would not be noticeable to anyone unaware of its presence.

(tone)

He began to get cold feet, wondering whether he would

actually have the nerve to go through with it. He'd lost count of the times he had gone over it, visualising the possible snags. He recalled the feeling of inspiration when the idea had first occurred to him, although its audacity had filled him with apprehension. Set in his ways, he was perhaps a little old fashioned – he certainly wasn't cut out for this sort of thing. He would draw attention to himself. Naturally reticent, he'd always shunned the limelight – going out of his way to avoid any kind of fuss or confrontation. But it was rather late in the day to harbour second thoughts now. One thought outweighed the rest, helping him overcome his hesitation. It's now or never, Jim – you won't get another chance. If he didn't grasp the opportunity, he would always regret it. He must think positive. It was quite feasible that he would achieve his objective. And if he didn't? If truth were told, he was past the point of caring. He would at least have the consolation of knowing that he had tried. He fought the bitterness that threatened to overwhelm him. Why on earth should he be placed in this position? Things should never have been allowed to get so out of hand. It didn't seem fair. Life wasn't fair.

(tone)

"Jim, could you pop into the library for me?" Dorothy was slowly coming down the stairs. Quickly he checked the living room for any telltale evidence. He thought it was better that Dorothy didn't know. Her health was failing rapidly and, on top of everything else, their son David's breakdown had been the final blow. She'd already suffered too much. If he pulled it off, she'd know soon enough. He put on his spectacles and studied his face in the mirror above the fireplace. The last eye test he'd had resulted in a prescription change and the thick-rimmed frames had certainly helped to change his appearance a little. As extra insurance, he picked up his cap and pulled it well down over his face. He mentally ticked off his checklist. A growing anger helped to strengthen his resolve – he would do it for Dorothy. It was purely by accident that he had found out what was going on.

(tone)

He arrived early, but quite a large crowd had gathered outside. She was already there. Fortunately, he saw her first and was able to dodge out of sight before she spotted him. The crush of people afforded him plenty of cover. It was essential that she remain ignorant of his presence and what he planned to do, otherwise his careful plan would be jeopardised. He found a seat towards the back, on the end of a row. The interior of the hall was warm and there was a noisy buzz of conversation. His new glasses misted over and he removed them to wipe the lenses. It was essential that he could see as clearly as possible. He patted his pocket, reassured by the shape tucked away inside. A display of colourful pictures on the nearest wall caught his attention and, for a moment, his thoughts started to drift. How he wished things had been different. They could never have foreseen the outcome. She had become totally vindictive, seeming to delight in all the heartache and unhappiness she'd caused. He sighed. It was too late now for regrets ... the damage was done. The lights dimmed. Once the interior was dark, he'd feel safe enough to remove his cap. There was a strong smell of peppermint. A fat woman sat next to him chewing, an open bag of sweets on her huge lap. She glanced at him and looked about to start a conversation. It was no good, that was the last thing he needed. He'd have to move. Turning round, he could see a small group of people standing at the back – they'd obviously arrived too late to get seats. He decided that perhaps it would be better to join them. Standing up would also give him a much better vantage point. Anxious to draw as little attention to himself as possible, he rose quietly and edged his way towards the back. She was clearly visible, seated several rows back from the stage, her dark, wavy hair contrasting with the pale cream collar of her coat. Was she conscious of his gaze? He used to joke that she had eyes in the back of her head. Carefully, he removed the expensive purchase from his jacket pocket. It had cost a lot of money, more than he could really afford, but he considered it worth all the expense. It seemed an ideal solution to the problem. He then checked his line of vision to ensure that nothing was blocking his line of fire and tried to keep his hands as steady as possible. He aimed towards the stage area, his finger tensed.

(tone)

The hall lights went out and the red stage curtains began to open. The moment he was waiting for had arrived. Just for a second he thought he had fluffed it. His hands felt clumsy and wooden, and he nearly dropped it. But then he regained his composure. A feeling of elation swept over him. He could do it. He *would* do it. She was completely off her guard. And now it was too late – there was absolutely nothing she could do to stop him. He pressed the zoom switch on the tiny camcorder and directed it at the brightly lit stage. Pressing the record button on the miniature camera, he focused on his objective. It was a struggle to contain his emotion. The bitterness and frustration were forgotten as the elderly man concentrated on the actions of the children and, in particular, one small boy. The old man's heart swelled with pride. It was Jamie, their beloved grandchild. Their only grandchild. Their estranged grandchild. Dorothy would be thrilled when he showed her the recording. She would be able to see how much Jamie had grown. She'd be so proud, watching his role in the end of term school play ...

Key

2 Possible answers: apprehensive, hesitant, bitter

3 Dorothy – in poor health, has a son, upset by her son's nervous breakdown

   Jim – wears spectacles, has a son, keeps a secret from Dorothy

   1 elderly

   2 husband and wife

6 Jim and Dorothy are an elderly couple whose son has suffered a nervous breakdown probably due to the failure of his marriage. Their estranged daughter-in-law has made it difficult for Jim and Dorothy to stay in contact with their grandson.

✳ Writing

> **Aims**
> To practise writing a review of a book or film.
> To practise a CAE Paper 2 (Writing) Section B task.

As preparation for this task, discuss with students what elements are usually included in a review of a book, film, TV programme etc. Bring in some examples in English or in their own language for them to look at and discuss.

You could ask students to choose their own book or film for review. Alternatively, if you use a class reader system or have access to a school library, you could ask students to select, read and review one of the class readers or library books. The completed reviews could then provide a useful guide for fellow students when selecting a book. Another approach would be to ask students to write a review of a book or film the whole class has agreed to read or see. If possible, display or publish the reviews for the benefit of a wider audience.

Vocabulary summary

> **Aims**
> To revise the main vocabulary fields of this unit.
> To have fun playing a game.

1 This paragraph describes the court system of Britain and many other countries. Discuss any differences students may be aware of between this system and that which operates in their own country.

2 This is a commonly played word game known as 'Hangman'. It can be an enjoyable way of filling a few leftover moments at the end of a class, and is a useful way of reinforcing correct spelling and the pronunciation of the letters of the alphabet. The game can be played in pairs, small groups, or as a whole class.

Key

1
1 *crime*
2 *trial*
3 *jury*
4 *prosecution*
5 *defendant*
6 *defence*
7 *Witnesses*
8 *evidence*
9 *judge*
10 *sentence*

C

Paper 3 (English in Use): Section B

> **Aims**
> To familiarise students with the content and format of CAE Paper 3 Section B.
> To practise identifying and correcting errors in a text.
> To raise awareness of the role of style in the choice of vocabulary and structure.
> To practise choosing stylistically appropriate words and phrases to complete a text.
> To review common spelling and punctuation conventions.
> To practise Paper 3 Section B tasks.

Introduction

Emphasize to students that being able to recognise and correct errors and inappropriacies in written work is a valuable skill:

a) when producing your own written material; or

b) when handling material written by other people.

For this reason, the skills students develop and practise in this section are useful not only in the context of preparing for the CAE examination, but also in general use.

Identifying and correcting errors in a text

1–5 These activities focus on different types of errors found in written text, and on the importance of correct spelling, punctuation and sentence structure. Opinions may vary on how important it is that a text should be error-free. Ask students how they personally feel when they meet errors in a text.

It is probably fair to say that errors of spelling and punctuation rarely interfere with comprehension, but they can nevertheless cause annoyance on the part of a reader and may give an impression of carelessness or ignorance on the part of the writer. Errors which result from disrupted sentence structure, however, can interfere more seriously with comprehension, and can even cause a reader to give up in frustration. The accuracy of a piece of writing may therefore be one factor which contributes to its achieving its intended goal.

Key

1–3

aged 32	→ aged 32,	missing comma
bite	→ bit	wrong form of the verb
sons	→ son's	missing possessive apostrophe
bournemouth	→ Bournemouth	capital letter missing in name
yesteday	→ yesterday	missing letter in a word
two year	→ two-year	missing hyphen

4 Most lines contain an extra word.

5 Unnecessary words: *he, the, did, all, be, when*

Exam practice 1

1–2 Encourage students to use the approaches identified and discussed in previous activities.

After completion of the exercises, discuss with students any difficulties they had and try to identify with them what caused the problem(s). Explain that in this type of exercise they really need to read the text very carefully, almost analytically, in order to spot some types of error. All too often we see what we expect to see, and not necessarily what is printed on the page. As a result we may fail to spot an error (e.g. *yesteday*).

Key

1

1	*their*	4	*chaos. People*	7	*delivered*
2	*thousands*	5	*hit",*	8	*additional*
3	✓	6	*Hatch*	9	*$150,000*

2

1	*the*	5	✓	9	*that*
2	*when*	6	*was*	10	*more*
3	*from*	7	*of*		
4	*which*	8	*at*		

Choosing appropriate words and phrases to use in a text

1–5 These activities focus on the importance of stylistic appropriacy when using vocabulary and structure in written English. They illustrate the way that vocabulary and structure can be used to reflect a degree of greater or lesser formality in what we write.

Activities 4 and 5 highlight the differences between the more informal language of a personal letter to a relative or friend, and the more formal language of a newspaper report intended for a general audience.

Remind students that the degree of formality or informality required in a piece of writing will largely be determined by the reason for writing and by the intended audience.

Key

1 C and A, B and D

2 A a personal letter to a friend – informal
 B a car park notice – formal
 C an official letter – formal
 D a short note to a friend – informal

3

Formal	Informal
immediate settlement	*clear straight away*
account	*bill*
legal proceedings initiated	*take to court*
loss or damage	*pinched or bashed*
cannot accept liability	*college won't want to know*

4 *broken into – burgled*
 got home – arrived home
 found – discovered
 'd smashed – had forced
 got in – gained access to
 cheque book and credit cards – valuables
 £25 in – £25 worth of
 worth – valued at
 couple of rings and a brooch – items of jewellery
 gone – stolen
 a terrible mess – considerable damage
 put out – issued
 had something to do with – been involved
 a couple of characters – two young males

5

(1)	*burgled*	(8)	*£25 worth of*	
(2)	*arrived home*	(9)	*items of jewellery*	
(3)	*discovered*	(10)	*stolen*	
(4)	*had forced*	(11)	*considerable damage*	
(5)	*gained access to*	(12)	*issued*	
(6)	*valued at*	(13)	*two young males*	
(7)	*valuables*	(14)	*been involved*	

Exam practice 2

This task gives students the chance to work through another CAE-type exercise. Encourage them to use the approaches identified and discussed in previous activities. Remind students that all the gaps can be completed using no more than two words. After completion of the exercise, discuss with students any difficulties they had, and try to identify with them what caused the problem(s).

Key

(1)	*quarrels/arguments/ disagreements*	(9)	*job/task*
(2)	*started/begun*	(10)	*keep things/keep everything*
(3)	*individuals*	(11)	*an answer/a solution*
(4)	*organisations/agencies*	(12)	*suits*
(5)	*answer*	(13)	*keen/eager*
(6)	*sides*	(14)	*more information*
(7)	*fix (up)*	(15)	*a ring/a call*
(8)	*talk about/talk through*		

Nine

A

Recognising feelings

Starter activities

> **Aims**
> To consolidate and/or extend vocabulary related to the topic of feelings.
> To raise awareness of the meaning of intonation patterns.

1 Encourage students to look carefully at the posture of the people in the photos as well as their facial expressions. Posture can reveal a lot about how people are feeling. Check the meaning of the words before doing the matching exercise, or during the exercise itself as gaps in students' knowledge become clear. Students may also need help with the pronunciation of some of these words – particularly the stress. Try some repetition practice if necessary.

2 Don't let students worry about whether they understand every word. They won't need to in order to do the task. You could ask them to repeat some of the extracts – this could be fun as well as being good pronunciation practice.

Tapescript
2 1 It makes no difference to me, whatever you say.
   2 That's fabulous, the best news I've heard in years.
   3 I'm not very sure, I really can't decide, you know.
   4 It was my favourite pen – I'd had it for years – my grandfather gave it to me when I was a child – where on earth can I have put it?
   5 This wretched computer – why can I never get it to work properly?
   6 I don't know, I don't really – I've tried and tried and it hasn't got me anywhere, has it?

   7 I'll do it, I've absolutely made up my mind – I don't care how long it takes me.
   8 Mm, I like your suit. I'd give an arm and a leg for a suit like that.

Key
2 1 *indifference*
   2 *delight*
   3 *uncertainty*
   4 *sadness*
   5 *frustration*
   6 *weariness*
   7 *determination*
   8 *jealousy*

3 *fright, downheartedness, elation, boredom, loneliness, reluctance, aggression/aggressiveness, confusion, fury, fascination,*

frustrated, angry, desperate, uncertain, delighted, sad, irritated, determined, depressed, jealous, weary, indifferent

✳ Speaking

> **Aims**
> To practise a CAE Paper 5 (Speaking) ranking task.
> To continue vocabulary extension work on the topic of feelings.
> To think more about the topic of feelings.
> To give fluency practice.

This activity follows the format of Phases C and D of Paper 5 (Speaking), i.e. a communicative activity followed by a more abstract discussion.

Make sure each student numbers the feelings without consultation before they start working with a partner.

If you wish to give students exam practice, carry out this activity in pairs (possibly with a third student listening in as audience/assessor).

🔊 Listening

Aims
To practise CAE Paper 4 (Listening) tasks from Section C.
To practise listening both for gist and for detail.
To continue the work on intonation begun in the Starter Activities.

1 Make sure students understand the expression 'having a row' before they start listening.

✱ 2 Students may need to hear the extract twice.

3 Before you begin this activity, check that the students know the meaning of all the words.

4 Encourage students to repeat the extracts as expressively as possible by getting into the thoughts and feelings of the people speaking.

Tapescript
1–2

Daughter: It's not fair. Why can't I go?

Mother: We're not saying you can't go; we just want to make sure that you're going to go in a safe way.

Daughter: Oh well, it is safe. I know loads of people who've done it and had a really good time. You're just ... you're just being ... you're just being spoilsports. You never let me do what I want to do.

Father: Charlotte, you're not serious anyway.

Daughter: I am serious. I've saved up all the money to go. I'm not asking you for any money. It's not like I'm trying to sponge off you or something.

Father: It's going to cost you a fortune. Anyway, why would you want to go to the States?

Daughter: It's not going to cost me a fortune, that's the whole point; the flights are cheap, and then this bus trip's really, really cheap. That's why young people go on it.

Father: [What bus trip?]

Mother: All sorts of people will be travelling on that bus, you know, any ... any number of undesirable people ...

Father: [Just a minute, I didn't know anything about a bus trip.]

Daughter: [You're such a snob, mum.]

Father: You're not seriously thinking about going on a bus around the States!

Mother: It's got nothing to do with being a snob [yes]! I just would much rather you stayed in one place, and just had a holiday in one spot, and didn't keep travelling around all over the place.

Daughter: ... we do that every year, like when we went before and I had to do exactly what you said, and it was ... I just ... I just want to do something on my own. I'm 16; it's about time I was allowed a bit of my ... you know a bit of my own freedom.

Father: Who are you thinking of going with?

Daughter: Clare. And her mother and father are fine about it, not like you.

Mother: Yes, but Clare ...

Father: Clare ...

Mother: Yes, but Clare's that bit older than you.

Daughter: No, she's not; she's only six months older than me.

Father: Wasn't it Clare that you went to Brighton with only three months ago, and took a lift off some stranger when you'd ... when you'd missed the last bus home?

Daughter: Yes, but

Father: This is the sort of thing you get involved in

Mother: Now look, don't [It's ridiculous] try and stay calm, shall we?

Father: She's useless in this country; I can't imagine her going all that way.

Daughter: Well, I'm going anyway, I don't care what you say.

Mother: Now, Charlotte, Charlotte, if you just ...

Father: You're not, my girl.

Daughter: I am.

Mother: Charlotte, will you listen to me now. Now look, if you want ... if you're prepared to just go to Los Angeles and stay with Bob and Carol, then that's absolutely fine with both of us, isn't it?

Father: Exactly [no]

Daughter: There's no way I'm going to stay with them; there's no way ...

Father: Well, you get on with their children ... Ted and Alice, they're lovely. [they're awful]

Mother: Look, Los Angeles, there's so much to see and do there, you know, you can stay in the one place and just move around from there. Then you can go to Disneyland and you can ... you know you can lie on the beach

Daughter: But you can't see nearly as ...

Father: And Bob taxies you round everywhere; he's so good to you.

Daughter: You can't see nearly as many places as cheaply as you can on this bus trip.

Father: And you can't get into trouble, that's the thing, isn't it?

Daughter: It's not. Look, it's advertised in all the student magazines. It's advertised in the newspapers; ... it's you know ... the green tortoise, you know, it's famous; loads of people ...

Mother: Well, I've never heard of it.

Daughter: Well, that's not surprising, is it?

Father: My daughter's turning into a teenage mutant ninja turtle before my very eyes. [It's ridiculous]

Daughter: No dad, it's a play on words; you know ... Greyhound bus; it's the opposite of that ... green tortoise. Oooh, get real!

Mother: Well, obviously it doesn't go very fast, does it?

Father: Let's talk about this some other time when we've all calmed down. Alright, Charlotte.

Daughter: That's the whole point .... (fade)

4
1   It's not fair. Why can't I go?
2   Oh well, it is safe.
3   You're just being spoilsports.

4 It's not like I'm trying to sponge off you or something
5 What bus trip?
6 You're not seriously thinking about going on a bus?
7 I just want to do something on my own
8 This is the sort of thing you get involved in
9 Well, I'm going anyway, I don't care what you say.
10 You're not my girl.
11 There's no way I'm going to stay with them; there's no way
12 Ooh, get real!

Key

1 Possible answers:
(a) a daughter, a father, a mother
(b) It's about the daughter's wish to go with a friend on holiday to the States and to travel round while there.
(c) The daughter wants to go on holiday with her friend and travel round the USA. The mother doesn't mind her daughter going but doesn't want her to travel around. The father seems unhappy about her going at all, especially with her friend Clare; he doesn't want her to travel around.

2 1 F 2 M 3 D 4 D 5 F 6 M,F 7 M 8 D 9 F

3 Possible answers:

rude – D, F	furious – F
firm – D, F	appalled – F
frustrated – D	reasonable – M
angry – D, F	worried – M
resentful – D	

Reading

> **Aims**
> To read a slightly different kind of text – a report of a psychological experiment.
> To stimulate thought and discussion on the topic of feelings.
> To practise reading for gist and reading for detail.
> To encourage deduction of meaning from context.
> To practise a CAE Paper 1 (Reading) multiple choice.

✱ 1 You could set a time limit (e.g. 3 minutes) to encourage students to read for gist.

2 Encourage students to use all the clues in the text to try and decide the meaning of these words. The purpose of asking the students to explain the meaning of the words in groups is to encourage them to explore the meaning as much as they can.

Key

1 e

2 Possible answers:
1 affecting the functions of the body
2 a hormone that induces fear, anger etc.
3 red
4 covered in sweat

5 a neutral substance given as medicine that is intended to work because the patient believes it is effective medicine
6 salt solution
7 a 'pretend' participant
8 very happy/ecstatic
9 initiate/cause/set in motion
10 to consider

3 1 D 2 B 3 B 4 D

Grammar analysis: phrasal and prepositional verbs

> **Aim**
> To raise awareness of the differences in behaviour between phrasal and prepositional verbs.

Key

1 a T
   b T
   c T
   d F – they generally occur in informal language
   e F – it is normally unstressed in prepositional verbs and stressed in phrasal verbs
   f T

2 1 phrasal
   2 prepositional
   3 phrasal
   4 phrasal
   5 prepositional
   6 phrasal
   7 prepositional

3 There are no fixed answers to this activity.

Vocabulary summary

> **Aims**
> To revise some of the topic-related vocabulary from Section A.
> To personalise the vocabulary for students.

1 It doesn't matter which ten feelings students write down. What matters is the process of reading through the section and selecting relevant vocabulary. Encourage students to notice the differences between their lists so as to bring as much vocabulary to their attention as possible.

2 Initially this activity focuses on the form of these words. Students often gain confidence through an opportunity to focus on form. It is also important, however, to reinforce the meaning of these words, hence the final activity in 2. Encourage students to explain how they feel and why.

Key

2

Noun	Adjective	Negative Adjective	Adverb	Verb
happiness	happy	unhappy	happily	
delight	delighted		delightedly	to delight
determination	determined	undeter-mined	determinedly	to deter-mine
irritation	irritated		irritatedly	to irritate
desperation	desperate		desperately	to despair
boredom	bored			to bore
guilt	guilty	not guilty	guiltily	
frustration	frustrated		frustratedly	to frustrate
contentment	content	discon-tented	contentedly	to content
fright	frightened			to frighten
depression	depressed			to depress

B

Expressing your feelings

Starter activities

> **Aims**
> To start thinking about the topic of expressing feelings.
> To get students thinking about when they express feelings, and their attitudes towards the expression of feelings.
> To revise and extend vocabulary related to feelings.

Before doing the questionnaire tell students that it is about feelings, and that the aim is to try to work out how 'emotional' they are. Check they understand the meaning of *emotional*. Students should do the questionnaire individually. As they do it, walk round checking that students have understood the vocabulary in the questions.

After the students have done the questionnaire, ask them to score their answers and then read the interpretation.

Listening

> **Aims**
> To listen to a story so that students can both experience and discuss feelings.
> To practise a CAE Paper 4 (Listening) task.
> To extend students' descriptive vocabulary.

1 There is no correct answer. Different students will react to the story in different ways. The purpose of the task is to encourage students to talk about their reactions and so work on their comprehension of the story. Encourage students to discuss as thoroughly as possible.

 2 This is an exam-format task. Please note, however, that listening texts in the exam are not as long as this one, and they are never a story as this one is. This story was included here to develop the topic of feelings and to provide absorbing listening.

3 The task is designed to encourage students to use context to try to deduce the meaning of words in a text.

Tapescript
Amy stood at the school gates under the shelter of her umbrella. She looked at her watch. Rosie was very late. Wherever could she be?

All the other children had spilled out, laughing and talking several minutes ago. Now the playground was

deserted and it had started to rain. But there was no sign of Rosie.

Amy peered anxiously up and down the road. Rain drummed on her umbrella and splashed to the pavement. Her feet felt uncomfortably damp. She checked the time again, frowning in puzzlement. A small boy ran down the street to where his mother stood waving beside a car, his school bag jolting rhythmically at his side.

'Excuse me!' cried Amy. 'Have you seen my daughter anywhere? Rosie Lister, she's called.'

The boy stopped, panting for breath. 'Ah, Sorry,' he said, 'she's not in my class.'

Amy drew her coat more closely around her and went through the gates, across the empty playground and into the main entrance.

Could it be that Rosie had stayed behind for some reason? It would soon be Easter. Perhaps she'd wanted to finish drawing her a card or a picture.

Maybe Miss Edmondson had stayed behind too, to help her. She was such a conscientious teacher. And Rosie liked to make a proper job of things. That must be the answer. Why hadn't she thought of it before? Rosie would be quite safe with Miss Edmondson.

Amy fondly imagined her daughter's Easter offering – eggs and chicks and rabbits, all in crayon with big, uneven writing. She would pin it on the kitchen wall with the other drawings when they got home.

But the school was empty except for the cleaners and a teacher Amy didn't know. They hadn't seen Rosie and seemed anxious for Amy to leave so they could go home.

Fighting her rising panic, Amy sat on a desk and tried to think clearly. Rosie had never before left school alone, but supposing, just supposing that today as a surprise, she'd gone to the newsagent's on the corner to buy her mother an Easter egg? Sometimes they called in there on the way home, so she'd know the way.

Mr. Phillips, the young owner of the shop, was as jovial as ever. 'Hello there; Mrs Lister, and how are you this wet and weary day?' 'Has Rosie been in just now?' asked Amy, scanning the empty shop, checking behind the tall stand of cards.

He shook his head, his smile fading. 'I'm sorry, I haven't seen her, I'm afraid.' 'I don't know what to do, she's missing!' Amy's hands were icy cold and trembling. She found it almost impossible to think straight. Where could Rosie be?

Deep in her mind something was stirring, like a foreboding, a certainty that this wasn't going to be alright, a mother's instinct crying out to be heard and urging her to do something quickly before it was too late.

'Now calm down,' said Mr. Phillips. 'Don't get all worked up. It won't do you any good. It's bound to be alright, you know, kiddies being what they are.'

But Amy wasn't reassured. 'I'm going,' she said, trying desperately to keep her voice steady. 'Perhaps we've missed each other and she's there waiting for me. Yes, that's what I'll do.'

Outside it was raining harder than before. Amy splashed heedlessly through the puddles, her heart racing. And then she saw Rosie! She was standing on the corner of the High Street holding Miss Edmondson's hand. She was skipping on the spot in excitement and waving. Her hood was down and raindrops glistened on her chestnut hair. 'Mummy,' she called, 'Mummy I'm here.' Thank heavens she was alright! Tears of relief filled Amy's eyes and spilled down her cheeks. Oh, what a fuss, a silly, silly fuss she'd been making. She started forward desperate to reach Rosie and hold her safely in her arms again.

But something was wrong. Her feet wouldn't move properly. She felt breathless and dizzy. Rosie was running towards her now, getting closer and closer, but swirling and shimmering before her eyes. And then, as the little girl reached her, the world slid gently away into the blackness.

Mr. Phillips stood, white with shock, mumbling replies to the policeman's questions. He couldn't take his eyes from the slim bundle lying on the pavement, over which someone had mercifully draped a coat. 'It's Mrs. ... er ... Mrs. Lister. She'd just been into the shop. I can't believe it. I was talking to her a few minutes ago, that's all. Are you quite sure we can't do anything for her, officer?'

The policeman shook his head. 'I'm sorry,' he said. 'There's no response at all. I think it must have been a heart attack. That's what it looks like anyway. We'll know for sure when the ambulance gets here.' 'She was in a bit of a state in the shop,' said Mr. Phillips. 'Quite upset. I suppose that could have brought it on.' The policeman frowned. 'What was she upset about?' Mr. Phillips pulled out a large handkerchief and blew his nose self-consciously. 'Er, Rosie, her daughter,' he said at last. 'The little girl died, you see, in a tragedy at that school around the corner. Rosie and a teacher, both killed outright.' He shook his head. 'Mrs Lister's got a bit confused recently,' he said, 'wandering around the streets looking lost, hunting for her little girl. She used to wait outside the school for her sometimes. It was pathetic to see her.'

Rain dripped on to the policeman's notebook, making round, swollen blotches on the paper. 'Poor lady,' he said quietly. 'Yes,' said Mr. Phillips. 'It's awful. All these years ... I wasn't even born when it happened, you know. Rosie and her teacher had stayed behind after school for some reason and a gas boiler exploded, right next to their classroom.'

For one last time, and to reassure himself that nothing more could be done, he lifted the rain-splashed coat and gazed down at the pale, wrinkled face with its frame of soft, white hair. It was then he noticed the old lady was holding something in her hand ... a child's drawing, it looked like, in bright crayon and with big uneven words. He could just make out the letters – 'HAPPY ... EASTER ...'

And Mrs Lister, at peace at last, was smiling.

Key

2 F D A I B H C E G

3 Possible answers:
   spill out – to come out in an unorderly way; as the children left school

peer – to look closely or intently; Amy looking up and down the road

drum – to thump; the rain on Amy's umbrella

jolt – to bump; the boy's bag against his side

scan – to glance briefly; Amy looking round Mr. Phillips' shop

stir – to begin to move; Amy's feelings

glisten – to sparkle; the raindrops on Rosie's hair

swirl – to whirl about; Rosie running towards her mum

shimmer – to glisten and shine; Rosie running towards her mum

mumble – to speak indistinctly; Mr. Phillips talking to the policeman

frown – to look puzzled or discontented; the policeman talking to Mr. Phillips

gaze down – to look in a non-focused way; Mr. Phillips looking down at Amy

Grammar reminder: *as* and *like*

> **Aim**
> To revise the differences between as and like when used to describe.

Key

a	*as*	f	*like*
b	*as*	g	*like*
c	*as*	h	*like*
d	*like*	i	*as*
e	*like*	j	*as*

Speaking: speculating

> **Aims**
> To raise awareness of the language of speculation and give practice in its use.
> To give fluency practice.
> To give students an opportunity to talk about how they would feel and react in particular situations.

1 Students could start this activity as a whole class so you can check on correct usage. Then they can continue in pairs.

2 After students have finished, invite them to tell the whole class any particularly funny or interesting answers they gave.

Reading

> **Aims**
> To further explore the topic of expressing feelings.
> To present students with a slightly provocative text to react to.
> To practise reading for gist, detail, and cohesion.
> To practise a CAE Paper 1 (Reading) gapped paragraphs task.
> To practise deducing meaning from context.

1 The headline, captions and photo all give plenty of clues as to what this article is about. Encourage students to exploit these clues to the full to predict content, as people do when reading outside the classroom.

2 Make sure students list their answers in note form.

✱ **3** This is an exam-format task. Make sure students use both grammatical and vocabulary clues. It is useful for them to gist-read the paragraphs to see at a glance what might fit where before going on to further investigate their hunches.

4 This activity encourages students to explore the meaning of words through context and through discussion with one another. Let the students try to work meanings out for themselves. It doesn't matter if their understandings are inaccurate initially, providing they become more accurate as the task goes on.

Key

2 • women found to have greater verbal fluency, prefer amicable solutions, be non-competitive, be better at arithmetic, be capable of storing more random information and better at identifying matching objects in a hurry
   • men found to be more decisive, aggressive and driven by money, more mechanically-minded, better at activities which require spatial reasoning
   • different levels of testosterone in men and women
   • babies thought to be born with mental gender differences
   • evidence suggesting that three-year-old boys are better than girls at targeting objects

3 1 E   2 A   3 D   4 B

4 Possible answers:
   1 a clue that can't be missed
   2 the slightest suggestion of a breaking of the voice
   3 a wrinkled brow
   4 not to hide your feelings, be up front with your feelings
   5 be slightly better than
   6 make you consider a problem from a new perspective
   7 people who take part in experiments
   8 add seriousness to
   9 aim at and hit
   10 from the complete beginning
   11 straightening out an imbalance

✳ Writing

> **Aims**
> To practise a CAE Paper 2 (Writing) task.
> To consolidate language found in the reading article.
> To give students an opportunity to express their own opinions about the topic.

Explain to students that letters to the editor are quite a tradition in English language newspapers. If this is also the case in their country, you could discuss the kinds of letter that get written, why, and the style they can be in.

Before students start writing this letter (whether they do it for homework or in class), discuss the style they are going to write the letter in, the level of formality of language they are going to use, and any useful letter conventions they may want to employ, such as:

Dear Sir/Madam/Editor, With reference to your article of (date) *on* (subject)

Dear Sir/Madam/Editor, I am writing to …

Students could also write out a short plan of their letter, outlining the order in which they will make their points.

Vocabulary summary

> **Aim**
> To revise the main vocabulary from the unit.

1 Students could read the unit to find their ten words. The teams may need help in devising crossword-like clues. You could give them examples beforehand (e.g. from the vocabulary quizzes in Units 4 and 7 (pages 56 and 98). Don't forget to keep the score as the quiz progresses. You might want to write the answers on the board as the students guess them. Then at the end you could check the meaning of the words and/or do some pronunciation work.

C

Paper 4 (Listening): Section C

> **Aims**
> To familiarise students with the aims and content of CAE Paper 4 (Listening): Section C.
> To think about the reasons for the different ways we listen.
> To practise for Paper 4 (Listening) Section C.

Introduction

Section C of Paper 4 probably contains the kind of listening – and listening task – which is most common in EFL materials, so students should be quite familiar with the formats.

Use this activity to fully address any doubts or queries students may have about Section C of Paper 4.

An example of CAE Paper 4, Section C

You could carry it out as an exam task, and then relate it back to the information in the Introduction by asking students to identify the kind of task, listening skill(s) and listening text it contains.

Tapescript

Presenter: At 9 a.m. on the 24th of July Yvonne Lawrence was going to the post office to buy a pint of milk. A woman rushed up and stopped her as she reached the door

Yvonne: She told me she'd seen an armed man inside.

Presenter: Seconds later, Yvonne spotted a man, wearing an anorak with a hood hiding his face, dash inside.

Yvonne: It suddenly dawned on me that I was witnessing an armed robbery.

Presenter: Peering through the windows of the post office and general store, Yvonne recognised a friend trapped inside with the two raiders. As the seconds ticked by, she became more frightened. Then the raider wearing the anorak backed out of the door with a shotgun. Yvonne watched him dash across the road. Moments later she heard a car starting up. Then a second man raced out of the post office.

Yvonne: Without stopping to think what I was doing, I swung at him with my shopping bag, then I thought to myself 'You're not getting away with this,' and I went for him!

Presenter: Startled shoppers looked on as plucky Yvonne grabbed the robber. Collapsing to the ground, he was pinned down by her 200 pound frame.

Yvonne:	I held him by his pullover and an elderly man trapped him by his legs.
Presenter:	Then they were joined by another woman who helped to hold on to him until the police arrived. Mother of three, Yvonne, was determined to keep hold of the robber.
Yvonne:	I knew his accomplice had a gun and there was a good chance he was armed, too. But it didn't cross my mind at the time. At first he struggled, but after a while he seemed to realise it was hopeless and just lay on the road.
Presenter:	The full impact of it all hit Yvonne when she heard sirens and saw the police van pull up.
Yvonne:	I started shaking then. I thought about what I'd done and I was really frightened!
Presenter:	As the police bundled the robber into their van, they found a gun lying beside him and the post office cash box which he had dropped as he tried to flee. Yvonne was even able to give the police the number of the getaway car. When she arrived home later, her children were shaken by their mum's brush with danger – and very proud.
Yvonne:	My eldest son, Kevin 23, who's a bus driver, kept asking 'Are you really a hero, mum?' – he'd heard about it from his work mates. For once my 200 pound build was an asset! I'm always thinking about dieting, but this time I think my weight actually helped!
Presenter:	The Metropolitan police praised Yvonne's bravery, but a senior police officer warned the public to be wary of trying to apprehend an armed criminal because it could end in disaster. He added that she did really well, though, and was quite a hero. The post office owner, James Concagh, is also full of praise.
James Concagh:	I was still inside the post office when Yvonne helped catch the robber. She was so brave. I just can't thank her enough.

Key

1 C   2 D   3 D   4 A   5 C   6 D

Ways of learning: different ways of listening

Make sure that students understand that in real life we usually listen in different ways according to what we are listening to and why. You could ask students to list different things they have listened to recently in their own language, and write beside each how they listened and why they listened, and then use these lists as a basis for discussion.

Encourage students to realise that listening for the exam is in some ways no different to listening in everyday life, in that you don't always listen to – or for – everything, and you don't always need to understand everything.

Students frequently feel nervous about Paper 4, even though their worries are not borne out by the examiners' information on performance. They need to be encouraged to listen to anything and everything they can in English: passers-by, English TV and radio programmes, taped stories (from a library) etc.

Exam practice

Tapescript

Interviewer:	So Jason, I understand from erm, you know, various newspaper clippings that I have read that you're a bit of a parachute freak on the quiet [oh yeah]. Do you want to … can you tell me a bit … how did you get into that?
Jason:	Well, I first parachuted when I was in the air cadets; I mean, you know, long before starting up the singing; erm so, I did a jump, and we did like about 4 days' preparation; it was just brilliant, and erm … I tried to then every six months or so go back to the same place, because if you stayed with the cadets you could keep doing two jumps a year; and then eventually I had to leave the cadets, erm, but then, once I started getting a bit of money from the singing, it's something I started looking into again; and I joined this club which is down at Bigginhill [yes]; and that's where, that's where I go sort of every weekend now.
Interviewer:	Every weekend you do it [absolutely, yeah]; my goodness, that must be quite … I mean it's not a cheap thing to do, is it, parachuting?
Jason:	No, but er, well, with the two records in the charts at the moment [well obviously, mm, mm], money's no object at the moment; we don't just jump from there, I mean we go out to … we've been … we've jumped in France and we're going out to America next year; [yes] we're going to jump off the canyon. [My goodness] … you know, down into the Grand Canyon.
Interviewer:	It must be terrifying, though?
Jason:	Well, it's, sort of, it's … I think that's the appeal of it; it's like … I can't imagine being quite as frightened as you are before you jump, but then once you've jumped then, it's just the most amazing feeling, 'cause … the fear sort of transcends into something else [yes] … which is, which is the greatest excitement I think you could ever have really.
Interviewer:	I've always, I've always wondered … is it very, when you first jump out, is it very noisy or is it very quiet?
Jason:	Yes, no, it's very, well, that again is a funny thing, if you, well there's a book written, I can't remember the guy, but he wrote this book about parachuting last year, and he said; it is incredibly noisy in a literal sense,

but at the same time it's a feeling of great calm as well; especially when you jump out the plane, and obviously there's the noise of the wind in your ears, but ... you know, there's just you and the elements [yes] and the ground underneath you, and if you're like at ten thousand feet or something, I mean you can't even see it moving, and it's like, it's like you're suspended above the earth; it's marvellous.

Interviewer: And when your parachute opens, is there ... is there an enormous change?

Jason: Oh yeh, yeh, it's a big, big jerk.

Interviewer: And it actually, does it pull you up?

Jason: It feels as if ... because you're not aware by that time that you're actually falling, so it suddenly feels that you've been hoiked upwards; whereas in fact, of course, it's just a deceleration; you're slowing down quickly [I see, yes] and it feels as if somebody's just pulled you up on a piece of string; but a ... it's a very violent sensation, but at the same time it's a good sensation because you know well the parachute's opened, so [which must be a relief] yes, yes, yes.

Interviewer: And have you ever had any, any bad falls?

Jason: Yes, there was a time when I was jumping with Mark who's also in the group, and erm, we were ... we were quite close together in this jump, and er his parachute opened up early, and er, some of it sort of got attached to me, or was wrapping around me in the wind; and I thought I've got to get away from this; and erm, and then mine went off; I don't know what happened, I must have been struggling to try and get the ... his cord away from me and pulled my ripcord; and so the two chutes were sort of then tangled up, and er, you know, I could see him looking at me, wondering what to do, and erm, we just followed really what is the basic procedure, which is to get rid of your main chute and then rely on your reserve [yes]; and we were at a good height; there was no danger of hitting the ground or anything, so we, we ... I released mine and he released his more or less at the same time; and then we separated and then er opened the reserve chutes and that was fine; down we went; and you know it was a bit of a shaker at the time; [I bet] a change of clothes when we got down (laughter) but that's the most dodgy thing that's happened, yes.

Interviewer: And, er ... have you erm, have you got any you know, any future plans? Is there anything that you ... as far as the parachuting goes?

Jason: Well, we're doing the Canyon thing next year, we hope [yes, yes, lovely]. Yeh, but me mother wants me to give it up, She ... but I'm going to keep doing it.

Interviewer: It must be quite hair-raising for those nearest and dearest to you ...

Key

(1) *was a member of/belonged to*

(2) *a parachuting club*

(3) *he makes money from his records/gets money from singing*

(4) *before you jump*

(5) *excited*

(6) *hoiked up/jerked up*

(7) *a friend's/Mark's*

(8) *the Grand Canyon*

Ten

A

What is assertiveness?

Starter activities

> **Aims**
> **To start students thinking about the topic of assertiveness.**
> **To check on and develop students' understanding of assertiveness.**
> **To give students an opportunity to gauge their own level of assertiveness.**

1 Discuss the situation portrayed in the cartoon before asking students to apply the adjectives, to be sure they all understand what the cartoon is about.

2 Ensure students distinguish between weakly stressed and strongly stressed syllables when they pronounce these words. Ask them to listen out for this.

4 The purpose of this activity is to give the students a chance to work out what assertiveness means before they read the reading passage (where a definition is given). You could get the students to compare definitions across groups to see which is the best one.

5 You may want to develop the findings of the questionnaire into a general class discussion.

Key
1 Some possible answers:
for the person under the umbrella: *victimised, rejected, defensive, uptight*
for the person behind the counter: *threatening, humiliating, angry*

2 '*threatening, re'spectful, re'jected, re'bellious, 'victi'mised, clear, 'equal, de'fensive, 'self-'confident hu'mili'ating, 'angry, 'up'tight, di'rect, 'fed-'up,*

3 The person under the umbrella is passive and the person behind the counter is aggressive.

Reading

> **Aims**
> **To further understanding of assertiveness.**
> **To practise reading for detail.**
> **To practise CAE Paper 1 (Reading) matching task.**
> **To extend vocabulary and to practise deducing meaning from context.**

1 Students may have to read the text quite carefully to get the right answer. Ensure they are not reading it word for word, though.

2 Warn students before they do this activity that the answers will often depend on the meaning of the word in the particular context.

The purpose of writing the names of people beside the adjectives is to help students build up associations with the words.

 3 This task, multiple matching, regularly occurs in CAE Paper 1 (Reading) as the first and last task in the paper. It can also be a double-barrelled task in the exam as this one is here, i.e. with two different matching tasks on the same text.

Key
1 c
2 *powerful – wimpish*
strong – small
effective – ineffectual
communicative – uncommunicative
calm – angry
easy – stroppy
good-tempered – grumpy
appropriate – maladroit
at ease – anxious
passive – aggressive
aggressive – passive
respectful – manipulative

3	1	C		7	A
	2	F		8	C
	3	D		9	C
	4	B		10	D
	5	A		11	D
	6	E			

Grammar analysis: modal verbs for speculation and deduction

Aims
To raise awareness of the meaning of modal verbs used for speculation or deduction.
To practise using present and past tense forms of these verbs.

3 Encourage students to come up with as many explanations and predictions as they can about these situations. In this way, they will get a lot of practice using modal verbs for deducing and speculating.

Key

1 1, 2, 3, 6, 7, 8, 10, 11

2 (a) *can, may, might, must*
(b) *'have'*
(c) *certainty in the speaker's mind*
(d) *a degree of doubt in the speaker's mind*

Listening

Aims
To listen for gist and detail.
To practise a CAE Paper 4 (Listening) note-taking task.

1 Encourage discussion of what the best title could be, so as to explore comprehension of the text.

* 2 This activity is typical of a Section A task in Paper 4 (Listening). Ensure that students' answers are short. Longer answers are not required and tend to be wrong. Don't forget that students are marked for the accuracy of their spelling (except in proper nouns).

Tapescript

Lecturer: Most 'unassertive' people take no for an answer much too easily. There is a growing awareness in our society that this tendency is jeopardising the rights of large numbers of people. For example, in recent years there has been an upsurge in consumer protection organisations and pressure groups. This is a welcome development as there will always be a need for such organisations to protect the interests of individuals and minorities in a competitive society. The danger is that we become over-dependent on professional workers for our rights and lose the art of asserting ourselves. It is better for your self-esteem and relationships with other people if you can learn the art of persistence for yourself.

Now, we have to learn to ignore some of the not-so-pleasant messages that may be ringing in our unconscious minds, such as:

'If you ask once more, I'll flatten you'
'You're a nagger – just like your mother'
'Don't make a scene'
'Anything to keep the peace'

The main technique that we use in assertiveness training to practise the art of persistence is called Broken Record. When a record is scratched we hear one sentence over and over again until we reach screaming pitch and jump up to turn it off.

Broken Record is the skill of being able to: repeat over and over again, in an assertive and relaxed manner, what it is you want or need, until the other person gives in or agrees to negotiate with you.

Now, this technique is extremely useful for:
☐ dealing with situations where your rights are clearly in danger of being abused
☐ coping with situations where you are likely to be diverted by clever, articulate but irrelevant arguments.
☐ situations where you are likely to lose your self-confidence because you know you could be affected by 'digs' and 'put-downs' to your self-esteem.

The beauty of using Broken Record is that once you have prepared your lines you can relax. You have nothing more to worry about because you know exactly what you are going to say, however abusive or manipulative the other person tries to be.

As with most assertive techniques, it must be used appropriately. It is a self-protective skill and is not designed to foster deep, interesting conversations and friendships with people! It is primarily of use in situations where your time and energy is precious.

For example:
☐ when a persuasive colleague rings you up at tea time and you don't want to spend hours explaining why you cannot help with doing some shopping for him.
☐ and when it's your only free shopping day in the month and you want your money back on unsatisfactory goods so that you can quickly replace them elsewhere.

When you've mastered the first Broken Record exercise, you can then move on to practising a more sophisticated variant. You can practise conveying the same message but using slightly different words each time.

Key

1 Possible answers:
Broken Record; An Assertiveness Technique;
A Step towards Assertiveness etc.

2 (1) *consumer protection organisations*
(2) *dangerous*
(3) *messages*
(4) *repeating*
(5) *gives in*
(6) *agrees to negotiate with*
(7) *don't change/stay the same*
(8) *time and energy*
(9) *slightly different*

Speaking: making your point

> **Aims**
> **To extend students' use of language for making points.**
> **To give fluency practice.**
> **To give students an opportunity to try out some assertiveness techniques.**

1 These phrases could come in handy for students in Paper 5 (Speaking) and Paper 2 (Writing), as well as in their everyday use of English.

2 This activity is taken from a book on assertiveness techniques. When students have finished, you could discuss what they thought of the activity and whether they think you can really train people to be assertive.

B

Being assertive

Starter activity

> **Aims**
> **To start thinking about the topic.**
> **To give students practice in varying their intonation.**
> **To begin the section with an entertaining activity.**
> **To provide an introduction to the listening task which follows.**

You might want to start this activity with the whole class to make sure they are on the right tracks, and then continue in small groups to give them all practice.

Listening

> **Aims**
> **To practise listening for gist.**
> **To raise awareness of and practise intonation.**

1 Students should listen for gist, and their answers should only be brief notes. Encourage discussion of answers, and replay the recording if necessary to build up students' awareness of intonation.

3 This activity is designed to give students practice in introducing range into their intonation – something they sometimes find difficult. If they relax and treat the activity as a game they will probably be more successful at it.

Tapescript
1 Get out of my way, will you?
2 Brown ... made of leather ... wheels on it ... it's got a big scratch on top of it and my name, of course, on the name tag.
3 I bought these shoes here last week and I'm afraid they've split already. Could you change them for me, please?
4 Erm, excuse me, erm, sorry to bother you, it's these shoes, you see, well, erm, I'm afraid ...
5 Oh ... erm ... well ... erm ... well ... not really ... I
6 No way, definitely not.
7 I'd just like to talk for a bit about your work. I know you've been getting a bit behind of late.
8 Erm ... sorry ... excuse me ... er ... could you pass me the sugar please?
9 Excuse me, could you pass me the sugar, please?

Key
1 1 asking someone to get out of the way
2 describing a lost suitcase
3 complaining about split shoes
4 complaining about shoes

5 refusing
6 refusing
7 discussing someone's performance at work
8 asking someone to pass the sugar
9 asking someone to pass the sugar

2

	Formal	Informal	Assertive	Passive	Aggressive
2 description	✓				✓
3 complaint	✓		✓		
4 complaint	✓			✓	
5 refusal	✓	✓		✓	
6 refusal		✓			✓
7 criticism	✓		✓		
8 request	✓			✓	
9 request	✓		✓		

Speaking

> **Aims**
> **To give students practice in being assertive.**
> **To practise varying intonation patterns.**
> **To develop awareness of body language.**

You could do this activity in threes with one student acting as a 'language analyst' and giving feedback to the others on their use of voice, body language etc.

Reading

> **Aim**
> **To help students realise that they can be assertive in writing as well as in speaking.**

The reading and integrated tasks might be better carried out in pairs to encourage participation and discussion of language and style.

Key
'Correctness' and context

The following go with one another:

really fantastic/had a ball/smashing/great/a lucky so and so/look us up/quite a riot/See ya!

very enjoyable/had a good time/lovely/nice/very lucky/come and see us/a lot of fun/All the best

most entertaining/was quite enchanted/particularly agreeable/ charming/most fortunate/allow us to return your hospitality/a pleasant little occasion/Warmest regards

Being consistent

Possible answers:
1 *inflicted on my property – you've done to my place*
2 *a fag – a cigarette*
3 *Furthermore, I require – and*
4 *O.K. – acceptable*
5 *were possessed by a feeling of intense consternation – suddenly became very anxious*

✱ Writing

> **Aims**
> **To practise a CAE Paper 3 (English in Use) rewriting task.**
> **To give students further practice in using language appropriately.**

Make sure students understand what a mail order catalogue is and how the writer attempted to buy the computer.

Ask students what style both of the letters are in and what style their answers should be in. See if they remember what the general features of formal and informal language tend to be (see Unit 7 Section C page 100).

Students could do this activity individually in class or for homework. It may be useful for them to look at how other students have filled in the blanks, and discuss which answers are best and why.

You could give students a copy of the correctly completed letter and ask them to compare it with the original letter. They should decide which the computer firm would rather receive, and which might produce what action or reaction.

Key
Possible answers:
(1) *complaint*
(2) *several*
(3) *receipt*
(4) *managed/was able*
(5) *However/Unfortunately*
(6) *broke down*
(7) *highly/clearly/quite*
(8) *considerable*
(9) *refund*
(10) *inconvenience*

Grammar reminder: adjectives + prepositions

> **Aims**
> To consolidate students' use of prepositions after certain adjectives.
> To encourage students to explore the meaning of prepositions.
> To build up awareness and knowledge of collocation.

1 You could do this activity individually at first, before moving on to pair or group work to encourage discussion of the answers. You might want to ask students when it is that different prepositions are used with the same adjective. To answer this they could work with the key.

2 Encourage students to make up as many sentences as possible about the cartoon.

Key
1 (Possible answers)

with	at	for	to	about	of	in
indignant	indignant	responsible	reluctant	hostile	capable	interested
rude	astonished	pleased	rude	kind	ashamed	bad
sensitive	angry	thankful	sensitive	ashamed		deficient
angry	discontented	bad	kind	bad		
discontented	pleased			right		
fed up	capable			doubtful		
pleased	bad					
hostile	deficient					
kind	fed up					
capable						
bad						

Vocabulary summary

> **Aim**
> To revise the meanings and forms of key vocabulary in the unit.

1 You may need to explain the aim of this activity to students.

2 You could make a short team game out of this activity when students have completed it. Each team reads out a word. The first team to change the adjective into its corresponding noun correctly gets a point. The team with the most points at the end is the winner.

C

Paper 5 (Speaking): Phase B

> **Aims**
> To familiarise students with the aims and content of CAE Paper 5 (Speaking): Phase B.
> To point out the usefulness of assertive behaviour in Paper 5.
> To continue to build up awareness of appropriate language.

As well as reading the information in the Student's Book, you can tell your students that Phase B is designed to give each participant a chance to talk uninterruptedly. The tasks are usually some kind of 'describe and identify/match/draw/order' activity. Students are <u>not</u> marked down for giving the wrong answer, i.e. identifying/ordering/drawing etc. incorrectly. The examiners mark the quality of the communication and language only.

Introduction

Depending on what answers your students give to this activity, you could use them to dispel their worries, or to try to overcome their reluctance towards any aspect of Phase B.

How should candidates behave?

This activity aims to show students that passive or aggressive behaviour will not help them in Paper 5, but assertive behaviour certainly will, particularly as students are assessed for their interactive abilities.

Key
1 passive

2 assertive

3 aggressive (probably)

4 assertive

5 assertive

6 passive (possibly)

7 assertive

8 aggressive

Exam Practice

Students need to get used to being assessed by two examiners, so it is useful for them to carry out this activity in groups of four. Acting as interlocutor and assessor also helps them to understand the procedure followed in the exam, and the assessment criteria used.

Ways of learning: situations in which we use different styles of language

Students may find it easier to understand the uses of appropriate language if they discuss instances of it occurring in their own language. See Unit 7, Section C page 100 for an outline of the characteristics of formal and informal language.

Key
2 topic of conversation, setting of conversation, status of participants in relation to one another, how well the participants know one another.

Revision Exam Practice 2

The following activities have been included in the course for two reasons:

- **to provide further practice in the language of the topics of the preceding five units.**
- **to give further exam practice in the tasks that have been featured in Section C of the previous five units.**

All the activities are presented as they would be in the CAE exam.

You may choose to use these activities for homework, for practice in exam-like conditions in class, or simply to work through and discuss in class.

Paper 1 (Reading)

This task is taken from the multiple matching section of the Reading Paper. For information on how to approach this section of Paper 1, see the information and the facsimile questions on pages 86–90 of the Student's Book. The answer sheet for the Reading Paper is reproduced on page 138 of this Teacher's Book.

Allow approximately 20 minutes for this task.

Key

1	A, B, C	8	B, C
2	D, E	9	B
3	A, B, C	10	E
4	A	11	A, B, C, D
5	F	12	D, E
6	B, C	13	D, F
7	C	14	A

Paper 2 (Writing)

This task is taken from section A of the Writing Paper. For information on how to approach this section of Paper 2, see the information and the facsimile questions on pages 99–100 of the Student's Book.

Allow approximately one hour for this task. See the Marking guidelines on page 47 of this Teacher's Book.

Key
Possible answer:

1. **Letter**

Dear Sir or Madam,

I've just read your ad for camp helpers, and I'm really interested in applying for one of these jobs. In your ad you ask for details of my experience, qualifications and personality. Let me give them to you.

I'm 20 years old and I come from Spain. I finished school two years ago, and since then I've been working as an assistant in a sports shop selling all kinds of sports goods and advising customers on the kinds of things that would be best for them. So as you see, I have constant contact with the world of sport. I also play a lot of sport – I've belonged to a tennis club for the last 8 years, I play basketball, and in the summer I go to the sea and do all the usual sea sports: swimming, water skiing, canoeing etc. In fact, last year I helped out at a beach sports club.

As for my personality, well, I suppose I'm quite extrovert. I love being with other people. Generally I'm quite patient and I like to think I'm understanding.

Could you give me some further details about the job? I'd like to know about what kind of accommodation there would be, whether I'd receive any pay, and also what kind of working hours I'd be expected to do each day and for how many days a week. Many thanks.

I look forward to hearing from you and hope that you will be able to offer me a job.

Yours faithfully,

2. Postcard

Thanks a lot for the card and the ad – that was a great idea. I've written off already and hope to hear soon. So we should be working alongside one another in a couple of months' time. Keep your fingers crossed.

Cheers,

Paper 3 (English in Use)

This task is taken from Section B of the English in Use Paper. For information on how to approach this section of Paper 3, see the information and the facsimile questions on pages 109–112 of the Student's Book. The answer sheet for the English in Use Paper is reproduced on pages 139–141 of this Teacher's Book.

Allow approximately 30 minutes for this task.

Key

1	1	accepted	8	✓
	2	✓	9	shops
	3	paid	10	worth
	4	reduce	11	✓
	5	crime	12	help
	6	presence	13	arranging
	7	security	14	vision/visibility

2   Possible answers:
   (15)   resident/residing
   (16)   not accept
   (17)   to establish/to determine
   (18)   essential
   (19)   unoccupied
   (20)   valuables
   (21)   unattended/unsupervised
   (22)   a personal/an individual
   (23)   admission/entry
   (24)   be reported
   (25)   regulations
   (26)   be obtained
   (27)   advisable
   (28)   to purchase

Paper 4 (Listening)

This task is taken from Section C of the Listening Paper. For information on how to approach this section of Paper 4, see the information and the facsimile questions on pages 122–124 of the Student's Book. The answer sheet for the Listening Paper is reproduced on page 142 of this Teacher's Book.

Allow approximately 10 minutes for this task.

Tapescript

Mr Buckhurst: Now Flora erm sit yourself down. I've been talking to Mrs Petts er and as as you already know she has a few problems with you.

Flora: Just a few. Well er I've got a few problems with her as well.

B: Well that's what I wanted to hear.

F: Well I don't really want to go first because then I feel I have to put my neck on the line. Er, it's just er I don't feel I'm being given enough responsibility at the moment.

Mrs Petts: I think part of the problem is is is that you haven't really shown yourself really capable of taking any more responsibility.

F: Er but that's because you're not giving me the chance.

P: Ah well there are plenty of opportunities for you. Let me give you an example Mr er Buckhurst. [hm hm] Erm we we we recently have as you know been having training sessions with the new computer software. Now as far as I know according to Miss Beatty anyway, Flora didn't actually show up for the main for most of [yes, why is that?] she wasn't actually there.

F: Because I had to got to the Doctor's. I phoned you and it was all okayed.

B: Well Miss Beatty er

P: Fair enough on one occasion but I think I think as far as far as I can see there were four different occasions where you didn't actually show up for these sessions.

F: Yes but I had to make appointments because I had a series of tests being run and I had to go back for the results. I can't help that.

B: Yes but Flora does it sound to you as though someone that's doing this sort of thing is that interested in promotion?

F: Ha, well quite honestly I'd just given up the idea of promotion because every time I gave suggestions then they were just knocked on the head. I I mean I've got qualifications. I've got skills in Wordperfect, I've got all the right you know things for this job and I'm not being given the opportunity to use them and these training things they're just lip service as far as I can see. I've been asking and asking and by that time I've just had enough, because aw for me to go along to the training sessions would just mean that I would had had the training and then be left in the same place because that's what's happened before. That's what happened when I went away on that course last year.

P: The thing is though you see at the moment your job description says that you are a secretary therefore your skills are those of a secretary. Now it seems to me [yeah] that what you are saying is [want to] you actually want to be doing a different sort of job, which is not the job [I want] that is not the job which you are being employed to do.

F: No, I do not do not want to be doing a different sort of job. What I don't want is to be called into the office and asked to take memos all day and just type letters because quite frankly [Miss Mac] you could employ a pet dog to do that.

B: Miss MacDonald please please ...

P: But that's what you're employed to do.

B: Exactly that is part of your job description.

F: I I I

B: You surely understood that when you took the job.

F: Yes I do understand that, but what was specified at that interview was that there would be a chance to move onwards and upwards possibly for promotion in the ...

B: By impressing Mrs Petts and Miss Beatty ...

F: Why

P: She

F: But

P: How long have you actually been here?

F: Three months.

P: Well exactly – three months – and what are you expecting you're expecting now to be to be doing to having the sort of responsibility that somebody who'd been here a year wouldn't have, and the other thing is that your whole attitude is that of somebody reluctant, surly bad tempered. You never come to er er brer er group meetings you know and you ...

F: I do come to group meetings.

F: I don't come to group meetings as often as I should because all I do is get shouted down by you and I don't think that it's fair just because you're in a position of authority over me that all that you do is crush my ideas and it comes to a point when any employee is in a position where they get tired of giving ideas and giving of themselves and just come in and do the job and leave and and hence you end up with employees bored and fed up and they've had no challenges and no responsibilities which is how I feel and I've been made to feel like that (fade)

Key

1	P	6	B
2	B	7	B
3	F	8	P
4	F	9	F
5	B		

Paper 5 (Speaking)

This task is taken from Phase B of the Speaking Paper. For information on how to approach this section of Paper 5, see the information and facsimile questions on pages 133–134 of the Student's Book.

Marking guidelines

See 'What are the examiners looking for?' on page 133 of the Student's Book.

Eleven

A
Learning at school

Starter activity

> **Aims**
> To start students thinking about the topic of learning at school.
> To give fluency practice.

Make sure students tick the thoughts they agree with. It would probably be better to carry out the discussion with the class as a whole, so that you can monitor students' knowledge of the vocabulary area and feed in any new items.

Reading

> **Aims**
> To encourage further thought on the topic.
> To practise a CAE Paper 1 (Reading) multiple matching task.
> To practise reading both for gist and specific detail.
> To extend students' vocabulary range.

1 You could set a time limit, e.g. 4 minutes, for this gist-reading.

3 This is a mixture of a comprehension and a vocabulary extension activity. It doesn't matter if students get the wrong answer. What matters more is that they discuss and give reasons for their answers before checking the texts.

Key
1 The schooling in the United States is unusual because it is undertaken by Brazilian students who come to the

States for a short time to live and study. St. Christopher School, Letchworth, is unusual because it is a boarding school and it also has a particularly relaxed and supportive atmosphere.

✱ **2** A 1, 2   B 1, 2   C 1   D 1   E 1, 2
  F 2   G 1   H 1, 2   I 1, 2   J 2

  3   1   budget, cramming, host family, curfew, tough, lug, economize, the target, reimbursed
      2   a soap, gossip, wave machines, strict, the loo, roller skates, clay, trainers, snooker, a chore

✱ ## Writing

> **Aims**
> To practise a CAE Paper 2 (Writing) task.
> To consolidate the language and content of the reading articles.

Before students write their letters – for classwork or homework – discuss with them who the target reader of the letter is, what style would be best for the letter, what effect the letter should have on the reader, and the organisation of information in their letters.

Key

Content: This should cover all the points mentioned in the rubric.

Register: This will probably be neutral to informal as it is a letter home.

Effect on target reader: This is likely to be positive in as much as the letter will be friendly. It could also worry those at home if the content showed that the writer wasn't settling in very well.

Language: This should be accurate and show as much range as is demanded by the letter (possibly not much in this case). Wording should not be lifted inappropriately from the rubric.

Grammar reminder: indirect questions

> **Aim**
> To revise how and when to use indirect questions.

You could elicit the rules about how to make indirect questions before students read them. They could then check their answers against the Student's Book.

Key

1 (1) *if I was/am enjoying my stay*
  (2) *how long I had/I've been here*
  (3) *if I liked/like American food*
  (4) *why I had come/came to the United States*
  (5) *what I would/will remember most and best about the United States*

Listening

> **Aims**
> To practise listening both for gist and for detail.
> To practise a CAE Paper 4 (Listening) task: deciding who holds which opinion.

NB Some of the answers to these questions are not stated explicitly.

Tapescript

Woman: Well I always thought I wanted to be a hairdresser; you know, because I thought, I thought I wanted to do that from the age of about 5 and then I did it for my work experience.

Man: Oh, I did work experience as well.

Woman: Did you?

Man: Yeh, I ... I did it in a lift factory of all places [oh, Cor]. I don't ... I do know why ... because it was really really close to my house, so I thought [oh, right] ... well, I might as well (yeh) kind of thing and it was O.K.

Woman: Did you go on and work in the factory?

Man: No, I didn't really. Well the only reason I did it was because it was so close to my house [yeh]

that I could kind of get home early [yeh] and it would be better than going to school.

Woman: So, what sort of things did you have to do for that then?

Man: Well, I don't know, you just kind of join in on lots and lots of tea-making really. Erm, but you join in, just see how it works, walk around and become a part of it. What ... did you actually cut people's hair?

Woman: Oh no, I mean it was really boring. I worked at this place called Raimondo's, and I thought I'd be like washing hair and stuff like that [yes], and all I ended up doing was sticking the towels in the tumble drier, erm mopping up a bit of hair [yeh] and putting the ... filling up the conditioner bottles. It was really boring [yeh], so that put me off for life. So I'm going to do physiotherapy now.

Man: Oh, that's good, but I mean, was it worth doing do you think I mean ...?

Woman: Well, it was a good laugh and I ... I met my boyfriend there [oh], and we're getting engaged. [that's alright] That's that's the only good thing I'd say about work experience really

Man: Hm, I haven't got many good things to say about it really, but then it did introduce me to the workings of a factory [right] erm, so I've got a bit of insider knowledge now. [right, yeh]

Key

1 The woman worked in a hairdresser's doing things such as cleaning and filling up bottles. The man worked in a lift factory making cups of tea.

✱ 2 A–W B–M C–W and M D–W E–W F–M G–W

✱ Speaking

> **Aims**
> To practise a CAE Paper 5 (Speaking) Phase D task.
> To give students fluency practice.
> To consolidate and round off the topic of learning at school.

You could organise this activity in groups of four students, with two acting as assessors and two as candidates. Then reverse the roles.

B

What makes us learn?

Starter activity

> **Aims**
> To start thinking about the topic of hothousing.
> To prepare for and introduce the listening text.

NB Hothousing is a way of bringing up children. It involves intensively teaching very young children to do all kinds of things that are usually taught much later, e.g. language, reading, writing, maths.

Add further questions if you wish to get the discussion going.

Listening

> **Aims**
> To practise listening both for gist and for specific information.
> To think further about what makes us learn.

This extract is taken from a true story.

Tapescript

Presenter: There was little that was conservative about Aaron Stern when thirty-five years ago, he gathered the media at a Brooklyn hospital for a remarkable event. Stern was about to launch perhaps the most flamboyant and brazen hothousing experiment of all time. 'Gentlemen of the press,' he announced as he was photographed by the cot of his infant daughter, 'I'd like you to meet my daughter, Edith. I am going to make her a genius and a perfect person.'

Edith was to be a human experiment. Her father, who now lives in Miami, had developed a theory that the world's evil was nothing more than the result of barbaric stupidity. If men and women could be made more intelligent, he reasoned, they would henceforth be less likely to follow another Hitler. Edith was to be the incarnation of his ideas, and in our cynical world, of course, something of a hostage to fortune.

Aaron Stern could not work as he was disabled, so he began to devote his time to teaching and developing his child. He spoke to her constantly, holding forth on philosophy and explaining the theories of Darwin and Freud as he fed her from a bottle. His wife Bella was not permitted to nurse the baby.

That, said Stern, was valuable learning time; Edith could read by the time she was two. He purchased second-hand volumes of the Encyclopaedia Britannica and placed them in her cot. By the time she was four she'd read them. Aaron Stern took Edith to museums and operas. In fact, he took her everywhere he might want to go, reading, training, explaining, even when he could not tell if she understood.

She was able to speak in full sentences by the time she was a year old. From that moment onwards, while living in conditions of some deprivation (one room without a window) he conducted a running dialogue with her; she could read at two, play music at three, chess at four.

School was not a happy time for Edith. One teacher called her arrogant; another said she knew a lot of stuff, but had a mediocre mind. Her father withdrew Edith from state school at the age of nine to educate her full time at home. She had made no long-term friends, and entered college at twelve. At fifteen, Edith became an assistant professor of mathematics – the youngest in American history – at Michigan State University, while she studied for a doctorate.

Edith was not, Stern now stresses, a natural Einstein, but today she has an IQ of 203 and works for IBM in secret computer software research and development.

In most respects it would seem that as an adult, Edith Stern comes near to her father's ideal, though he sometimes complains now that she does not really love him. 'She doesn't have the love she should have for a father with a pacemaker,' he says. ('Do you love him?' we asked. 'Sometimes, yes,' Edith replied.)

Now thirty five, with shoulder length brown hair and glasses that constantly slip down her nose, Edith is softly spoken but blunt and impatient, and does not suffer fools – or journalists – gladly.

Edith and her husband, a computer programmer, live in a house full of books, with one entire room full of science fiction. Her father thinks her preoccupation with science fiction is a waste of time; she regards it as a wonderful mental exercise and both she and her husband are active in the local sci-fi society. Edith is the mother of a six-year-old son, whom she teaches and hothouses much as her father taught her.

* Key

2

> **A portrait of Edith Stern**
> 1 Father's name: Aaron Stern
> 2 Father's occupation: none; unemployed because of disablement/full-time hothouser
> 3 Mother's name: Bella
> 4 Methods employed by father to 'develop' his child: Constantly talking to her on advanced subjects, taking her to museums, operas etc., always giving her challenges, always exploiting any situation for its learning potential, full-time education at home
> 5 Age at which accomplished the following:
>   read: 2
>   read the *Encyclopaedia Britannica*: 4
>   spoke in full sentences: 1
>   played music: 3
>   played chess: 4
>   went to college: 12
>   became an assistant professor of mathematics: 15
> 6 IQ: 203
> 7 Current job: researcher in secret computer software
> 8 Physical description: brown shoulder-length hair, wears glasses
> 9 Character description: impatient, direct
> 10 Age: 35
> 11 Marital status: married (with one child)
> 12 Interests: science fiction

Reading

> **Aims**
> To practise reading for gist, deducing meaning, and reading for detail.
> To practise CAE Paper 1 (Reading) gapped paragraphs and cloze tasks.

1 You could give students a time limit, e.g. 2 minutes, to encourage them to read for gist.

2 Encourage students to work out the meaning of the vocabulary items from the context of the article.

3 Students could do this activity individually, and then pair up to check and justify their answers before checking with the class as a whole.

* 5 This is a cloze task as in Paper 3 (English in Use). You could ask students to do it individually, in pairs, in groups, or for homework.

Key

1 It seems to suggest that both are strong.

2 *talent will out* – special abilities will reveal themselves
startling – amazing
to discern – to notice
to track down – to hunt
determining – deciding
a mapping technique – a way of showing where things are

a riddle – a puzzle
innate – inborn
a brain scanner – a machine that reads cerebral activity
distinctive – special
lateralisation – a process involving the development of one side of the brain
all-round – general
to give ammunition – to strengthen

3 a T
b F (she believes talent will out)
c F (he hopes he may have)
d T
e T
f F (she hasn't proved it; her studies seem to indicate that this is true in the States at least)
g F (lateralisation seems to occur more strongly in boys than girls; when it is extreme it seems to aid the ability to do mathematics)
h F (proportionally, Chinese boys seem to be better at maths than Chinese girls; however there seem to be more Chinese girls than American girls who are good at maths)
i T

4 1 E   2 A   3 D   4 F   5 B

5 (1) spend
(2) parental
(3) cause
(4) both
(5) style/way
(6) However
(7) sure
(8) guarantee

Grammar analysis: the present perfect and present perfect continuous tenses

> **Aim**
> To raise awareness of the differences in meaning between the present perfect and present perfect progressive tenses.

Key

1 (1) *present*
(2) *past*
(3) *influence/effect/results*
(4) *duration*
(5) *finished/terminated*

2 1 *have been studying*
2 *have never read*
3 *have really enjoyed/have really been enjoying*
4 *has marked*
5 *has always had*
6 *have been sending*
7 *has always believed*
8 *have been studying*

Vocabulary summary

> **Aim**
> To revise the form and meaning of the main
> vocabulary fields in the unit.

You could do this activity as a competition. It is possible that students will come up with different opposites for certain words. This is because the precise meaning of a word will depend on the context it is used in. You could ask students to find contexts to justify their choice of particular opposites.

Key
Possible answers:
ambitious – unambitious
tough – lenient
temporary – permanent
cosy – cold
strict – lenient or tolerant
ahead – behind
tolerant – intolerant or strict
dull – bright
fresh – stale
protest – acceptance
ban – allow
gifted – ungifted
exaggerated – normal
distinctive – ordinary
innate – cultivated
stimulating – boring
alert – dull
clear – unclear or confused
shoot ahead – lag or trail behind
fascinate – bore
narrow-minded – open-minded

Ways of learning: different reasons for reading

> **Aim**
> To further explore different ways of reading.

This section should reinforce students' confidence in the fact that it is not necessary to read in the same way for all tasks, and indeed that to do so can be counter-productive. How you read depends on why you are reading.

Key
2 understand the general meaning of the text: Section A, page 143, activity 1; Section B, page 148, activity 1

understand each word in the text: none

understand the details of particular parts of the text: Section A, pages 143 and 144, activities 2 and 3; Section B, page 148, activity 3

understand the general meaning of particular sentences: Section B, page 148, activity 4

C

Paper 1 (Reading): Gapped paragraphs

> **Aims**
> To familiarise students with the aims and content of CAE Paper 1 (Reading): gapped paragraphs.
> To provide strategies for dealing with gapped paragraph tasks.

Using lexical and grammatical clues

1 Make sure that students note down what they are doing as they make their decisions. This will help them do activity 2.

2 It is not always obvious how to complete a gapped paragraph task. Students should try to develop a systematic way of approaching this task, as they would for e.g. multiple choice. Some gaps are usually easier to fill than others, and students could begin with these and then tentatively try to complete the others by a process of elimination. What students need to do is get a feel for the argument/chronology/development of the text, so they can almost predict what will come next. Although reading for detail can play a role in carrying out this kind of task; especially when making final decisions, what helps most initially is understanding the sequence of the text at paragraph level. See the key to activity 4 for discussion of the various strategies.

3 Not all the clues in this text are circled – there are so many of them! This activity is designed to show students the range of clues that can occur and also their position in the text – i.e. before and/or after the gap, and sometimes at a considerable distance from the gap.

Key
1   1 A   2 E   3 C   4 D   5 B   6 G

3   1   *my first week at university*
    2   *a first*
    3   *he slept late in the mornings*
    4   *adult life*
    5   *the sketchiest of weekly timetables ... defining time*
    6   *a book/a few pages*
    7   *lecture notes*
    8   *strategy*

4   a   is not a good idea. Detailed understanding of the whole text is rarely required for this kind of task.
    b   is not a good idea. It will be quite possible to carry out the task without understanding every word. Reading on this level is also very slow and would eat up valuable time.
    c   is a good idea. Probably the best thing to do first with these texts is to read them for gist.

d may be a good idea but not necessarily. If some answers seem obvious from the beginning, it will be useful to note these down to act as clues for the rest of the answers. Be careful though, these answers may be wrong. They will need to be confirmed by further reading of the text and the completion of the other blanks.

e No, don't make final decisions as you go through. Just make tentative decisions which will need to be confirmed or otherwise once you have finished. All the text is so interdependent that if one answer is wrong at least one other answer will also be wrong.

f This can be a good idea, and some people certainly like to work in this way. Don't end up underlining everything though, as this could be quite confusing.

g There will probably be more than one clue for each gap. These may be before and/or after the gap.

h Yes, definitely.

i This can be a good idea, as it is quite easy to forget what you have decided should go where. It also helps you to read through the text in order when looking for further clues.

j This can be useful, especially if you aren't very sure of your answers, as it will help you to get into the development of the text.

Exam practice

Key

1 D   2 C   3 E   4 A

Twelve

A

Time off

Starter activities

> **Aim**
> **To start students thinking about the topic of leisure
> activities.**

1–2 Students could have access to dictionaries if they
wish. Remind them to check the correct pronunciation
of any new vocabulary.

Key
**1   surfing, watching a football match, going to the
theatre, hill-walking**
**2   Possible answers: reading, eating out, playing chess,
attending a pop concert, taking a coach tour, drinking
with friends.**

Speaking

> **Aims**
> **To stimulate discussion of trends in leisure activities
> at different ages and in different cultures.**
> **To practise using contrastive conjunctions.**

1   Write the four age-ranges on the board while
students keep their books closed. This will encourage
them to think of their own ideas first before consulting
the table.

2   Encourage students to practise using contrastive
conjunctions as they discuss the statements about
leisure.

Listening

> **Aims**
> **To practise inferring information or views.**
> **To practise a CAE Paper 4 (Listening): Section D task.**
> **To stimulate discussion about favourite times of day.**

1–✳2   Explain to students that there is inevitably
some degree of overlap between the time-periods
listed, but that in general they are seen as being fairly
distinct in English. (*The small hours* is the term often
used to describe the early hours of the morning, any
a.m. time between about 1 and 3.)

Warn students not to expect the speakers always to use
the words in the answer options. They may paraphrase
them, or provide clues by which it is possible to infer
the time of day being referred to and the reasons for
a speaker's preference. This is often a feature of the
Section D listening extracts, and students need to be
actively listening for relevant clues.

Tapescript
V1: I think my favourite time of day is probably first
thing after breakfast ... I like the feeling of the day
still stretching out in front of you ... and it's probably
because I like to feel I have everything ahead of me
properly organised, sort of neatly planned out ... er you
see, I'm not too good at coping with the unexpected!
V2: Yeah, funnily enough the best time of day for me is
the middle of the night ... um, I'm often awake for
two or three hours in the very early morning, but I
don't really mind because, that's the time when I do
a lot of my thinking or reading, things I rarely have
time to do during the rest of the day. I'm the sort of
person who needs plenty of time and space to myself
so, you know, perhaps it's just as well!
V3: I find it takes me a while to get going ... and I'm
terrible first thing in the morning so that's not my
best time at all ... but after lunch I'm usually raring
to go and really keen to pack as much as I can into
what's left of the day ... and from then on it takes a
lot to wear me out!

V4: I suppose I'm what you'd call a night-owl ... by the time everyone else is ready for bed, I'm ready to get up and go ... which doesn't always go down too well with my friends and family. I've always been a bit unconventional in the hours I keep but then I've always been confident enough to do my own thing, and not be forced into a so-called "normal" routine.

V5: I think the end of the day is probably my favourite time ... you know, when the working day is over and everyone's at home enjoying a meal together or just relaxing. Summer evenings at home in the garden ... just as the sun's going down ... that's the time when I get a real sense of contentment and well-being ... I wouldn't want to be anywhere else!

Key

2	1	B		6	B
	2	H		7	F
	3	D		8	D
	4	G		9	C
	5	E		10	A

Your thoughts

You might like to follow up with a class survey to find out which are the most popular times of day, and why. Ask students to write a short report on their findings with illustrative diagrams (e.g. bar charts etc.) and encourage them use contrastive conjunctions when they describe the results.

Reading

> **Aims**
> To practise reading for detail.
> To practise identifying a writer's opinions.
> To extend vocabulary relating to work and leisure.

1 As usual, students do not need to read and understand every word in the text to answer the initial questions. Set a time limit if necessary.

2 Ask students to organise any new vocabulary from these two fields so that it becomes easier to learn and remember.

For example, they could draw a pair of cartoons: one – a miserable man at work surrounded by think-bubbles containing illustrations and vocabulary for the different leisure activities he wishes he was doing; the other – the same man, but much happier now because he's shown enjoying one of the leisure activities and is surrounded by think-bubbles illustrating aspects of the working life that he's temporarily left behind.

You could ask students to work in small groups on different parts of the overall design, and then display the results for the benefit of the whole class.

✱ 3 Students will need to read the text more carefully to answer the multiple choice questions. Refer them back to the guidance given in Section C of Unit 1 (page 26) if necessary.

Key

1 senior business executives; to take the services of a 'leisure adviser'

2 a *corporations, captain of industry, workers, tycoon, board of directors, schedule of appointments, senior executive, burnout, the office, faxes, overseas subsidiaries, deal, bankers, lucrative client*

b *ease up, luxurious yacht, beach house, play golf, climb mountains, ride river rapids, go scuba diving, play tennis, holiday home, leisurely walk*

3 1 C   2 C   3 C   4 A   5 B

Grammar reminder: *would* and *used to*

> **Aims**
> To revise the use of would and used to to talk about the past.
> To practise using would and used to.

Key

1	1	*used to*
	2	*used to/would*
	3	*used to*
	4	*used to/would*
	5	*used to/would*
	6	*used to*

B

Moving images

Starter activity

> **Aim**
> To start students thinking about the topic of film, television and video.

1–2 Set these activities as homework in advance of the lesson. Alternatively, do the activities in class, but make sure that students move around to interview people.

Reading

> **Aims**
> To practise reading for detail.
> To develop and extend knowledge of phrasal verbs.

1–2 The whole of the quiz could be done in class, but the reading, scoring and analysis may take up quite a lot of time. An alternative would be to ask students to read and respond to the quiz (1) in advance of the lesson, and then to follow up with the scoring and analysis (2) in class. Remind students that this type of popular quiz is designed for fun and shouldn't be taken too seriously. You might like to go on to discuss with them the value or otherwise of such a quiz.

3 These activities focus on some commonly-used phrasal verbs in English.

After compiling with students a list of all the phrasal verbs from the two texts, you may want to focus attention on those particular phrasal verbs which your students are less likely to have encountered. This may depend partly on whether you have a monolingual or multilingual group.

To help students learn new phrasal verbs you could make up a class display with examples or illustrations. Alternatively, keep two boxes in the class – one containing cards with the new phrasal verbs and the other containing cards with explanations and illustrations for the verbs. From time to time, ask a student to pick out a card from one of the boxes and then challenge the rest of the class to give or find the matching phrasal verb/explanation.

Key

3

turn on	*work out*
tune in	*send off*
find out	*finish off*
settle down	*fall into*
get to	*get out (and about)*
glaze over	*lie back*
put together	*guard against*
get off (to sleep)	*flake out*
jot down	*nod off*
look forward to	*miss out on*
flick between	*rush off*
jump at	

Grammar analysis: time clauses

> **Aims**
> To revise and analyse the use of time clauses.
> To practise using time clauses.

Key

1 2 *until*   3 *when*   4 *before*   5 *after*

2 1 b   2 e   3 d   4 a   5 c

3
a *before, prior to*
b *while, whilst, during, at the same time, as, whenever*
c *after, subsequently*
d *when, the moment, once, as soon as, immediately*
e *since, until, till, by the time*

5 *... I dislike being interrupted while watching my favourite programmes ...*
... when watching a debate ... I often work out what I'd say ...
I am annoyed when my favourite programmes are being shown at the same time ...
... when I watch a travel or holiday programme I'm transported into another world ...
I usually have the TV on in the background while I do jobs around the house
I often bring work home and finish it off while watching TV

Listening

Aims
To practise listening for gist.
To practise listening for speakers' opinions.
To stimulate discussion on violence in films.
To raise awareness of the role of hesitation techniques in spoken English.

1 Make sure students have a chance to discuss the eight statements thoroughly before listening to the extract. This will help to activate relevant vocabulary and aid their comprehension while listening.

2 The discussion on tape is quite long. Reassure students that when they first listen they don't need to hear and understand every word, but should instead focus on identifying the topic of the conversation.

3 Students should now concentrate on the various opinions expressed. Explain that they may still not understand everything, but that this need not stop them from picking out the different speakers' opinions.

4 This time focus students' attention on the way in which speakers' comments are punctuated with hesitation expressions. Point out that hesitating is a very natural feature of native speaker English. Play the first quarter of the conversation to illustrate this (*in fact*, *um*, *you know*). Then go on and ask students to listen to the rest of the conversation and tick the other phrases used.

Explain to students that hesitating allows the speaker valuable time to organise their thoughts, restructure what they are saying, maintain their turn in the conversation etc. Learning to hesitate properly in English may help to make a non-native speaker sound more fluent.

Tapescript
V1: ... I remember actually seeing previews and trailers when I'd gone to see other films at the cinema, and I was completely put off because I don't especially like going to sit through a violent film, if I'm forewarned then I won't go and I really didn't want to go and see what; what I think really upsets me more, if I go to see a film – and I've not been prepared in any way for the violence that actually happens [yes] within the film, that upsets me more; in fact I went to see, I think it was a Clint Eastwood film and it was a cowboy, and I just, I left, I actually walked out because I – I thought that I've been given the choice, had I've gone in with the knowledge that this was going to be a violent film – fine, but I wasn't, and I felt really subjected to something that I hadn't chosen and *that* upset me more ...

V2: Didn't, weren't you a bit naive to see [No!] to go into a Clint Eastwood cowboy film and not imagine you're going to see violence?

V1: No I think not because I think with those sort of cowboy films they, you do expect a certain level of, um, high action [mm] and I'm prepared for that and they are action films and you know, the nature of sort of one character going through the entire film you come into these sort of violent sequences but a lot of people were meeting very very nasty ends and ...

V2: But, but I mean, I think I know the film that you're talking about and the thing is what you'd call high action is when you see, when guns go pop pop pop and people just get killed and you're objecting to a film where you actually see the consequences of of a gun being shot at close range [No ...], and surely that makes the violence more real and more horrible, yes, but it makes you realise that it isn't just cowboys and indians; I mean people talk about cowboys and indians films and they're about killing [yeah, I ...], but they're just bland entertainment, and a film that makes you realise what real violence is [mm, I know, I know this ...] how offensive you find it I think it's ...

V1: Yeah, I know this Nick, and I appreciate what you're saying there but what I feel in this instance is actually I was drawn in to see a film that had been portrayed as being a sort of a wholesome action film – and, and I went in and to me what I saw was a completely different type of film.

V3: Don't you think the directors could do so much more by just leaving things to the imagination?

V1: I think, I mean, I think the power of, of a good film is when you see something happening on the screen and then maybe there is a cut away and you realise something has happened and they don't actually have to spell it out and show all the blood [but I ...] ...

V3: Do you think the censors could do more? I've ...

V2: I think the censors are a waste of time, really because it's like any form of prohibition, once the cat's out of the bag, so to speak, once there're violent films or whatever you're talking about you're trying to prohibit, once it's there people are going to get to it whatever [mm] and prohibition really just blurs the issue [yes, I ...]

V3: But it, but it certainly stops a lot of outlets, if you, if you had a, if you had um censorship for videos for, you know as we do which are largely the same as censorship for films in the cinema, um, surely that would stop certain younger people getting hold of the wrong [no, not at all ...]

V1: Well I actually saw the news only the other night and what's happening now, apart from the censorship that's already seemingly implied on video, you know, video nasties so-called shouldn't be available to, um, people below a certain age, but I mean older children or whichever video outlet is making it accessible for young children to actually see these things, but now there is a telephone line as well, so you can even just over your telephone tap in a certain number and pick up computerised images [mm], um, of all manner of porn and violent films, and the big worry in fact, it was on the news only about a week ago, the big worry is that children are going to have easy access to this.

V3: Mm, so isn't that then the case for banning them

all together?

V2: Well I don't, I just think, talking of banning and censorship is going down a blind alley because all it does is glamorise the things that you're trying to prohibit and people will get their hands on them whatever, and they'll be more inclined to try and see them when you, when you censor them than if you, you know, it's very difficult because you're in a position where you've gone this far, you've made the films, the films exist, and therefore people'll want to see them (fade) …

Key

2 c

3

Opinion	Speaker's view
1 It's better to know if a film contains scenes of violence before you go and see it.	✓
2 Cowboy films don't usually show the real effects of violence.	✓
3 Violence on screen encourages violent behaviour in society.	
4 A good film is one where the audience is encouraged to use their imagination.	✓
5 Young people need to be protected from seeing certain films and videos.	✓
6 Censorship is unfair on both film-makers and the viewing public.	
7 There is a case for banning all pornographic and violent films.	✓
8 Censorship can simply make things appear even more attractive.	✓

4 *um, er, well, in fact, you see, you know, sort of, I mean, I think, so to speak*

Ways of learning: checking back over written work

> **Aims**
> **To encourage students to check back over their written work.**
> **To remind students of the assessment criteria for CAE Paper 2 (Writing) tasks.**

1–2 These activities encourage students to consider features of written work which can contribute to achieving a good mark. There is no 'correct' answer for activity 2. Use the students' ratings as the basis for a discussion and ask them to justify their views with evidence from the piece of written work.

3–4 This could be set as a homework activity, but in a follow-up lesson try to go over with each student

personally their list of the sorts of mistakes or problems that occur in their written work and the steps they could take to improve. This discussion could then lead to either individual checklists or a checklist for the benefit of the whole class. If possible, display or distribute copies of the 'best' checklist for everyone to look at.

Remind students that it is always worth checking back over work, not just in the context of the classroom or of an examination, but also in ordinary day-to-day writing activities. It will ensure that a piece of writing achieves its desired goal, and will have a positive effect on the reader.

✱ Speaking

> **Aims**
> **To practise using hesitating techniques in spoken English.**
> **To practise a CAE Paper 5 (Speaking) Phase C task.**

This activity gives students a chance to discuss further the issue of censorship. Encourage students to try and make use of the hesitating expressions from Listening activity 4.

In a monocultural class it may be possible to focus discussion on specific examples of violent films, books, videos etc. which have caused public concern. In a multicultural class, be aware of possible sensitivities over the issue of moral (and political) censorship which plays a much greater role in some countries than in others.

✱ Writing

> **Aims**
> **To practise writing a formal letter of complaint.**
> **To practise a CAE Paper 2 (Writing) Section B task.**

Encourage students to make use of some of the ideas and language previously encountered during this unit. Before they write, review appropriate beginnings and endings for a formal letter of complaint.

✳ Vocabulary summary

Key

2	1	C		6	D
	2	B		7	B
	3	A		8	D
	4	C		9	A
	5	B		10	C

C

Paper 2 (Writing): Section B

Introduction

Remind students that they have already carried out a number of writing tasks similar to those included in Section B of Paper 2. Here much of the work on writing done in earlier units is reinforced, and important features relating specifically to the preparation and execution of Paper 2 Section B tasks are highlighted.

The three steps – identify, select and connect – reinforce and build upon approaches studied in Unit 7 Section C. Many of the activities here are designed to be done in pairs or small groups, but make sure that you check the progress of the groups after each activity to resolve any problems or confusions.

Key

(1)	*4/four*	(4)	*purpose*
(2)	*1/one*	(5)	*intended audience*
(3)	*content*	(6)	*250*

Identifying the task

1–3 These activities give students a chance to revise and practise identifying the important elements in any writing task: audience, purpose, content, organisation, style. There are no correct answers for activity 3, but students should be able to justify the suggestions they make.

Key
Possible answers:

1   • Who am I writing for?
    • Why am I writing?
    • What am I going to include?
    • How am I going to organise it?
    • What sort of style am I going to adopt?

2   1 an English friend
    2 to respond to his letter and offer some useful advice

3   thanks for the letter and enthusiastic response to the idea, ideas on places to visit, means of travel, places to stay, possible work, invitation to visit

4   order as in 3

5   friendly, positive, encouraging, helpful

Selecting the format

1–5   These activities highlight issues relating to format and layout in writing tasks, and give students relevant practice. There are no correct answers for activities 3, 4 and 5, but again students should be able to justify the suggestions they make.

If possible, show students examples of English language newspapers, magazines, travel brochures, entertainment guides, information leaflets etc. This will help them develop a sense of the variety of formats and layout features which are possible, and the different effects which they create.

Key

1   1 B   2 C   3 A

2

Layout features	A	B	C
section headings		✓	
numbering	✓		
shorter paragraphs		✓	
longer paragraphs			✓
instructions	✓		
letter layout			
note form (rather than full sentences)			
short, simple sentences	✓		✓
longer, more complex sentences		✓	
illustrations/diagrams			✓

Connecting the ideas

1–4   Encourage students to work in groups fairly independently for this, but go round the groups regularly offering advice and checking progress.

In activity 4 remind students to check that the finished text doesn't look as though it has been written by four or five people. Ask them to check that the style is consistent, that appropriate referring expressions (e.g. pronouns) have been used where possible, that appropriate link words are used to help paragraphs run smoothly, that information is consistent from one paragraph to another etc.

Ways of learning: understanding the instructions for a task

1–4   These activities show students the importance of carefully reading and understanding the instructions for a writing task. The annual CAE Examination Report regularly states that students need to be encouraged to read the questions carefully and consider what type of writing is being asked for. The task instructions are skilfully designed to supply candidates with sufficient information about the context of a task to enable them to select an appropriate style and register. They also give precise guidelines on the necessary content.

Advise students that in the examination they should always choose sensibly from the selection of tasks on offer. For example, it might be unwise to choose a work-related writing task if you have little or no experience of work.

Key

1   1   choose one task only

2   follow the instructions given

3   write about 250 words

2   the reader is a friend (i.e. informal style)

the format should be notes (i.e. not a report or an essay)

the purpose is to provide useful/helpful information (and avoid anything irrelevant)

the content should include how ..., where ..., who ... etc.

3   there is no correct answer for this activity but suggestions could include: *place in your own country, good holiday destination, account of how to travel, where to stay, what to see, anything else of interest*

4   they highlight essential information for the writer concerning the context and content of the task

Exam practice

Students will already have done a certain amount of preparation for all the writing tasks. This could be set as a timed activity in class (45 minutes to an hour depending on how much preparation has already been done). Alternatively, set this exam practice for homework and use the writing tasks from Revision Exam Practice 3 (Student's Book page 203), as a class-based practice test. Use the marking guidelines given in Revision Exam Practice 3 (Teacher's Book page 129) to mark the students' work.

Thirteen

A

It's a weird world

Starter activities

> **Aims**
> To start students thinking about the topic of weird phenomena.
> To begin to elicit vocabulary and structures related to the topic.

2 Students are quite likely to have 'weird tales' to tell. Encourage them to share them. They may prefer to work in small groups initially. Any really interesting stories could then be related to the whole class.

Reading

> **Aims**
> To further reflect on the topic of weird phenomena.
> To practise reading both for gist and detail.
> To practise deducing meaning.
> To practise a CAE Paper 1 (Reading) multiple choice task.

1 This text is a factual account, i.e. it does not come from a fictional text. If students come from a non-Christian background, it may be useful to explain to them after they have answered the task that the Virgin Mary was the mother of Jesus Christ, and that in many Christian countries it is common to find shrines to her on roadsides.

2 Encourage students to use supporting text (i.e. the words surrounding any one word) as well as individual words to help them find the answers.

Key
1 The weird phenomenon is the different movements made by the statue.

2
a	*wayside*	g	*a shrine*
b	*tilted*	h	*swaying*
c	*shivering*	i	*shrugging*
d	*intrigued*	j	*untoward*
e	*grotto*	k	*dissipated*
f	*to witness*	l	*a gasp*

✱ 3   1 A   2 D   3 D   4 A   5 A

Grammar reminder: cohesion through substitution

> **Aim**
> To give further practice in recognising and using cohesion.

Key
1
- a *the shrine*
- b *Virgin Mary*
- c *passers-by*
- d *to worship*
- e *to worship*
- f *the statue*
- g *witness a miracle*
- h *moving her head*
- i *move her head*
- j *the situation*

The main function of these words is to avoid repetition and to make the text stick together.

2
- a *it*
- b *it*
- c *do*
- d *did too/so did other people/did so too*
- e *did (it/so)*
- f *do*
- g *does*
- h *it*

Pronouns and auxiliary verbs.

📼 Listening

Aims
To provide an opportunity to listen to and enjoy a 'good story'.
To practise listening both for gist and for detail.
To provide fluency and accuracy practice in speaking.

Fictional texts are not used in the CAE exam. This one is included here for students' pleasure and to encourage them to enjoy listening to English.

2 The answers to this question will vary from person to person. The activity is designed to get students talking about the story, and to explore comprehension through the discussion.

3 Students will need to understand these words to get the most out of activity 4.

4 You could do this activity as suggested in the Student's Book. Alternatively, it lends itself well to a jigsaw listening approach in which students only note down those parts of the story you designate to them.

Tapescript

Story teller: The night was clear and fine above us. The stars shone cold and bright, while a half-moon bathed the whole scene in a soft, uncertain light. Before us lay the dark bulk of the house, its serrated roof and bristling chimneys hard outlined against the silver spangled sky. Broad bars of golden light from the lower windows stretched across the orchard and the moor. One of them was suddenly shut off. The servants had left the kitchen. There only remained the lamp in the dining-room where the two men, the murderous host and the unconscious guest, still chatted over their cigars.

Every minute that white, wool plain which covered one half of the moor was drifting closer and closer to the house. Already the first thin whisps of it were curling across the golden square of the lighted window. The farther wall of the orchard was already invisible, and the trees were standing out of a swirl of white vapour. As we watched it the fog-wreaths came crawling round both corners of the house and rolled slowly into one dense bank, on which the upper floor and the roof floated like a strange ship on a shadowy sea. Holmes struck his hand passionately on the rock in front of us and stamped his feet in his impatience.

'If he isn't out in a quarter of an hour the path will be covered. In half an hour we won't be able to see our hands in front of us.'

'Shall we move further back upon higher ground?'

'Yes, I think it would be as well.'

So as the fog bank flowed onwards we fell back before it until we were half a mile from the house, and still that dense white sea, with the moon silvering its upper edge, swept slowly and inexorably on.

'We are going too far,' said Holmes. 'We dare not take the chance of his being overtaken before he can reach us. At all costs we must hold our ground where we are.' He dropped on his knees and clapped his ear to the ground. 'Thank Heaven. I think I hear him coming.'

A sound of quick steps broke the silence of the moor. Crouching among the stones we stared intently at the silver-tipped bank in front of us. The steps grew louder, and through the fog, as through a curtain, there stepped the man whom we were awaiting. He looked round in surprise as he emerged into the clear, star-lit night. Then he came swiftly along the path, passed close to where we lay, and went on up the long slope behind us. As he walked he glanced continually over either shoulder, like a man who is ill at ease.

'Hist!' cried Holmes, and I heard the sharp click of a cocking pistol. 'Look out! It's coming!' There was a thin, crisp, continuous patter from somewhere in the heart of that crawling bank. The cloud was within fifty yards of where we lay, and we glared at it, all three, uncertain what horror was about to break from the heart of it. I was at Holmes' elbow and I glanced for an instant at his face. It was pale and exultant, his eyes shining brightly in the moonlight, but suddenly they started forward in a rigid, fixed stare and his lips parted in amazement. Lestrade gave a yell of terror and threw himself downwards upon the ground. I sprang to my feet, my inert hand grasping my pistol, my mind paralysed by the dreadful shape which had sprung out upon us from the shadows of the fog. A hound it was, an enormous coal-black hound, but not such a hound as mortal eyes have ever seen. Fire burst from its open mouth, its eyes glowed with a smouldering glare, its muzzle and hackles and dewlap were outlined in flickering flame. Never in the delirious dream of a disordered brain could anything more savage, more appalling be conceived than that dark form and savage face which broke upon us out of the wall of fog.

With long bounds the huge creature was leaping down the track, following hard upon the footsteps of our friend. So paralysed were we by the apparition that we allowed him to pass before we had recovered our nerve. Then Holmes and I both fired together, and the creature gave a hideous howl, which showed that one at least had hit him. He did not pause, however, but bounded onwards. Far away on the path we saw Sir Henry looking back, his face white in the moonlight, his hands raised in horror, glaring helplessly at the frightful thing which was hunting him down.

But that cry of pain from the hound had blown all our fears to the wind. If he was vulnerable, he was mortal, and if we could wound him, we could kill him. Never have I seen a man run as Holmes ran that night. I am reckoned fleet of foot, but he outpaced me as much as I outpaced the little professional. In front of us as we flew up the track we heard scream after scream from Sir Henry and the deep roar of the hound. I was in time to see the beast spring upon its victim, hurl him to the ground and worry at his throat. But the next instant Holmes had emptied five barrels of his revolver into the creature's flank. With a last howl of agony and a vicious snap in the air, it rolled upon its back, four feet pawing furiously, and then fell limp upon its side. I stooped, panting, and pressed my pistol to the dreadful, shimmering head, but it was useless to pull the trigger. The giant hound was dead.

Sir Henry lay insensible where he had fallen. We tore away his collar, and Holmes breathed a prayer of gratitude when he saw that there was no sign of a wound and that the rescue had been in time. Already our friend's eyelids shivered and he made a feeble effort to move. Lestrade thrust his brandy-flask between the baronet's teeth, and two frightened eyes were looking up at us.

'My God!' he whispered. 'What was it? What, in Heaven's name, was it?'

'It's dead, whatever it is,' said Holmes. 'We've laid the family ghost once and for ever.'

In mere size and strength it was a terrible creature which was lying stretched before us. It was not a pure bloodhound and it was not a pure mastiff; but it appeared to be a combination of the two – gaunt, savage and as large as a small lioness. Even now, in the stillness of death, the huge jaws seemed to be dripping with a bluish flame, and the small, deep-set cruel eyes were ringed with fire.

Key

1   Yes it is successful, as they get rid of the Hound of the Baskervilles for ever and also solve the mystery of what the monster is.

✳ Writing

Whether students carry out this task at home or in class, you could have a useful classroom discussion beforehand about its contents and layout.

Reports don't have a fixed layout, but they do often make use of headings, so you could encourage students to do so too. The headings in Lestrade's notes are probably the most useful ones to use.

Discuss how formal the report should be, how detailed, the effect it should create, and what sequence it should follow.

Key

Content: to cover all points outlined in the instructions

Register: neutral or formal

Target audience: a chief inspector in the police

Effect on target reader: precision and efficiency

Range of language: as appropriate to the task – in this case, quite detailed

Speaking: illustrating your point

Key

2   The answers to this will depend on your students' opinions.

B

It's a damaged world

Starter activities

> **Aims**
> **To start thinking about the topic of pollution.**
> **To consolidate and/or extend use and pronunciation of vocabulary related to the topic of pollution.**

1 By comparing their answers students will see a broader range of vocabulary items.

3 Some of these words may be difficult to pronounce, particularly from the point of view of word stress. Ensure that students get this as accurate as they can.

Tapescript

2 fossil fuels, plastics, chemicals, domestic waste, industrial waste, gases, car exhausts, air pollution, water pollution, soil pollution, chemical pollution, acid rain, transport pollution, water contamination, energy production, noise pollution.

3 plastics, chemicals, domestic waste, industrial waste, gases, car exhausts, soil pollution, chemical pollution, acid rain, transport pollution, water contamination, energy production, noise pollution.

Key

2 Pollutants: fossil fuels, plastics, chemicals, domestic waste, industrial waste, gases, car exhausts

Pollution: air pollution, water pollution, soil pollution, chemical pollution, acid rain, transport pollution, water contamination, energy production, noise pollution

3 'plastics
'chemicals
do'mestic 'waste
in'dustrial 'waste
'gases
'car ex'hausts
'soil po'llution

'chemical po'llution
'acid 'rain
'transport po'llution
'water contami'nation
'energy pro'duction
'noise po'llution

🔲 Listening

> **Aims**
> **To practise a CAE Paper 4 (Listening) note-taking task.**
> **To practise listening for specific information and detail.**

This text is taken from Rachel Carson's book *Silent Spring*, a book about how people are destroying the world through polluting it. This book came out in the 1950s and was very influential in developing the environmental movement.

1 Encourage students to describe as much as possible of what they can see before they listen to the extract. In this way listening serves to check rather than to give answers.

✳ 2 Point out to students that they must try to keep within the word limit in their answers. In the exam it tends to be the overlong answers in note-taking that are the wrong answers – generally because they contain more room for inaccuracy of comprehension or spelling.

Tapescript

1 There was once a town in the heart of America where all life seemed to live in harmony with its surroundings. The town lay in the midst of a chequerboard of prosperous farms, with fields of grain and hillsides of orchards where, in spring, white clouds of bloom drifted above the green fields. In autumn, oak and maple and birch trees set up a blaze of colour that flamed and flickered against a backdrop of pines. Then foxes barked in the hills and deer silently crossed the fields, half hidden in the mists of the autumn mornings.

Along the roadsides flowering bushes and wild flowers delighted the traveller's eye through much of the year. Even in winter the roadsides were places of beauty, where countless birds came to feed on the berries and on the seed heads of the dried weeds rising above the snow. The countryside was, in fact, famous for the abundance and variety of its bird life, and when the flood of migrant birds was pouring through in spring and autumn, people travelled from great distances to observe them. Others came to fish the streams, which flowed clear and cold out of the hills and contained shady pools where trout lay. So it had been from the days many years ago when the first settlers raised their houses, sank their wells, and built their barns.

2 Then a strange blight crept over the area and everything began to change. Some evil spell had settled on the community: mysterious maladies swept the flocks of chickens; the cattle and sheep sickened and died. Everywhere was a shadow of death. The farmers spoke of much illness among their families. In the town the doctors had become more and more puzzled by new kinds of sickness appearing among their patients. There had been several sudden and unexplained deaths, not only among adults but even among children, who would be stricken suddenly while at play and die within a few hours.

There was a strange stillness. The birds, for example – where had they gone? Many people spoke of them, puzzled and disturbed. The feeding stations in the backyards were deserted. The few birds seen anywhere were moribund; they trembled violently and could not fly. It was a spring without voices. On the mornings which had once throbbed with the dawn chorus of scores of bird voices there was now no sound; only silence lay over the fields and wood and marsh.

On the farms the hens brooded but no chicks hatched. The farmers complained that they were unable to raise any pigs – the litters were small and the young survived only a few days. The apple trees were coming into bloom but no bees droned among the blossoms, so there was no pollination and there would be no fruit.

The roadsides, once so attractive, were now lined with browned and withered vegetables as though swept by fire. These, too, were silent, deserted by all living things. Even the streams were now lifeless. Anglers no longer visited them, for all the fish had died.

In the gutters and on the roofs, a white granular powder still showed a few patches; some weeks before it had fallen like snow upon the roofs and the lawns, the fields and streams.

No witchcraft, no enemy action had silenced the rebirth of new life in this stricken world. The people had done it themselves.

Key

2 1 *sickness and death*   4 *apple trees*
   2 *illness and death*   5 *roadsides*
   3 *disappearing*   6 *lifeless*

Grammar analysis: the future

> **Aim**
> **To raise awareness of the differences in meaning conveyed by different ways of expressing the future.**

2 So as to build up a good discussion, ask students to do this activity individually first, and then to compare their answers.

4 Students should compare and discuss their answers to give themselves further practice.

Key

1 going to a   will/shall d, e, f   present continuous c
present simple b

2 1 *will come in/is coming in/comes in*
   2 *I will recycle/am going to recycle*
   3 *is going to get bigger*
   4 *won't be*
   5 *am going to take part in/am taking part in/will be taking part in*
   6 *will go on*
   7 *will become*
   8 *will stop/are going to stop*
   9 *will ban*
   10 *change/will change*

3 (letters refer to views of future given in 1)
   1 f/c/b
   2 e/a
   3 a
   4 d
   5 a/c
   6 d
   7 d
   8 f/a
   9 d
   10 b/f

✳ Reading

> **Aims**
> **To practise CAE exam tasks: gap-filling at phrase or sentence level (Paper 3 – English in Use) and multiple matching (Paper 1 – Reading).**
> **To practise reading for detail.**
> **To practise reading diagrams.**
> **To reinforce work on vocabulary related to the topic.**

1 Give students an opportunity to look at and talk about the diagram before they begin the task. This type of task appears in Paper 3 (English in Use), and is studied in detail in Section C of this unit. You could point this out to students.

2 Students may know the answers to some of these items from their general knowledge. They should nevertheless read the diagram to check or confirm their answers. This activity provides practice with the multiple matching format without making heavy demands on students' powers of comprehension.

NB Answers designed to call on general knowledge do not appear in the exam.

Key

1 1 E   2 B   3 F   4 C   5 A   6 G   7 H   8 I

2 1 F   2 D   3 C   4 A   5 E   6 B

📼 Vocabulary summary

> **Aim**
> **To revise key vocabulary from the unit.**

Students should be accustomed to the procedure of this quiz by now, as it is the same as those in Units 4 and 7. Ensure they read through the unit first. You could end by doing some pronunciation work.

Tapescript
Number 1.
What 'm' is a wild stretch of open country?

Number 2.
What 's' is a man-made figure often made of stone?

Number 3.
What 'w' is an injury?

And number 4.
What 's' means shaking with cold?

Number 5.
What 'a.r.' is caused by atmospheric contamination?

Here's number 6.
What 't' is a spotted, fresh-water and edible fish?

Number 7.
What 'l' is a long and sudden jump?

Here's number 8.
What 'g' shines softly in the dark?

Number 9.
What 'i' means you're puzzled?

Number 10.
What 'h.w.' is stuff we throw out from our homes?

Followed by number 11.
What 'f.f.' are made from ancient organisms?

Number 12.
What 's' moves your shoulders?

Try number 13.
What 'd' is an animal that usually lives in forests?

Number 14.
What 'r' is found at the edge of roads?

And number 15.
What 'c.e.' are the harmful thing that car engines produce?

Number 16.
What 'h' do chicks do at birth?

Number 17.
What 't' fires a gun?

Here's number 18.
What 'l' often made of glass helps you see better?

Number 19.
What 's' means you've got the strength to continue to live?

And finally number 20.
What 'w' means very, very strange?

Key

1	*moor*	11	*fossil fuels*
2	*statue*	12	*shrug*
3	*wound*	13	*deer*
4	*shivering*	14	*roadsides*
5	*acid rain*	15	*car exhausts*
6	*trout*	16	*hatch*
7	*leap*	17	*trigger*
8	*glow*	18	*lens*
9	*intrigued*	19	*survive*
10	*household waste*	20	*weird*

C

Paper 3 (English in Use): Section C

> **Aims**
> **To familiarise students with the aims and content of two CAE Paper 3 (English in Use) tasks: gap-filling at phrase or sentence level, and note expansion.**
> **To provide strategies for approaching these tasks.**

Gap-filling at phrase or sentence level

Gap-filling at phrase or sentence level is similar to cloze in that finding the right answers depends on looking for lexical and grammatical clues both before and after the gap. Items which provide cohesion within a text (e.g. conjunctions, punctuation, relative pronouns, pronouns, words within a lexical field, substituted words etc.) are particularly important clues in this type of task. This kind of task may be easier for students than gapped paragraphs. The sense of the text remains stronger because less is removed from it.

Notice that there are always more removed sentences or phrases than gaps, and the removed sentences or phrases all start with either lower case letters or capital letters, so the case of the letter doesn't act as a clue to where the sentence or phrase belongs.

1 Ask students to reflect on how they approach this activity and to note their strategies down.

3 This activity aims to build up students' awareness of the range of lexical and grammatical clues available to them, and also of the position of these clues before or after the gap, and close to or further from the gap. Pair or group discussion of answers would help increase this awareness.

Key

1   (1) D   (2) C   (3) F   (4) H   (5) I   (6) A

3   D   *they* = Eskimos; *less* = short; *surface area* = arms and legs

    C   *enabling* = larger blood volume (i.e. grammatical clue); *them* = people living in the tropics; *more* = than other people (implied)

    F   *sweat* = sweat

    H   *they* = Nigerians; *start* = start; *sweating* = sweat glands; *more* = than British men (implied)

    I   *for* = tendency (grammatical clue); *salt* = salt; *sweat* = sweating

    A   *salt* = salt

Exam practice 1

Key
(1) G   (2) H   (3) I   (4) B
(5) E   (6) A   (7) J   (8) F

Notes expansion

The questions are designed to cover the kinds of
problems and queries students have about this task. It
is important to realise that this task is marked at item
level and not at text level, i.e. each numbered item is
marked by itself. How the sentences join up to the
sentences in the next item is not taken into consideration.
It is cohesion within the item that students should
concentrate on.

Key
1   no
2   articles, auxiliary verbs, prepositions, conjunctions,
    relative pronouns
3   there can only be one
4   no, they change if necessary
5   no
6   neutral in this case, as is fitting for the poster
    presentation
7   not always

Exam practice 2

Key
Possible answers:
(1) At home we're going to always turn out the lights
     and we're going to avoid using spray cans.
(2) Seven people in our class smoke which is harmful
     to them and to others, so they're going to give up.
(3) Instead of asking for or accepting any more lifts
     from our parents, we're going to start walking,
     cycling or using public transport, which is better
     for our health too.
(4) As for litter such as sweet papers, drinks cans,
     burger wrappings etc. etc., well, they'll be going
     in the bin.
(5) We want to tell other people about environmental
     dangers as well by using posters, debates, articles
     in the press and campaigns.
(6) And finally, we're going to be collecting lots of
     money that we'll be sending to environmental
     projects.

Reflections

Students could work in groups. One member of each
group could then give a mini-presentation to the class
on the advice they have chosen. This could lead to a
class discussion on the best advice to give.

Fourteen

A

Personal relationships

Starter activities

> **Aims**
> To start students thinking about the topic of personal relationships.
> To activate vocabulary to do with weddings.
> To stimulate discussion of wedding traditions around the world.

1–2 If possible, bring into the lesson any wedding pictures of friends or relatives you may have, especially any which illustrate differences in fashion or culture. Ask your students to bring in any pictures they might have.

In a monocultural class, you may be able to discuss regional traditions associated with weddings. Alternatively, you may like to consider the way wedding traditions in your country have changed over the last 50 years. In a multicultural class, encourage students of all the nationalities represented to describe to others the wedding traditions in their country.

Key

1 **Possible answers:**
   bride, bridegroom, bridesmaids, best man, church, bouquet, wedding ring(s), marriage service, wedding reception, wedding cake, toasts, wedding presents

2 1 e   5 a
   2 f   6 b
   3 g   7 c
   4 h   8 d

Reading

> **Aims**
> To stimulate discussion on the status of marriage today.
> To practise reading for factual details.
> To practise pronouncing expressions with numbers.
> To practise a CAE Paper 3 (English in Use) Section A open cloze task.

1 Check that students are sure about the meaning of the terms *increasing*, *decreasing* and *remains stable* before they have to use them. In a multicultural class some sensitivity may be necessary, since different cultures take different moral positions on divorce, remarriage, living together and having children outside marriage. Also try to be aware of any individuals in the group for whom these may be personally sensitive issues.

✱ **2–3** Students are not supposed to read this text word by word. They should read it superficially at first to find those sections which are relevant to their task, and from which they can extract the information necessary to answer the questions. They will need to read the questions before consulting the text.

 4 Dates, large numbers and fractions often present difficulties even to quite advanced students, largely through lack of practice. Focus on stress and rhythm to improve fluency.

✱ **5** This activity is in the form of an open cloze task and is similar to the second task in Paper 3 (English in Use) Section A. Remind students that each gap must be filled by only one word, and that they should pay careful attention not only to the words immediately before and after the gap, but also to the way that meaning is built up throughout the text as a whole.

Tapescript

4   in the early nineteen seventies
since eighteen ninety one
eighty-five per cent of men
ninety-one per cent of women
eleven point six per thousand
fourteen point nine per thousand
one hundred and forty-three thousand six hundred
and sixty-seven
three hundred and forty-eight thousand four hundred
and ninety-two
between nineteen seventy-nine and nineteen eighty-
eight
from two point seven per cent to seven point seven
per cent
fifty fifty
two and a half times
two thirds of marriages

Key

2   1 B   2 A   3 A   4 A   5 A

3   1 H   2 I   3 D   4 I   5 E   6 C

5   (1) *with*
(2) *the*
(3) *that*
(4) *what*
(5) *if*
(6) *is*
(7) *as*
(8) *in*
(9) *their*
(10) *such/these*

✳ Speaking

> **Aims**
> **To stimulate discussion about stress arising from personal relationships.**
> **To practise reporting the outcome of a discussion.**

You may need to be aware of students in the class for whom the life events being discussed are an especially sensitive issue.

Grammar analysis: 'empty' *it*

> **Aims**
> **To revise and analyse the use of 'empty' *it*.**
> **To practise using 'empty' *it*.**

Point out to students that having a subordinate clause as the subject or object in a sentence can be unwieldy. Substituting *it* produces a much neater sentence structure. Putting the adjective first in the sentence as in example 1 gives it greater emphasis. You may like to refer back to the grammar sections on substitution (Unit 5 page 66) and cleft sentences (Unit 6 page 85).

Key

1   1 c
2   b
3   a

2   1   It is much easier now to get a divorce than it was fifty years ago.
2   It has become much more common in recent years for children to be born outside marriage.
3   The Family Policy Studies Centre finds it worrying to see so many marriages ending in divorce.
4   It is widely accepted by the experts that on average married people tend to live longer than unmarried people.

▭▭ Listening

> **Aims**
> **To practise listening for detail.**
> **To practise identifying speakers' opinions.**
> **To stimulate students to talk about someone who has influenced their life.**

1   Reassure students that they will not need to understand everything the speakers say in order to answer the question.

✳ 2   Give students time to read the notes about Claire and Philip, and to identify the sorts of information and opinions they are listening for (e.g. ages, academic subjects etc.). Emphasise that they can write the answers using no more than three words for each gap.

Tapescript

Speaker 1:   When I was a little girl, um, my best friend was was called Beverley, and er her father was um a guy called Simon Hardcastle, and er he was he was actually a war correspondent for the for the Times, and um he was a very glamorous figure to er to both of us, I mean he was absent a lot of the time, and er, often you know in exotic places – he was sort of in Beirut during that particular conflict, and er Uganda and places like that, and um, and my dream as a child was to become a war correspondent like him and he had a profound influence on many decisions that I made. When I went to university I studied er history and languages, um with the intention of becoming a journalist, and er in fact I did, I started working um a local paper in East Sussex where I lived, and um and then I went on to er work for the Independent which is what I'm doing now; um and er funnily enough Simon er is er has become a friend of mine. He now works for the ITN news, um but er we're still in touch and um he's really become a very close friend as well as being an influence on my life ...

Speaker 2:   Um I think one person who had a particularly strong influence on me was um a master where I was at school. Where I went to school there was a lot of er discipline and I was brought up in quite a strict family too; um but this master, he was very young, to us he looked old – he was actually only about 22 but um I was 15 at the time and he appeared a much older person. He came into the school to take over the Music Department, but he then opened up all sorts of other areas and he he challenged us to challenge the authority that the school and possibly our upbringings had er imposed on us; um and up until that point I'd I'd never questioned anything like that, um, I'd accepted what I was er told to do; and um he made me ask why um I behaved like that and whether the instructions I were given were valid; um it completely broke broke all um barriers for me really; it was a new area, and um he also opened up a musical area in my life and I found that I wasn't particularly academically very strong but suddenly there's another area in which you can um move forward and it gives you a confidence of a different kind; um and we used to go several of us used to go for long walks um with this master and we'd start these um very animated and philosophical discussions which we often used to get lost on but he'd keep us all up and um make us question everything that came our way and it was a very refreshing way to think; and um I still think back to him when people tell me to do things and er I feel it's my right to question them.

Key

1   b and d

2   (1) *a little girl/a small child/still very young* (etc.)
     (2) *war correspondent/journalist*
     (3) *exotic/exciting/dangerous places* (etc.)
     (4) *glamorous/exciting/exotic figure/person* (etc.)
     (5) *history and languages*
     (6) *journalism*
     (7) *(still) at school/a teenager/only 15* (etc.)
     (8) *challenge/question*
     (9) *accepting/doing*
     (10) *thinking about/looking at things/life*
     (11) *musical*
     (12) *sense of confidence/self-confidence*

Your thoughts

This activity could be followed up by asking each student to write a short piece reflecting on the person they chose. If possible, compile the accounts into an anthology. If you have a class or school magazine, then publish some of the accounts in that.

B

Working relationships

Starter activities

> **Aims**
> To start thinking about the topic of relationships at work.
> To activate vocabulary relating to working relationships.
> To stimulate discussion about the nature of teamwork.

Key

2   Possible answers:
     cooperation, acceptance of leadership, awareness of the skills of others, trust, honesty, sense of humour, sense of a shared goal, etc.

Speaking

> **Aim**
> To stimulate thought and discussion about different personality types and their effect on teamwork.

1–3 These activities encourage students to reflect on their own personality in a very general way. Students should not be tempted to take any analysis or comparisons with others too seriously.

Listening

> **Aims**
> To practise listening both for gist and for detail.
> To practise listening for speakers' opinions.
> To stimulate discussion on personal experience of being part of a team.

1 Reassure students that, as usual when they first listen to an extract, they don't need to understand everything the speakers say. They only need to identify the experiences of being part of a team referred to by the two main speakers.

2 Give students enough time to read and understand the ten opinions listed. Discuss and clarify any confusion. Explain to students that this time they will have to listen more carefully in order to identify which speaker(s) express(es) which opinion(s). Point out that a speaker does not always state an opinion explicitly, but may express it by implication by agreeing with or endorsing the opinion put forward by the previous speaker. Tell students to listen for examples of this.

With less confident students you could ask half the class to concentrate on the opinions expressed by Pam while the other half concentrates on those expressed by Neil. Play the extract a third time with the groups reversed, and then ask students to compare their answers.

Tapescript

Interviewer:

I think er a sense of achievement is something that we all like to feel, um but I think probably coming first in a race or winning a competition [mm] isn't always the most important [mm] thing, I think the taking part seems to be the chief the chief element, that actually "being part of a team" factor, I mean, would you would you say that being part of a team is something that you particularly enjoy, Pam?

Pam: Um, yes, I think so, I think um the the experience that um that I most remember is about ten years ago, I travelled to New Zealand, [mm] and I was there for about a 9-month period and I, I decided to do a survival course which was [yeah] [oh] um quite out of character really, but er, um and it was extraordinary, I mean meeting you know absolute strangers, [mm] um who'd all got together for one reason or another and we were together for a week and we were split into two teams we had to get from A to B in the best way we could [yes] and obviously we had all various pieces of equipment, you know ropes and stuff like that, um and we also did some white water rafting which was pretty exhilarating [oh yeah] I have to say it was just quite it was the most exhilarating thing I think I've ever done in my whole life more or less, um but the thing about it was we we um it was extraordinary it was I think the thing I learned from it was it was kind of an inroad into into people's personalities really because um people were in the teams you know who from all different walks of life I mean you know business people [yes], accountants, teachers, um nurses, and [so] the more cautious ones [yes] um given a situation where you know they really had to you know like your life in their hands sort of thing I mean came to the fore and their sort of leadership qualities came out in extraordinary ways you know some people who you'd never think in a million years would be able to to get something like that together ...

Neil: Um, barriers come down quickly [yes] don't they [yes, barriers do come down] yes I know what you mean [was that your experience as well?] yes yeah you it's a great leveller isn't it being part of a team ...

P: Absolutely, yes [yes].

N: If you have if you want to survive in it you've got you have to kind of throw all your judgements and um inhibitions and things out the way [yes]

Int: And of course you're thinking of the survival not only of yourself but of people around you you know [yes] say in a situation in which you can help

another person [exactly] that's also part of the [exactly] ...

N: That I found an interesting thing I was on a similar sort of thing to you it was a it was a naval um selection test to go into the navy [mm] and we were put together and very often there's a personal survival instinct which you have to almost sacrifice to remain part of a team [yes, yes] and you have to think on a bigger scale instead of just thinking well I know what I'm going to do I'm going to get across that bridge and go this way [yes] [yes] you have to think about how as a group you you're going to work.

P: Yes [yes] and in some instances there are certain people who are who are you know very obviously weaker [mm] than others [yes] and and it's it's amazing how how the ones who are caring and have got more concern [yes] that comes out to the fore as well [mm] because they're concerned about you know they take care [yeah, I ...] if you like play the mother goose rather ...

Int: I wonder did you ever worry about the particular skills that you personally could bring to a team, did you ...

P: Oh absolutely, absolutely!

N: Yes, oh yes.

Int: Did you think oh is my contribution enough [yes]? [yes, oh yes]

P: Yes but I think that er you you soon began to realise that, that that really didn't matter I mean um it was extraordinary I mean um everybody was very supportive of each other I mean there were moments where you know we had a few little sort of hysterical outbursts [yes] you know people just sort of said I can't do this I can't do this and ...

Int: ... and they were coaxed on by the others in the group who ...

P: ... and yes, then they were sort of reassured um by the others and then suddenly found that they were able to do it something you know because you're coming up against fears as well [yes].

N: Did you did you find that that taking decisions whereas in the past you may have only taken them for yourself the responsibility of taking a decision for the group is really quite worrying?

Int: [Yes] Yes that's something else isn't it [yes] because it's all right some people feel very cosy being a part of a team [yeah] but when it comes to something that only you can bring and you have to make a decision [yeah] um obviously that's you're putting a number a number of other people's well in that case lives at stake [yes absolutely yes] aren't you.

P: Yes it's it it brings out all sorts of different elements I think um especially when you're with um it's different when you're with absolute strangers [mm] I mean if you've been in a team you know [yes] with with with people that you've known for a long time [mm] then that's quite different.

Int: I think it is so I mean so would you say then in general that actually what is important is being part of a team or being recognised as being a champion being a winner of a race would you say that both of you very quickly, being a part of a

team is the most important thing?
P: I think taking part ...
N: Taking part – learning to listen but not being afraid to speak out too ...
P: ... yes flexibility, [yeah] flexibility and adjusting.
Int: Thank you both very much.
N: Thank you.

Key
1 a ... a survival course (in New Zealand).
  b ... a naval selection test (to get into the navy).

2 1 P
  2 P, N
  3 P, N
  4 N
  5 P
  6 P, N
  7 P
  8 P, N
  9 P
  10 N

Your thoughts

You may like to follow up the discussion with a small class survey to find out which are the most common team experiences and which the most unusual.

Reading

Aims
To stimulate discussion of problems that can arise in relationships at work.
To practise reading for gist and for detail.
To extend awareness of connotation.
To extend awareness of the use of negative prefixes.

1 Some students may have little personal experience of problems in the workplace. If so, ask them to draw on their general knowledge, e.g. the experience of friends or relations, newspaper reports of court cases, the portrayal of workplace relationships in film and TV etc.

2 Give students only one minute to glance through the text and decide the best title. Discuss the clues they used to arrive at their decision, and why the other two are unsuitable.

* 3 Give students more time to read the text in detail and complete the multiple matching task. If time is short, divide the class into three groups and ask each group to take responsibility for finding the answers to either **1**, **2** or **3**.

4 Part 1 focuses on positive and negative connotation in a selection of nouns, verbs and adjectives. Remind students that for certain words connotation is not necessarily permanently fixed, e.g. *superficial* in *he's a*

very superficial person carries a negative connotation, while the same word in *he sustained superficial injuries* (i.e. minor rather than major injuries) could almost be said to carry a positive tone to it.

Part 2 focuses on the use of negative prefixes. Point out to students that although the new adjectives created by adding a negative prefix are antonyms, they are not always negative adjectives, e.g. *informal*.

Key
1 Possible answers: jealousy, sense of superiority/inferiority, resentment, competition, misunderstanding, mutual attraction/dislike, sexual harassment etc.

2 B

3 1 A, C, D, E, G
  2 A, D, F, H
  3 A, B, C, D, E, G, I

4 1 Positive: *willing, compliment, cooperation, satisfaction, interesting, well-being, fair*
    Negative: *hypocritical, ignorance, conflict, denigrate, suspicion, problem, superficial, criticise, hostility*
  2 *uninteresting*
    inessential
    impersonal
    uncomfortable
    infrequent
    anti-social/unsocial
    unfair
    dissatisfied
    informal
    unspecific/non-specific
    abnormal
    uncooperative
    unwilling
    impossible
    unimportant

Grammar reminder: conditional sentences

Aims
To revise the use of conditional sentences.
To practise using conditional sentences.

Key
1 a 3 b 5 c 6 d 1 e 2 f 4

2 1 If they got to know him better they *would find* he's not so bad after all.
  2 You will see an improvement in your working relationships if you *follow* some basic rules.
  3 If he *had looked* me/*looked* me in the eye when we talked, I'd have a much better idea of what he really thought.
  4 If they'd both made more of an effort, they *would get on/would have got on* much better together.
  5 You spend a lot of your time talking to people if you *work/are working* in an office.

6 If the boss *had not criticised* his secretary in public, she never would have left the company.

7 If I lost interest in what she was saying, I *would transfer/transferred* my attention to the photograph on the wall behind her.

8 Life can be very difficult if you *share/are sharing* an office with someone you dislike.

✱ Writing

> **Aims**
> To practise checking and correcting written text.
> To practise an error-correction task from CAE Paper 3 (English in Use), Section B.
> To stimulate discussion about suitable rules for relationships in the classroom.
> To practise writing a set of rules for public display.

1 This activity is similar to the error correction task found in Section B of Paper 3 (English in Use). Students could refer back to the advice given in Section C of Unit 8 (page 109) either before or after doing the task.

2 By this stage in the course your students should have had considerable experience of working together, so this activity could generate some interesting comments. Ask students to share their views as sensitively as they can, and encourage them to write 'positive' (*Always/Try to …*) rather than 'negative' (*Never/Don't …*) rules. Encourage them to apply some of the skills they have practised in previous writing tasks. Display the suggested sets of rules for all to see and comment on. You may like to decide on a 'best' set for permanent display in the classroom.

Key

1 1 *it's*
   2 *John*
   3 *self-esteem'.*
   4 *affirm*
   5 ✓
   6 *(not*
   7 *suspicious*
   8 *usually*
   9 ✓

Vocabulary summary

> **Aim**
> To revise the main vocabulary fields of this unit.

Key

social skills	*single parent*
working conditions	*serious illness*
close friends	*dramatic rise*
divorce rate	*popular culture*
vital element	*significant proportion*
life expectancy	*family life*

C

Paper 4 (Listening): Section D

> **Aims**
> To familiarise students with the content and format of CAE Paper 4 (Listening) Section D.
> To highlight and practise listening techniques for identifying the topic.
> To highlight and practise listening techniques for identifying the speaker.
> To highlight and practise listening techniques for identifying a speaker's attitude.
> To highlight and practise listening techniques for identifying purpose or intention.
> To practise a Paper 4 Section D task.
> To consider different approaches to focusing attention while listening.

Introduction

1–2 These activities are designed to introduce students to the content and format of Section D of Paper 4 (Listening). Emphasise that this task is normally built around a series of short listening extracts, so students need to develop skills in quickly identifying such things as topic, speaker, speaking purpose etc. using all the clues provided.

Tapescript

1 **For Section D of CAE Paper 4 you will hear a series of short extracts, each of which will be between 10 and 30 seconds in length. All the extracts will be linked in some way and there will be a brief pause between each one. You will hear the whole series twice. The questions may test how well you can identify what topic is being talked about in each extract, what the purpose of each one is, who the speaker is in each extract, and what their attitude may be.**

Key

(1) *short*	(4) *linked*	(7) *purpose*
(2) *10–30 seconds*	(5) *twice*	(8) *speaker*
(3) *brief*	(6) *topic*	(9) *attitude*

Identifying the topic

1 Encourage students to think about the sorts of clues they might use, e.g. the vocabulary (especially any key words relating to a topic), aspects of the speaker's approach/style/tone, number of speakers involved etc.

2 Play the extract without giving any clues as to its content. Students should have no difficulty guessing what the topic is.

3 Point out the importance of the keywords related to a single idea: *showers, dry, cloud, rain, cooler, wind, temperatures*. Other keywords relate to geographical references. Point out too the approach of the speaker – friendly and informative. Draw students' attention to the pattern of tenses used – beginning with present perfect to describe the recent situation, and moving on to future tenses to describe what is to come.

Students will also have used their world knowledge, i.e. that weather forecasts are a regular feature of our daily lives, and that they are normally delivered in a standardised way by a single speaker. Point out that students may not have understood everything the speaker said, but that this did not stop them grasping the topic and purpose of the extract.

4 Before playing the next extract, tell students that it is a short sports report. They must identify the particular sport concerned using similar clues to those in activity 3.

Tapescript

2 (fade in) ... so let's put in the details for today then; let's start with the whole of southern England and the South Midlands. Well, there've been one or two showers around on the south coast, but basically it's been mainly dry; and for the first part of the afternoon there'll be further isolated showers, but then we're going to see cloud tumbling its way into south-west England bringing with it some more persistent rain; this cloud and rain will continue to move east during the afternoon; it'll feel cooler today with a breezy south-westerly wind and temperatures only reaching 21 degrees at best, perhaps nearer 17 to 18 in the south west of England ... (fade)

4 After so much English success in the pool over recent days, Northern Ireland and Scotland can both look forward to a share of the spotlight in the finals. Marian Maguire is third fastest for the 200 metres butterfly giving rise to hope of a first ever Irish medal. Helen Otter from Scotland goes in the 200 metres backstroke, while fellow-countrymen Graham Wilson and Peter Frith challenge the mighty Australians in the 1500 metre freestyle; and England, Wales and Scotland all contest the last event, the men's medley relay.

Key

2 the weather

4 swimming (key words: *pool, butterfly, backstroke, freestyle, medley relay*; also references to the distances)

Identifying the speaker

1 This time the focus is not on the topic but on the speaker. Explain that students will hear another short sports report and must decide who is speaking. Encourage them to try and be aware of the clues they are using to decide the answer.

2 Discuss with students the clues they were aware of using. These probably included the choice of words and the relationship to the topic – *my coach, I was in with a chance of getting a medal, I knew I was running well* etc. Perhaps also the style of speaking – slightly breathless after a race and as a result of excitement.

3 Play the second extract and ask students to apply a similar approach.

Tapescript

1 Well my coach always said I was in with a chance of getting a medal ... but even though I knew I was running well I still don't think I really believed it ... so to get gold ... well that was quite something ... it probably won't sink in until tomorrow!

3 The trouble is, Chris, if you don't start taking things more seriously, you're going to find yourself in real trouble before too long. Your other teachers tell me your marks leave a lot to be desired and you still haven't handed in that history essay I set for the class over 2 weeks ago – it's just not good enough – I want to see some improvement (fade) ...

Key

1 c

3 b (clues = *your other teachers, your marks, you still haven't handed in, history essay I set for the class*)

Identifying a speaker's attitude or opinion

1 Point out to students that, in addition to paying attention to the words a speaker chooses to use, we can often infer a speaker's attitude or opinion by taking account of other features of the person's speech (sometimes referred to as paralinguistic features). Although it is very difficult to describe in a simple way how different speech features convey different attitudes, it may be helpful to point out the following:

The pitch of a speaker's voice will move up and down in normal conversation, but a significant movement in pitch from high to low or low to high may signal a strong emotion such as anger, surprise, delight, frustration etc. Similarly, very little change in pitch may indicate disappointment, fear, annoyance, boredom etc. A raised voice may indicate excitement, anxiety, anger etc. while a lowered voice could mean sadness, seriousness etc. A slow speech tempo may convey an attitude of seriousness or thoughtfulness, while a fast tempo may indicate excitement, nervousness, or annoyance.

2 Replay the two extracts. This time ask students to try and suggest the attitude of the speaker.

Tapescript

2   Well my coach always said I was in with a chance of getting a medal ... but even though I knew I was running well I still don't think I really believed it ... so to get gold ... well that was quite something ... it probably won't sink in until tomorrow!

The trouble is, Chris, if you don't start taking things more seriously, you're going to find yourself in real trouble before too long. Your other teachers tell me your marks leave a lot to be desired and you still haven't handed in that history essay I set for the class over 2 weeks ago – it's just not good enough – I want to see some improvement (fade) ...

Key

2   Extract 1: a (fast tempo, raised voice, high pitch)
Extract 2: b (slower tempo, lowered voice, low pitch)

Identifying purpose or intention

1   Remind students that we usually use language to achieve a particular purpose or function, e.g. to ask for something, give praise to someone etc. Play the short extract so that students can identify the topic, and then ask them if they can explain what the speaker is actually doing. Tell them to imagine a scenario in which she might be saying these words. Play the extract a second time if necessary.

2   Point out to students the various phrases which are appropriate for (1) ('describing a new car'). Then help students decide on phrases they might expect if they overheard someone arranging to borrow a car from a friend (2), e.g. *I wonder if I could possibly ..., I need to ..., I'll make sure ..., I promise I'll ..., naturally I'll pay ...* etc. Ask them to do something similar for 3–5.

3   Play the two extracts on cars to give students practice in identifying the speaker's purpose/intention.

4   Discuss with students which of the words and phrases they thought of in activity 2 were actually used in the listening extracts for activity 3. It is quite possible that some of their suggestions were paraphrased, so look out for any examples of this.

Tapescript

1   Oh, I'm really pleased with it – it's a dark blue Toyota, a couple of years old, only one owner, erm, loads of room in the boot – I only picked it up from the garage yesterday and it feels like I've been driving it for ages already ...

3   I feel awful about it – I must've just caught the the concrete pillar as I was coming out of the car park and it's scraped a bit of paint off the wing – I'm terribly sorry, I should've been more careful. I just I do hope the garage will be able to match the colour and of course you must let me know how much it costs ...

It's in excellent condition as you can see – it's had regular services since it was new, but even so it's very reasonably priced, and of course we may well be able to arrange a part exchange deal on your existing car. Would you like to take it out on the roads for a test drive to help you decide?

Key

1   a   a car
b   to describe a new car which has been bought

3   Extract 1: 3
Extract 2: 5

Exam practice

Here students listen to a set of five short listening extracts and complete a task like those in Section D of Paper 4 (Listening). Encourage them to use the techniques discussed and practised in previous activities. They should write their answers, while they are listening, into the boxes provided in their book. Play the recording twice, and at the end of the task discuss with students any difficulties they had.

Tapescript

1   (museum assistant to school group)
Now if you come over here children, you can see several different instruments that were used by people in the past for telling the time, before mechanical clocks as we know them were even invented. Perhaps some of you have seen a smaller one of these in your kitchen at home – see how the glass can be turned upside down so that the sand runs through the narrow opening in the middle ... when all the sand had gone from the top half to the bottom half, people knew that an hour had passed ...

2   (elderly lady to antiques expert)
Now this has been in my family for as long as I can remember – I think it was originally bought by my great grandfather ...

Ah, now this is a very nice piece of work, probably made sometime during the nineteenth century by Thomas Goldsmith and Son in London – yes, look, you can see the maker's name on the clockface there. You know, it was quite common at that time for the door of the case to be made with a glass panel in it so you could actually see the pendulum swinging. In this condition I could imagine it fetching ooh erm, oh several hundred pounds at auction ...

3   (grandparent giving a present to daughter-in-law for her grand-daughter)

I got this for Sara's birthday – I know she's a bit young to be able to tell the time yet but I thought she might enjoy watching the figures move ...

Oh – how kind of you, it's lovely – it's ideal for her bedroom and it'll fit perfectly on the wall above her bed. Actually she's just beginning to recognise numbers so it's ideal ... oh, what a lovely idea – thank you so much, Mum!

4 (shop assistant to customer)
This one's got a second hand – and it's waterproof –
is that the sort of thing you're looking for?

Well, I'm not really sure that's going to be big
enough – the face is a bit small and I don't really
want something with a strap. What I really need is
something I can easily carry around in my pocket
and use to time the children's performances in the
pool – [what about this then?] yes, that's the sort of
thing I had in mind ...

5 (customer to shop assistant)
Excuse me, I bought this from you recently and I've
brought it back because the alarm isn't working
properly. Actually I'm rather annoyed because I
specifically bought it to take with me on a business
trip abroad and in the end I had to rely on the hotel
giving me an alarm call every morning ...

Oh I'm sorry to hear that madam – would you like
me to replace it or would you prefer a refund?

Key

1	E	6	G
2	C	7	H
3	H	8	F
4	A	9	B
5	G	10	C

Ways of learning: focusing attention in Section D Listening tasks

This final activity highlights the different approaches
which can be adopted when answering the questions
in the Section D task, given that the recording is heard
twice. Discuss with students what they were aware of
doing during the exam practice task, and the advantages
and disadvantages of each of the approaches.
Individual students may find they prefer to focus their
attention in the same way each time, or to vary their
approaches according to the nature of the task.

Fifteen

A

Let's peoplewatch

Starter activities

> **Aims**
> **To start students thinking about the topic of 'peoplewatching'.**
> **To help students understand the meaning of 'peoplewatching'.**

2 This activity may best be done as a whole class activity. As students give their answers write them up on the board. This will then act as a vocabulary extension/consolidation exercise.

Key
1 observing other people

Speaking: generalisations and exceptions

> **Aims**
> **To extend/consolidate vocabulary for describing facial appearance.**
> **To build up awareness of language used to generalise and make exceptions.**
> **To give fluency practice.**
> **To develop discussion of the link between appearance and character.**

2 You could draw two columns on the board headed 'generalisations' and 'exceptions'. Students could then tell you which expressions to write in which column.

4 You could carry out this discussion as a whole class or in groups to provide a contrast with activity 3. Activity 3 serves as a resource for a good discussion.

Key
2 Generalisations: *Generally speaking ... In general ... By and large ... As a rule ...*
Exceptions: *The exception is ... There are exceptions ... Apart from ... You can't really say that about ...*

Reading

> **Aims**
> **To practise reading for detail.**
> **To extend vocabulary related to the topic of 'peoplewatching'.**

1 Students may well recognise this face – that of Leonardo da Vinci's *Mona Lisa*. They should be able to carry out the activities whether they recognise the face or not.

2 Students will need to understand these words to get the most out of the next activity. The focus is on the connotation of these words, as the message of the text hinges on connotation.

3 This activity is intended to be light-hearted. As it is subjective there will be no fixed answers to it.

4 This activity extends students' comprehension of the text – again it is subjective and there are no fixed answers.

Key
2 positive: *witty, an unflinching gaze*
negative: *sinister, lose her temper, bawdy, callousness, flab, greedy, a spendthrift, fickle*
it depends: *plump, enigmatic, a glint in her eyes, a mole*

✳ Writing

> **Aims**
> To give students writing practice.
> To consolidate the language and theme of the section.

Prior discussion of the writing task(s) would probably be useful. As usual students should be thinking about the target reader, style, appropriate language, the effect on the reader, layout, sequencing of information, and accuracy of language.

Key

	First task	**Second task**
content	to cover all points mentioned in instructions	to cover all points mentioned in instructions
register	any	formal probably or neutral
target reader	general audience	author of *Mona Lisa* passage
effect on target reader	interesting	persuasive
range of language	good range of descriptive language, especially adjectives and nouns	good range of structures to match formality of tone

Grammar analysis: verbs taking two objects

> **Aim**
> To raise awareness of word order and passivisation with verbs taking two objects.

Key

1 Correct sentences: 2, 3, 4, 6, 7, 8, 9, 10

2 1 *I lent her a record/I lent a record to her.*
  5 *They offered them a drink/They offered a drink to them.*
  11 *I asked him a question.*
  12 *We owe them some money/We owe some money to them.*

[If the indirect object pronoun comes before the direct object, *to* is omitted. If it comes after, it must be included.]

3 *write, play, take, teach, send, grant*

4 a 4 b 3 c 5 d 5 e 4 f 1 g 2 h 1 i 3 j 2

  6 Our friend was promised some help/some help was promised to our friend
  7 He was read a story/A story was read to him
  8 I was saved some chocolate/Some chocolate was saved for me
  9 The ticket was handed to him/He was handed the ticket
  10 A job was found for me/I was found a job
  11 He was asked a question/A question was asked of him
  12 Some money is owed to them/They are owed some money

🔲 Listening

> **Aims**
> To practise listening for detail and for specific information.
> To practise a CAE Paper 4 (Listening) Section D task.

After students have carried out the activities, you could ask them what they notice and what they like or dislike in peoplewatching.

✳ Tapescript

Speaker 1: Watching people's faces fascinates me. I always wish I had a little miniature polaroid camera that I could carry round with me when I'm walking through the street or on a bus or whatever, and I could just whip round and take a picture of that wonderful expression on somebody's face, whether it's somebody being told off, somebody telling somebody off, somebody having an argument, somebody having a good laugh, and finding something very funny. The face can tell a very interesting story, I think.

Speaker 2: I like watching people watching other people. Er, I like to see people reacting to situations going on around them, because erm, it's something ... there's something very honest and erm unthinking about it. It's erm ... when it's erm an extreme situation, like er, I don't know ... somebody who's drunk getting on the er ... the tube train, and er it's just very interesting watching people react to that. Er, you often get people with some deep ... behaving in an extraordinary way right next to them, and they're desperately trying to pretend it's not happening, and I find that very amusing. Erm, so I ... I watch people watching other people.

Speaker 3: Well, er, yes, I have to admit, I do like peoplewatching; partly because I'm terribly short-sighted, and I'm always squinting, so I kind of think they probably don't think I'm looking at them anyway. Erm, but erm, it's normally mannerisms, 'cos I think I've got quite a few, so erm, and shoes, feet; if they're sort of kicking their legs out and things on trains, or erm facial expressions, flinches and erm, little ticks perhaps, what they do with their hands, erm I find that quite interesting; erm, and it's always good to see, see people on trains, because you're in such close prox ... proximity to people that erm erm they obviously don't like, normally like you to catch their eye, so I quite like the way people avert their gaze; that's always an interesting one.

Speaker 4: I don't really like watching people. Erm, I don't like eating outside, I don't like travelling on public transport. The trouble is, if you ... if you look at people you see them doing all sorts of disgusting things like picking their noses, and I just think that's really disgusting and I don't like it at all. And er ... I don't like watching people scratching themselves and things, because they always do that, and they're all passing, and you're trying to have a meal, and someone's scratching themselves in your face. I think it's just ... I prefer to stay indoors really.

Key

1

	1	2	3	4
feet			✓	
faces	✓		✓	
arguments				
hands			✓	
scratching				✓
people watching other people		✓		
people getting drunk				
mannerisms			✓	

2

Which speaker likes or dislikes watching ...?	1	2	3	4
people's disgusting habits				✓
people pretending not to notice something embarrassing		✓		
people watching other people		✓		
people on trains			✓	
people avoiding your glance			✓	
faces that tell stories	✓			
people's mannerisms			✓	

B

Reasons for peoplewatching

Starter activities

> **Aims**
> To start students thinking about the topic of clothes and the meaning they have.
> To consolidate and/or extend vocabulary related to personality and appearance.

2 Students will probably get most out of this activity if they do it individually or in pairs first. Make sure students know the meaning of all these words. You could also do some pronunciation work, focusing on word stress.

NB The answers to this activity are subjective.

Listening

> **Aims**
> To practise listening for detail and for specific information.
> To practise a CAE Paper 4 (Listening): Section D task.
> To further develop the topic of appearance and personality.

* Tapescript

Speaker 1: (laugh) I love the cool dude in the waistcoat – He has a very mad look about him. But I find him slightly intimidating. I'd probably be frightened to approach him. I wouldn't mind him approaching me, though! Clothes really affect how I feel about people. I can't stand shoes that are too shiny or falling apart. I'd be happy to take him to an office party though!

Speaker 2: She's really pretty – but in the pink she looks like a bimbo. The most attractive is the office outfit. I like women who dress smartly and you can tell she's high-powered and classy. She's probably got a nice car and she's certainly got a good brain. I wouldn't mind the number of her mobile phone!

Speaker 3: The one in the flowery dress. She's got all the qualities I find attractive in a woman – intelligence, smart appearance. The dress really stands out from the rest. It isn't too short, it isn't too revealing and her heels aren't too high. I can't say any more because my girlfriend will be here in a minute... !

Speaker 4: I wouldn't want to meet him in the waistcoat. All he'd have to say is 'Look at me.' But he looks much nicer in those jeans – neat, casual and trendy. I'd be quite happy to go out with him.

Speaker 5: The one in the jeans looks like a real human being. I'd definitely talk to her. She looks very natural, approachable, comfortable and confident. She isn't trying to be anything other than who she is. Even her make-up isn't over the top. She looks as though she dresses for herself.

Key

1 1 h   2 c   3 b   4 e   5 a

2 1 C   2 B, D   3 B, D   4 A, F   5 A, F, G

Grammar reminder: indirect statement

> **Aim**
> To revise and practise indirect statements.

1 You could elicit these rules from the students before they read them. They can check what they have said.

2 Play the sentences from the cassette, or give students further practice by playing other parts of the recordings.

Key

2 *She said she loves/loved the cool dude in the waistcoat.*

She said she can't/couldn't stand shoes that are too shiny.

He said he wouldn't mind/wouldn't have minded the number of her mobile phone.

He said his girlfriend would be there soon.

She said she'd be/she'd have been quite happy to go out with him.

He said she wasn't/isn't trying to be anything other than who she is/was.

Reading

> **Aims**
> To practise reading for gist and for detail.
> To practise CAE Paper 1 (Reading) multiple matching and multiple choice tasks.
> To develop the topic of appearance and personality.

This passage is taken from a book called *Manwatching* by Desmond Morris, a popular British sociologist. The book was published in 1978. If students are interested they may be able to get hold of the book, perhaps in a local library.

* 2–3 You could do these tasks in exam-like conditions, or as pair or individual work.

4 This is intended as a light-hearted activity to round off the theme of this section. Make sure students don't read their own pieces of paper out loud, as this would stop them guessing who was being talked about.

Key
1   The original title for this passage was D.

2   1 D   2 F   3 E   4 A   5 C   6 B

3   1 D   2 D   3 A   4 D   5 D

Vocabulary summary

> **Aim**
> To revise vocabulary from the unit.

Students may need help making up clues – the clues can be difficult, but they shouldn't be incomprehensible or too misleading! Check the clues as the students prepare them in groups. The final activities in Section B in Units 4, 7, 9 and 13 contain quizzes. Students may wish to look at these to find out how to make clues.

C

Paper 5 (Speaking): Phases C and D

> **Aims**
> To familiarise students with the aims and content of CAE Paper 5 (Speaking) Phases C and D.
> To present useful language for these phases.
> To give further exposure to the assessment criteria used for Paper 5, and the roles of the interlocutor and assessor.
> To reinforce students' awareness of interactional language.

Introduction

Phases C and D of Paper 5 (Speaking) need to be considered together, as Phase D develops out of Phase C. Phase C is a concrete communicative task, and Phase D is a more abstract discussion based on the theme of the Phase C task.

Students are not always asked to report back on their decisions in Phase D – this is at the discretion of the examiner. The examiners may use this phase to encourage less forthcoming students to talk, or to get more language from students whose mark is not yet clear. However, if students are asked to contribute during this phase they should not interpret this as meaning anything special. It may simply be that the examiner wishes to continue the discussion.

NB Dominant students must be careful not to be too forceful in these phases. They will lose marks for interactive communication if they play too strong a part. Less forthcoming students must do their best to hold forth. Examiners can only judge what they've heard – they cannot judge a candidate's potential. Remind students that the quality of their ideas is not assessed.

The role-play aims to give students an opportunity to become well acquainted with Phases C and D. They could take it in turns to play both roles with different partners.

Useful language for Phases C and D: Interacting with other speakers

There are of course other expressions useful for interacting with others and reporting decisions. These are given as examples for students to use as they wish. You could ask them what others they know. Appropriate use of these expressions will help students sound more fluent, and ease their ability to interact.

Key

A 1, 2, 3, 5, 8   B 4, 7, 11
C 6, 9, 11, 12   D 1, 10

Useful language for Phase D: Reporting your decisions

Key

A 2, 9, 10, 14, 15, 16, 17   B 3, 11
C 1, 8, 12, 15   D 4, 5, 6, 7, 12, 13

Exam practice

It is useful if students can carry out these tasks as assessors as well as candidates – this helps them to get a better idea of the assessors' role, the kinds of things the assessor is looking for, and what the candidate can do to improve their performance. Watch the timing on these activities.

Reflections

Encourage students to give one another constructive feedback during this activity, e.g. *You could have done X ... Why don't you try doing Y* etc.

Revision Exam Practice 3

The following activities have been included in the course for two reasons:

- **to provide further practice in the language of the topics of the preceding five units.**
- **to give further exam practice in the tasks that have been featured in Section C of the previous five units.**

All the activities are presented as they would be in the CAE exam.

You may choose to use these activities for homework, for practice in exam-like conditions in class, or simply to work through and discuss in class.

Paper 1 (Reading)

This task is taken from the Gapped Paragraphs Section of the Reading Paper. For information on how to approach this section of Paper 1, see the information and the facsimile questions on pages 151–155 of the Student's Book. The answer sheet for the Reading Paper is reproduced on page 138 of this Teacher's Book.

Allow approximately 20 minutes for this task.

Key

1	B	4	E
2	G	5	D
3	C	6	F

Paper 2 (Writing)

This task is taken from Section B of the Writing Paper. For information on how to approach this section of Paper 2, see the information and the facsimile questions on pages 165–168 of the Student's Book.

Allow approximately 1 hour for this task.

Marking guidelines

In assessing a student's written work, try to take account of the official assessment criteria used by CAE examiners. These relate to content (points covered), organisation/cohesion, range of vocabulary and structures, register (formality/informality), accuracy, and the effect on the target reader. On a rising scale of 1 to 5, give an impression mark based upon a combination of accuracy of language and task achievement. You may also want to mark up errors and add specific comments relating to accuracy, content, style etc.

The following questions may help focus your attention during the marking process:

Has the student thought about the purpose and the audience in terms of choice of appropriate language, style and layout?

The vocabulary and structure used should be relevant to the topic; the style should be appropriate to the target audience and purpose in writing; and the layout should be matched to the instructions.

Has the student succeeded in planning and organising their writing?

Well-planned and organised work leads the reader clearly through from start to finish and achieves its intended objective. Poorly planned and organised written work is usually confusing, exhausting to read and distracts from its purpose.

Has the student done everything the question asks within the specified word limit?

An underlength answer probably means that the task is incomplete in some way and that important elements have been omitted. An overlength answer could mean that irrelevant material has been included which may in turn have a negative effect on the target reader.

Has the student checked for accuracy of grammar, punctuation and spelling?

While occasional errors need not be heavily penalised, persistently poor spelling, grammar or punctuation can have a negative effect on the target reader and may adversely affect the achievement of the task.

Would the writing achieved the required objective?

Give an impression mark based upon a combination of accuracy of language and task achievement. Remember that clarity of handwriting can have an important effect on a target reader, so poor handwriting should be penalised.

Paper 3 (English in Use)

This task is taken from the Gap-filling and Note-expansion Section of the English in Use Paper. For information on how to approach this section of Paper 3, see the information and the facsimile questions on pages 176–179 of the Student's Book. The answer sheet for the English in Use Paper is reproduced on pages 139–141 of this Teacher's Book.

Allow approximately 30 minutes for this task.

Key

1	1	C	5	I
	2	G	6	A
	3	D	7	F
	4	B		

2 Possible answers:

(1) The description which is given of them is the same the world over and describes them as being about 2 metres tall and weighing about 300 kilograms.

(2) They tend to have different names in different places; for example the Abominable Snowman, the Yeti, the Wild Man and the Sasquatch.

(3) The proof of their existence comes from their footprints which have been found in snow and mud, and sightings of them that have been reported in different places.

(4) The best evidence of their existence has been provided by a Russian scientific expedition which took place near Lake Balkhash and reported two sightings as well as footprints and smashing sounds.

(5) The problem is that as yet no one has managed to take any photos or movies of them.

(6) Another expedition to prove the existence of the Ape Man is leaving soon, but it needs money, so please give generously.

Paper 4 (Listening)

This task is taken from Section D of the Listening Paper. For information on how to approach this section of Paper 4, see the information and the facsimile questions on pages 188–190 of the Student's Book. The answer sheet for the Listening Paper is reproduced on page 142 of this Teacher's Book.

Allow approximately 10 minutes for this task.

Tapescript

V1: Sports teacher (complimentary)
... well, all in all, we're really very pleased with his progress over the past year – especially his ball skills ... and as captain of the swimming team I think he was instrumental in their success at the schools championships a couple of months ago, they did tremendously well so I do hope he'll stay with the team, and perhaps even get involved in coaching some of the younger boys, you know he's a born teacher ...

V2: French teacher (disappointed)
... I have to say I find it rather a shame that James has shown so little interest in the subject recently – especially since he was doing so well in both his oral and written work last year – and it was a great pity he decided not to go on the school trip because he would have got such a lot out of it, it would have helped his pronunciation enormously ...

V3: Music teacher (cautious)
Well ... it's difficult to know quite what to say ... although James is making quite good progress with the theoretical part of the course, I'm not really so sure about his practical work ... perhaps if he were to practise on a more regular basis, maybe even join the orchestra, then I might feel a bit more confident that he'll do himself justice in the long term ...

V4: Chemistry teacher (critical)
I really think he's going to have to revise his attitude over the next few months if he wants to get a satisfactory grade – there's nothing wrong with either his understanding of the theory or his practical experimental work but his written projects are virtually always late and often incomplete ... and to be perfectly honest, his behaviour in the laboratories sometimes verges on the dangerous ...!

V5: History teacher (supportive)
I do realise that James has missed rather a lot of the course because of illness this year and that has had an effect on his performance ... it's made it rather more difficult for him to keep up-to-date with all the reading and so on, but we've had some extra classes together and, as a result, his essay on the causes of the American Civil War was a good effort and showed real understanding of the political and social conditions of the time ...

Key

1	E		6	D
2	F		7	B
3	A		8	C
4	D		9	H
5	H		10	G

Paper 5 (Speaking): Phases C and D

This task is taken from Phases C and D of the Speaking Paper. For information on how to approach this section of Paper 5, see the information and the facsimile questions on pages 199–202 of the Student's Book.

Marking guidelines

See 'What are the examiners looking for?' on page 133 of the Student's Book.

Map of the book

Unit and topic	Reading Listening	Writing	Speaking	Grammar
Starter Unit	**A Ways of learning** Reading: advertisements for methods of learning Listening: conversation about learning languages **B What does 'communicating' mean?** Reading: text about communication			
1 Introductions	**A The way we live** Reading: newspaper article about who does what in the house Listening: four excerpts from a radio programme about the way people used to live **B The way we are** Reading: a magazine article about someone's idyllic childhood Listening: various people describe what they were like as children	Letter: describing the way we live	Yourselves	**Reminder:** prepositions **Analysis:** the simple past and present perfect tenses
2 Travelling the world	**A Voyages of discovery** Reading: magazine article about Christopher Columbus Listening: discussion on why people go exploring **B Holiday travel** Reading: four short texts (postcard, holiday brochure, guidebook, novel) about holidays Listening: three short monologues on favourite types of holiday	Magazine article: views on why people go exploring today	Travel/exploration, holidays	**Reminder:** *so* and *such* **Analysis:** the present simple and continuous tenses
3 Living with other people	**A Family matters** Reading: newspaper article about sibling rivalry Listening: conversation about family relationships **B Habits and customs** Reading: four letters to a magazine about 'good manners' Listening: three short monologues describing surprising habits/customs	Personal letter: offering advice on appropriate behaviour at a wedding in *another* culture	Family relationships, different ways of behaving	**Analysis:** stative verbs **Reminder:** *-ing* or infinitive?

Vocabulary	Functions	Phonology	Style and register	Ways of learning	Focus of Section C
Word fields: • means of communication					The CAE Exam: general information
Prefixes and suffixes Word fields: • domestic chores • personality • physical description • childhood	Asking for personal information	Word stress		Approaches to reading	Paper I (Reading): multiple-choice
Word fields: • travel/exploration • holidays Positive adjectives	Discussing opinions Describing a situation	Stress and intonation in phrases	Choosing an appropriate written style	Choosing and using a grammar book	Paper 2 (Writing): Section A
Collocation Word fields: • family relationships • forms of behaviour Grammatical terms	Offering advice	Stress and intonation in phrases	Using appropriate words for a given context	Talking about grammar and vocabulary	Paper 3 (English in Use): Section A multiple-choice cloze and open cloze

Unit and topic	Reading/Listening	Writing	Speaking	Grammar
4 Good and bad health	**A Health on holiday** Reading: magazine article about how to beat holiday stress Listening: questions about illness on holiday **B Health around the world** Reading: article about exercise and health in the UK Listening: discussion about health in Algeria and the UK	Leaflet: instructions for avoiding holiday stress	Illness on holiday, general health issues	**Reminder:** modal verbs expressing obligation and permission **Analysis:** the definite article
5 Body language	**A Animal communication** Reading: extract from textbook about teaching animals to talk Listening: extract from radio discussion on animal communication **B Reading the signals** Reading: extract from book on communication skills Listening: extract from lecture on communication skills	Review of a lecture: on the subject of communication skills	Communication skills	**Reminder:** prepositions of position/direction/time/manner/purpose **Analysis:** substitution
Revision Exam Practice 1				
6 Everyday objects	**A Inventions** Reading: two magazine articles on new telephone inventions Listening: telephone conversation about an inventor **B The art of persuasion** Reading: extract from textbook on advertising Listening: two short conversations about making adverts	Article: discussing new telephone inventions	Important inventions, advertising	**Reminder:** order of adjectives **Analysis:** cleft sentences
7 Jobs	**A What about getting a job?** Reading: book extract about some unusual domestic help Listening: two young people talking about their jobs **B Will I get a job?** Reading: article about success Listening: three people talking about unemployment	Letter of reference: suitability for employment	Jobs and employment	**Reminder:** words for linking sentences/clauses **Reminder:** more words for linking sentences/clauses
8 Crime and punishment	**A Crime and society** Reading: newspaper report on a criminal court case Listening: short radio reports of crimes **B Crime and the writer** Reading: magazine article about writing/televising a crime novel Listening: short story	Review: of a book or film	Crime in society and in fiction	**Reminder:** reporting orders/requests/advice **Analysis:** relative clauses
9 Feelings	**A Recognising feelings** Reading: a report on an experimental study of feelings Listening: a family row **B Expressing your feelings** Reading: magazine article about the differences between men and women Listening: short story	Letter to a newspaper: personal response to a newspaper article	Feelings	**Analysis:** phrasal and prepositional verbs **Reminder:** as and like

Vocabulary	Functions	Phonology	Style and register	Ways of learning	Focus of Section C
Word fields: • good/poor health • expressions with numbers Collocation	Agreeing and disagreeing	Word and sentence stress		Dealing with listening in exams	Paper 4 (Listening): Sections A and B
Word fields: • communication skills Word-building Collocation	Introducing oneself/ someone else	Stress and intonation patterns		Being aware of body language	Paper 5 (Speaking): Phase A
Compound nouns and adjectives Connotation	Structuring information: ways of marking emphasis	Stress in compound words	Vocabulary of persuasion: using sentence structure for stylistic effect	Deducing word meaning from context	Paper 1 (Reading): multiple matching
Word fields: • jobs and employment Collocation	Ways of comparing	Word pronunciation and stress	Formality and informality in written English	Self-evaluation	Paper 2 (Writing): Section A
Word fields: • crime and punishment Word-building	Reporting orders/ requests/advice		Lexical cohesion Formality/ informality in text		Paper 3 (English in Use): Section B proofreading and text editing skills
Word fields: • feelings Word-building	Speculating	Expressing feelings through intonation	Elements of formality/informality in vocabulary	Different ways of listening	Paper 4 (Listening): Section C

Unit and topic	Reading/Listening	Writing	Speaking	Grammar
10 Assertiveness	**A What is assertiveness?** Reading: a leaflet extract about assertiveness Listening: part of lecture on how to be assertive **B Being assertive** Reading: an extract about the use of language Listening: conversational extracts discussing different degrees of assertiveness	Formal letter: complaint	Talking assertively	**Analysis:** modal verbs for speculation and deduction **Reminder:** adjectives + prepositions
Revision Exam Practice 2				
11 Learning	**A Learning at school** Reading: two articles about unusual kinds of schooling Listening: two teenagers talking about work experience schemes **B What makes us learn?** Reading: article about genes and intelligence Listening: radio documentary about a young genius	Personal letter: describing feelings and experiences	School and other learning experiences	**Reminder:** indirect questions **Analysis:** the present perfect and present perfect continuous tenses
12 Leisure activities	**A Time off** Reading: magazine article about leisure advisers Listening: short monologues about a favourite time of day **B Moving images** Reading: magazine quiz on television viewing habits Listening: discussion about film and video censorship	Formal letter: complaining about violence on TV	Leisure activities, film/TV censorship	**Reminder:** *would* and *used to* **Analysis:** time clauses
13 The world around us	**A It's a weird world** Reading: book extract about miracles Listening: extract from Sherlock Holmes story **B It's a damaged world** Reading: a book extract about environmental problems Listening: extract from a fable about the countryside	Report: account of an unusual incident	Unusual phenomena and environmental issues	**Reminder:** cohesion through substitution **Analysis:** the future
14 Relationships	**A Personal relationships** Reading: magazine article on the state of marriage in Britain Listening: two monologues about influential people **B Working relationships** Reading: extract from a book about relationships at work Listening: radio discussion about team-work	Leaflet: rules for relationships in class	Personal relationships at home and work	**Analysis:** 'empty' *it* **Reminder:** conditional sentences
15 People watching	**A Let's peoplewatch!!** Reading: book extract about *Mona Lisa* Listening: several people talking about peoplewatching **B Reasons for peoplewatching** Reading: a book extract about the role of clothes	1 Personal description 2 Letter: stating opinions	What people look like and clothes	**Analysis:** verbs taking two objects **Reminder:** indirect statement
Revision Exam Practice 3				

Vocabulary	Functions	Phonology	Style and register	Ways of learning	Focus of Section C
Word fields: • behaviour • approval and disapproval Opposites Adjectives and prepositions	Making your point	Word stress Expressing attitude through intonation	Selecting and maintaining the right style and approach for a situation	Situations in which we use different styles of language	Paper 5 (Speaking): Phase B
Word fields: • school • learning Word-building Opposites				Different reasons for reading	Paper 1 (Reading): gapped paragraphs
Word fields: • leisure Contrastive conjunctions Phrasal verbs	Making comparisons Hesitating	Word stress Hesitation techniques	Selecting appropriate layout features	Checking back over written work Understanding the instructions for a task	Paper 2 (Writing): Section B
Word fields: • unusual phenomena • environment • personal reactions	Illustrating your point	Word pronunciation and stress	Style	Remembering vocabulary	Paper 3 (English in Use): Section C gap-filling and notes expansion
Word fields: • personal relationships at home and work Connotation Collocation	Identifying topic, speaker, attitude and opinion in listening	Expressions with numbers		Focusing attention in a listening test task	Paper 4 (Listening): Section D
Word fields: • appearance • personality characteristics Connotation	Making generalisations and exceptions Interacting with other speakers Reporting decisions			Interactional language	Paper 5 (Speaking): Phases C and D

138

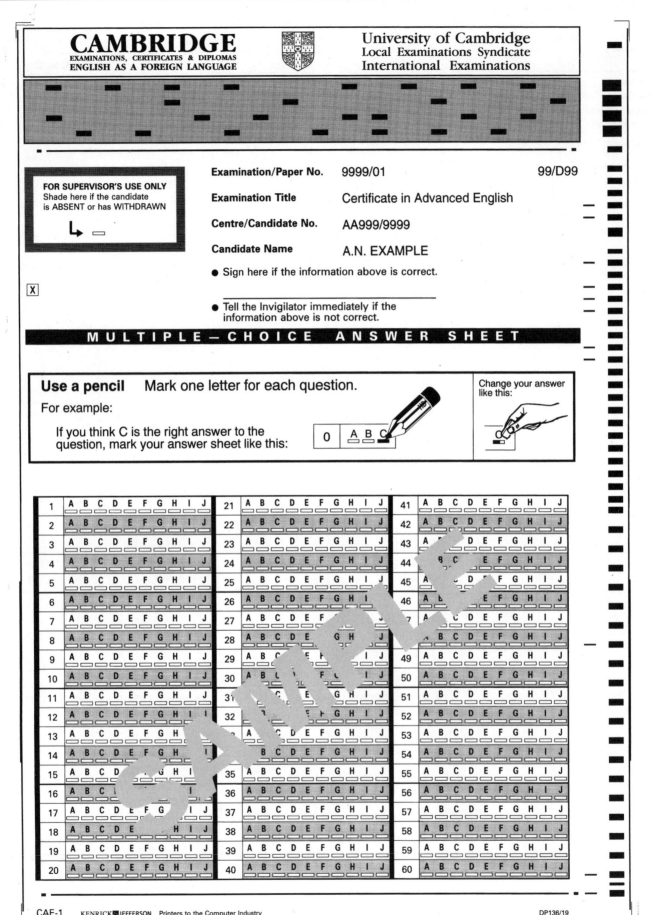

CAMBRIDGE
EXAMINATIONS, CERTIFICATES & DIPLOMAS
ENGLISH AS A FOREIGN LANGUAGE

University of Cambridge
Local Examinations Syndicate
International Examinations

FOR SUPERVISOR'S USE ONLY
Shade here if the candidate
is ABSENT or has WITHDRAWN

Examination/Paper No.	9999/03	99/D99
Examination Title	Certificate in Advance English	
Centre/Candidate No.	AA999/9999	
Candidate Name	A.N. EXAMPLE	

● Sign here if the information above is correct.

....

● Tell the Invigilator immediately if the information above is not correct.

CAE - PAPER 3 - ANSWER SHEET ONE

1		1	19		19
2		2	20		20
3		3	21		21
4		4	22		22
5		5	23		23
6		6	24		24
7		7	25		25
8		8	26		26
9		9	27		27
10		10	28		28
11		11	29		29
12		12	30		30
13		13	31		31
14		14	32		32
15		15	33		33
16		16	34		34
17		17	35		35
18		18	36		36

Continue on **ANSWER SHEET TWO** →

FOR OFFICE USE ONLY		
0 1 2	0 1 2	0 1 2
81	84	87
82	85	88
83	86	89

CAE-3 (1)   KENRICK■JEFFERSON   Printers to the Computer Industry   DP116/34

CAMBRIDGE
EXAMINATIONS, CERTIFICATES & DIPLOMAS
ENGLISH AS A FOREIGN LANGUAGE

University of Cambridge
Local Examinations Syndicate
International Examinations

FOR SUPERVISOR'S USE ONLY
Shade here if the candidate
is ABSENT or has WITHDRAWN

Examination/Paper No.	9999/03	99/D99
Examination Title	Certificate in Advance English
Centre/Candidate No.	AA999/9999
Candidate Name	A.N. EXAMPLE

● Sign here if the information above is correct.

● Tell the Invigilator immediately if the
information above is not correct.

CAE - PAPER 3 - ANSWER SHEET TWO

37	37	59	59
38	38	60	60
39	39	61	61
40	40	62	62
41	41	63	63
42	42	64	64
43	43	65	65
44	44	66	66
45	45	67	67
46	46	68	68
47	47	69	69
48	48	70	70
49	49	71	71
50	50	72	72
51	51	73	73
52	52	74	74
53	53	75	75
54	54	76	76
55	55	77	77
56	56	78	78
57	57	79	79
58	58	80	80

Continue on the OTHER SIDE of this sheet →

CAE-3 (2)   KENRICK JEFFERSON   Printers to the Computer Industry   DP118/36

81

82

83

84

85

86

87

88

89

UCAM59 GLYN 22-JUL-91 REVERSE DP118 & DP119
SEE INK REFERENCES

CAMBRIDGE
**EXAMINATIONS, CERTIFICATES & DIPLOMAS
ENGLISH AS A FOREIGN LANGUAGE**

University of Cambridge
Local Examinations Syndicate
International Examinations

FOR SUPERVISOR'S USE ONLY
Shade here if the candidate
is ABSENT or has WITHDRAWN

Examination/Paper No.   9999/04   99/D99

Examination Title   ANY CAMBRIDGE EXAM

Centre/Candidate No.   AA999/9999

Candidate Name   A.N. EXAMPLE

● Sign here if the information above is correct.

X

● Tell the Invigilator immediately if the
information above is not correct.

LISTENING COMPREHENSION ANSWER SHEET

ENTER TEST
NUMBER HERE →

FOR OFFICE
USE ONLY →

FCE	CAE	CPE
[1]	[5]	[3]

[00] [10] [20] [30] [40] [50] [60] [70] [80] [90]
[0] [1] [2] [3] [4] [5] [6] [7] [8] [9]

1		1	21		21
2		2	22		22
3		3	23		23
4		4	24		24
5		5	25		25
6		6	26		26
7		7	27		27
8		8	28		28
9		9	29		29
10		10	30		30
11		11	31		31
12		12	32		32
13		13	33		33
14		14	34		34
15		15	35		35
16		16	36		36
17		17	37		37
18		18	38		38
19		19	39		39
20		20	40		40